The Autobiography of
DONOVAN

❖

The Autobiography of
DONOVAN

❖

The Hurdy Gurdy Man

❖

Donovan Leitch

ST. MARTIN'S PRESS

New York

DISCLAIMER

The names and identifying characteristics of some of the
people in this book have been changed and some dialogue
from conversations long ago has been re-created from memory.

The haiku appearing on p. 251 is by Shiki from R. H. Blyth's
fourth volume of haiku titled *Haiku: Autumn–Winter*,
published by The Hokuseido Press, Tokyo, 1952, p. 24.

THE AUTOBIOGRAPHY OF DONOVAN. Copyright © 2005 by Donovan Leitch. All
rights reserved. Printed in the United States of America. No part of this book
may be used or reproduced in any manner whatsoever without written
permission except in the case of brief quotations embodied in critical articles
or reviews. For information, address St. Martin's Press,
175 Fifth Avenue, New York, N.Y. 10010.

www.stmartins.com

Design by Kathryn Parise

LIBRARY OF CONGRESS CATALOGING-IN-PUBLICATION DATA

Leitch, Donovan, 1946–
    The autobiography of Donovan: the hurdy gurdy man / Donovan
Leitch.
        p. cm.
    ISBN 0-312-35252-2
    EAN 978-0-312-35252-3
        1. Donovan, 1946– 2. Folk singers—Great Britain—Biography.
I. Title.
    ML420.D677A3 2005
    782.42164'092—dc22
    [B]   2005050964

First published in Great Britain under the title
The Hurdy Gurdy Man by Century

First U.S. Edition: December 2005

10 9 8 7 6 5 4 3 2 1

To She . . .

A theme I try to follow in this book:

I became an outsider when I left home at the age of sixteen. I realized that I resembled what author Colin Wilson had described as the "romantic outsider." In this book I explore the ways in which I faced the interior challenges of this form of rebellion. Then, when I read about Zen Buddhism, the answer to the problem of my alienation seemed to present itself to me. I became a musician and dedicated myself to sing to the teachings that can't be taught.

And always I am blessed with knowing She who was there in the darkness of the labyrinth. My lady of the lamp, my muse and wife, Linda.

Contents

Thanks to . . .

❖

Thanks to my father, Donald Leitch, for the poetry; to my mother, Winifred Leitch, for the power to stand my ground; to my brother, Gerald, for smiling through it all; to my other parents, Violet and Alec Lawrence, for the safety net; to my best friend, Gypsy Dave, for the wandering times; to Stewart Lawrence for being here always; to my two daughters, Astrella and Oriole, for constancy and love; to my son, Donovan Junior, for the understanding and his lady, Kirsty, for the fey; and to my dear daughter, Ione, for long-distance love; to Enid for the times. And thanks to my dear grandchildren: Sebastian for a second parenthood, Coco for the Humor, Joolz for the cool vibe, Katie for the bonding, and Violet for the future—I am enriched. And to my Welsh son and Brian's son, Julian, for the will to power; and especially to She, my muse and only wife, Linda Anne, without whom this book would never have been written.

Thanks to Jason Rothberg for the passion. To Carol and Ian Griffith for the "metta," to Mandy Aftel for the clear sight.

To Buddy Holly for the smooth; to Woody and Arlo Guthrie for the Lodestone's; to Derroll Adams for the Zen banjo; to Buffy Sainte-Marie for the shamanism; to Joan Baez for the chalice; to Pete Seeger for recognition; to Bob Dylan for the link; to George Harrison for silence; to John Lennon for the heart; to Paul McCartney for frabjuous joy; to Ringo Starr for the "Nod"; to Bert Jansch and Dirty Phil for the secret picking and to Mac Macleod and Mick Softley for the riffs; to Anita and Ashley Kozac for heart and soul; to Shawn Phillips for the duet of a lifetime; to Terry Kennedy for the first session; to Mickie Most for the amazing partnership in sound; to John Cameron for the perfect compliment to my song-tales; to John Sebastian for the long friendship and the grin of plenty; to Cathy Sebastian for tea and sympathy; to Roger McGuinn for the real folk-rock sound and square sunglasses; to Jimmy Page, John Paul Jones, Jeff Beck, Graham Nash, and to all my studio pals, diamonds all. Let's do it again! Thanks to my book agent, Sara Lazin, for confirmation.

Thanks to Sydney Maurer for the "art-cool" and Barbara for the parachute; to Ralph Peer Junior and all at Peer Music down the years; to Geoff Stevens and Peter Eden for discovery; to Clive Davis for the élan.

A special thanks to Pete Kameron for more than I can say.

I thank Rebecca Heller and all at St. Martin's Press for fraternity; I thank Beth Hannant for smiles and files.

To Stephen King for the salutation and John Mellencamp for the "hail."

To Andee, Rick, William, and Aya, for the magick.

The Autobiography of
DONOVAN

❖

Childhood

❖

Glasgow, 1954

I liked the danger wi' Harry. Ah was limpin', runnin' wi' Harry Cadbury across the back of St. Vincent Street. We were in a battle, lobbin' tin-can grenades over the line at the Anderson Gang. The cans were filled with cold ashes from the tenement refuse. We made the sound of explosions and felt brave.

Lots of the buildin's in Glasgow were skeletons from the bombing. Harry and me collected shell cases from the rubble of a World War: Spitfires and Hurricanes, Messerschmitts and Heinkels.

Oor wee battle over, we climbed the wall intae a ruined tenement—against the rules. The weak Scottish sun shone on the wallpapered bed-rooms, open tae the sky, the mouths of the dead fireplaces gaping.

I was in a bedroom wi' half a floor and the ceiling caving in. Balancing on a joist, I found a cupboard and opened it. Inside was an old flower vase which had escaped damage. Inside the vase was a collection of Victorian "scraps," printed scenes of cherubs and young ladies in long dresses and muffs. I was amazed at this find. Harry was a rough-and-tumble Catholic kid. I was a sensitive Proddie boy. Harry saw how much the scraps might get whilst I saw art and pretty girls to dream on.

Noo Harry was hanging oot a top-floor windae, tearin' the lead pipe from the eaves. His daddy had taught him this. Soon we had a fire in the back, splintered wood doors and windaes, paint bubblin' in the flames. Harry cut the lead into small pieces and smelted them in an old tin can. He poured the molten metal into ingots on a house brick. The company name came oot reversed. I was amazed.

The city night fell early in the northern wintery sky. Lights in the windaes shone in the dark tenements. Hungry yins (ones) called up to their mammies for a "piece 'n' jam." Bread spread with jam or butter and sugar flew doon from the kitchen sill, wrapped in newspaper. We crunched the sugar in our mooths, red-faced and hands tingling from the cold.

Efter a time, the windaes opened up again and the mammies called across the dark world.

"Are ye there, Harry?"

"Donovan, come up tae yer bed right now!"

I used to sleep wi' ma mammy. Daddy used to wake me up to kiss me good night, the smell of machine oil on his dungarees. He worked during and after the war as a tool setter in the Rolls-Royce factory that produced the Merlin engine for the Spitfire. He was a self-taught man. He might have made a scholar, had he not been born a poor boy, barefoot and underpaid. Mammy worked as a factory girl.

Donnie and Wynn had waited to begin a family, marrying in 1942, mammy at twenty-six and Daddy thirty. The ceremony was conducted in the side chapel of the Catholic church, as was the custom when a Protestant married a Catholic woman. Wynn was a young beauty who loved to dance, as did all the "Big Band Generation" and you could

See them doon the Barra-Land
Wi' frizzed and shinny hair

A blondie Ginger Rogers
And a skinny Fred Astaire.
—Donovan Leitch,
"Glasgow Town"

The Second World War ended in the spring of 1945, but it wasn't until Hiroshima and Nagasaki were vaporized that all the Earth stopped fighting. I was conceived the August of that nuclear holocaust.

In the disruption following the Second World War, three epidemics swept the city: scarlet fever, diphtheria, and polio. The children were hardest hit. The vaccines were too strong, and I was actually given the polio disease this way. So my right leg began to show signs of "wasting." An operation was performed, cutting the Achilles tendon in the foot, and I wore an ugly leg brace for some time after. It was a long boot made of a hard substance that I wore only at night to give the little leg support. Removing the device would tear the hairs and hurt so much that I cried each morning, painful for my mammy and daddy to watch.

My limpy leg did not hurt, but I could not run fast with the gang, so daddy bought a wee two-wheeled pram with a long handle and the boys whizzed me around the back screaming, "The injuns are comin', the injuns'll get ye."

I got battered by some boys. I didn't fight back. Harry had to fight for me. I jist hiftae find anither way tae beat the boys, I thought.

Daddy would cradle me in his arms and read poetry to me: Robert Service, W. H. Davies, and the Romantics, Shelley, Wordsworth, Coleridge, Byron, and the Visionaries, Blake, Yeats, and, not forgetting the Shakespeare of Scotland, our own Robert Burns. His uncanny memory retained long monologues and difficult poems, a traditional talent of the Celtic race. Oh, how my bardic father would intone magic poems of wandering. He opened a mysterious door to the other world of vision.

One day I turned from my game on the linoleum to see my silver-tongued daddy standing in the doorway, his lips pursed in a smile. He winked at me. I tried to wink back but closed both eyes instead. When I opened them again, he was dressed in a fur parka with sealskin boots and mittens, a mischievous twinkle still in his eye. The parlor had disappeared, snow-capped mountains gleamed in the distance. As my Klondike daddy spoke, poetry came out of his beard in puffs of frozen air, snatches of Robert Service. When he got to the bit about Sam McGee being cremated, I closed my eyes again. I was feart. But Daddy was not feart. He was brave enough to dream. He was telling me it is okay to dream.

At the age of five I stopped sleeping in Mammy's bed, and instead slept alone in the front room on a convertible sofa covered with brown "American" cloth. The high Edwardian room had a dark plywood dressing table and a wardrobe in the 1940s style, soft and curvy. I remember the tall sash windows and a mood of somber stillness as I lay alone in bed, watching the silhouettes of the passing trams in St. Vincent Street moving across the ceiling.

Across the tramlines was a comic store that sold *Superboy, Green Lantern,* and the mysterious *Mandrake The Magician,* and cousin Billy would come round to swop issues with me. I remember my cousin Billy was an artist and he made a drawing for me of a graveyard with old-fashioned soldiers burying an infantryman. I was fascinated to see the drawing of the soul leaving the body. This image is as clear to me now as when I first saw it.

There was a big cupboard in my room where Daddy went to make pictures in his darkroom. He liked to take pictures of weddings and something called a "bar mitzvah." I didn't go into the darkroom without knocking. Sometimes Daddy let me stand and watch the white paper in the china tray slip about in the thick water. The magic pictures came from nowhere, and I thought ma daddy so fine to do this. He never said a word. It was so peaceful in there, his secret place.

One night, when he was not making pictures, I slipped into the darkroom and took down a large manual from the shelves. The pages opened at a lovely young woman in the nude. She was smiling, her eyes laughing and her toes painted. I couldn't stop staring at her soft curves. She stepped out of the book and slid next to me in my bed, her long wavy hair falling over my face as she held me close to her wonderful breasts.

At the back of the posh row of flats at the other end of our street was a large walled garden called The Henney. One morning, Harry and I were peering into the garden through a hole in the old stonework. A little girl was playing on the lawn—we'd never seen grass anywhere else than the park. She was pretty and skipped up to see the scruffy boys. She lifted her skirt and we gave her a mud pack on her wee girl's willy. After school, Mammy was very serious and held my hand as we knocked on the posh door. I was told off for doing a bad thing. I didn't understand.

Two weeks later, unrepentant, I stood in the dark "close" while an older girl lifted her skirt and pulled her knickers down to show me her smooth quim, fine red hairs, sleek and silky. I was amazed when she then peed in a bottle. Afterwards, Harry said that one of the boys had got television. We all went up to see the wee shiny square of glass in the big wooden sideboard. It was just like the pictures but black and white and not so much fun. We got bored and played in the dark. I thought of the big girl and hoped no one told.

My mammy was the second eldest of seven sisters and two brothers. Her father, Michael Philips, had died soon after the First World War. Mustard gas had damaged his lungs and eventually killed him. They should have received the War Pension but the doctors insisted it was tuberculosis, so the family had only the Widow's Pension, and all the children had to work.

> They fought for country, fought for King,
> They won the war, it's true,
> Tae see Germany and Japan,
> Ye widnae think it noo.
>
> —Donovan Leitch,
> *"Glasgow Town"*

My daddy was the eldest of two brothers and two sisters. His mother had married twice and outlived both husbands and was known to me as Granny Kelly. She lived on the other side of town, and I remember her dark wee kitchen where we took tea and scones. Uncle Bill still lived with Granny. It was through handsome Uncle Bill that I first heard American folk music. Bill would dress in full tartan sometimes, a silver dirk in his hairy sock. I was surprised to hear later from Scottish comedian Billy Connolly that he knew Bill as "Postie," a figure of some renown in Glasgow.

I often stayed with my Granny Philips in Argyle Street. Sometimes on Saturday nights when Mammy and Daddy were out dancing, Granny held me over the windowsill two floors up over the street, which frightened my parents, but she did it with all the grandchildren.

Granny was a big woman with tattooed arms. I remember a name of a dead husband in a freckled heart. She had long black hair, streaked with silver. Below us the Saturday night drunks were raving. One night a man was crawling along the pavement, clawing the paving stones, absolutely "legless" as they say.

Another night, at a pub over the road, it was kicking-out time and a crowd had gathered in a circle to watch two women fight. Great roars were heard as one woman tore the peroxide hair from the other, bringing her opponent's head down on a knee to smash the teeth.

And after the street died down, Granny took me into her bed in the wall, which had doors and was next to the fire. Once inside I stared at the icon on the wall. It was Mary, Granny told me, and she prayed for *all* her children. During this prayer I let out an uncontrollable fart.

Granny said, "Do you know wit a fart means, Donovan?"

"No, Granny," I replied. I was a little scared of the big lady.

"It's a message from God tae say . . . you must go tae the toilet."

Granny's daughters were gorgeous. Aunt Frances and her two sisters, Kathy and Lena, left for America to get jobs as nannies in New York. Frances worked as a nanny for an American actress, Beatrice Strate, and looked after a wee boy named Willard.

One day a big parcel arrived from America. Inside were children's clothes. A wee leather jacket with a name on the back, all red and silver. A check jacket in a soft fabric. Then ma mammy pulled out a complete cowboy suit—waistcoat, check shirt, and chaps; a cowboy hat; and, best of all, a pair of Hopalong Cassidy six-guns in real leather holsters on a belt. I got all dressed up and stood for my daddy to take a "photay" with his Rolleiflex. We were something called poor, so all this was new to me, like Christmas in the "pictures."

Harry and I loved going to the Gaiety to see the Lone Ranger and Flash Gordon, Flash in his spaceship rolling across some planet of rocks and sand, trying to save the world. Sometimes it was Hopalong Cassidy. Then one day Hoppy came to Glasgow and rode down Sauchiehall Street on his horse, throwing silver dollars—but I didn't get one. It was like the weddings when the couple throws pennies out the windae of the car.

When I was seven, I woke up with a sore mouth and Mammy took me around to a big house in the posh row. In a funny-smelling room, a man put me in a big chair with shiny bits. He put a rubber thing over my mouth and asked me to count to ten. A horrible smell filled me up, and I forgot after seven what number I was at. I could hear the dentist counting, too, and a radio playing on the windowsill. After I woke up, I spat blood into a shiny bowl of water and he gave me an orange, a luxury at the time. I said, "Where's the radio?" "What radio?" he replied. There was no radio. I was shocked to see the black hole in my mouth when Mammy showed me. I was sick now and stayed in my room. Mammy told me stories of how I had slept so long in the big pram in the street when I was a baby that Mammy and Daddy had to hold a mirror in front of my mouth to see if I was still breathing. Not keen on waking life—reluctant to get involved, perhaps.

One October afternoon I sat quietly in the room. The door opened slowly and a thin man walked toward me. I froze with fear. He wore a suit of tails, a top hat, and a Chinese rubber mask. He silently lifted up his arms, white gloves on his hands. I couldn't speak. I couldn't breathe. The gloved hand rose up to the awful face and slowly pulled off the mask. The smiling face of my mammy shone down at me. I burst out crying. Mammy laughed and gathered me up in her arms. It was Hallowe'en and she was dressed for a party.

I remember being alone in the tall, somber room, watching the goldfish circle his ocean in a glass bowl. Mammy was cooking the rations or buying coal briquettes from the horse and cart in the street or, when there was no money, packing the coal-dross into newspaper bundles. She would soak them, dry them and burn them for heat.

> Three craws sat upon the wa'
> Sat upon the wa', sat upon the wa'-a'-a'-a',
> Three craws sat upon the wa'
> On a cold and a frosty morning
> —*Glasgow children's song*

I heard a man singin in "the back" and Mammy opened the windae. She threw him a coin as he made a sad sound with his voice. The coin went spinning down, and Mammy said he's a poor old bugger who needs a drink. She said it's nice tae hear a tune. She had been to the Steamy to wash all the clothes. Sometimes I went too, and all the mammies laughed and sang in the big place with all the clouds and carbolic soap bubbles.

Ma daddy said I sang my first song in the Steamy when I was four. It was Robbie Burns night and sometimes a band played there. I got up and sang with a blind man who played the piano. I sang "There Was an Old Lady Who Swallowed a Fly" all the way to the end and everybody smacked their hands. I liked the singing better than haggis.

I went to the Kent Road School, a Proddie one. I remember the first day Mammy took me. I was scared and cried and cried. I didn't understand why she was leaving me with those people. It looked like an army barracks, red-brick walls and barbed wire. The head teacher stood like a preacher at a big desk with a Bible on it, us kids all in rows like prisoners in a film.

One day I did a bad thing and the head teacher shouted at me. He had a thin leather strap with tails at the end, and he told me to put out my hand. I had been told about this, and so was shaking all over. The strap cut the air and lashed my hand and wrist. A terrible sting of pain hit me, and I closed my eyes. The red skin was throbbing as I sat humiliated at my desk. I would tell ma granny. She'd get him for this!

But that day I didn't go straight home. I wandered through the backyards of bombed tenements, clambering through the ruins, breaking glass, and getting lost. The police had to bring me home.

Granny Philips would have hurt that teacher if I'd told her. I heard a story of when her own son Michael had been beaten with the strap. She went down to the school and was shown into a class full of children.

"Ur you the teecher that strapped ma boy?"

"Well, Mrs. Philips, he was a bad boy."

The big Irish woman rolled up her sleeves and bowled him out with a punch. All the children cheered.

"If ah ivir catch ye hittin' ma boy agin, I'll kill ye, dae yer heer?"

I was at the seaside with my cousins and aunts. Every year Granny Kelly rented a wee hoose in Ayr, a yellow strand on the southwest coast of Scotland. We would shelter from the wind by the granite seawall, eating sandwiches and making sandcastles. I was fascinated by the rock pools, gazing at translucent fishes and scurrying crabs.

Swimming was the thing for the polio leg, apparently, and my daddy was a strong swimmer. He soon had me doing the crawl. "Watch out for the scary seaweed and the jellyfish," he would call. Daddy showed me a picture of himself standing by a pool with Johnny Weissmuller (whose real name was Tarzan). I wanted to swim like Tarzan. I wanted to swim the Amazon and ride elephants into the sunset!

Donkey rides on the wide dark sands, Punch and Judy, Victorian band-stands with Salvation Army Brass Band, and when the sun slipped into the sea I would lie in bed and marvel as Daddy read me Lewis Carroll. I dreamed of a sleepy yesterday of crinoline and parasol, walrus and griffin, seagull and seashell.

After the magic days by the sea, it was back to the city and the backyard battles in the bombed-out tenements, the itchy woollen swimsuits put away for another year.

I remember thinking it must be a party today 'cause Daddy was hanging flags out of my window over the street and everybody else was, too. The whole town was laughing and singing, the radio playing marching music, and the schools all closed. I didn't know what was happening and neither did Harry. The next day every window in the street was open and all the mammies and daddies and kids were hanging out, waving at a great crowd of people waving back. Down the street came a band playing really loud and a big shiny car with an old woman in jewels waving at everybody. Mammy said it was the Queen Mother and her pretty daughter just got a crown and now she's the real Queen. I had thought that pretty daughters went to America.

Our family had parties all the time. There was always a big one at Hog-manay, the last day of the year. Everyone sang a party piece. All the kids, cousins, brothers and sisters would sit under the tables with a "shandy"—a mixture of beer and fizzy lemonade—to listen and watch a slightly tipsy relative or friend do their bit. After much coaxing my mammy would sit on a chair in the center and sing her song.

I remember the sad sound of the Irish songs, filled with feelings of longing and leaving, and how they contrasted with the humor and vigor of the Scottish tunes. And, of course, the amazing verse readings and monologues that my daddy had memorized.

"Come on, Donnie, gi' us 'James' or 'Dan McGraw'—aw, come on, Donnie."

In truth *he* did not need much coaxing. He could thrill and tickle an audience effortlessly.

My daddy arranged and performed many amateur shows during and after the war. As a boy, his mother had taken him to see all the great music hall artists. His considerable memory and oratorical skill and his great love of books influenced my songwriting immensely.

When, in 1954, Daddy bought me the new record by Bill Haley and the Comets, my life received its first musical shock just as this first white rock-and-roll success—rockabilly—would open up the world of rhythm and blues to everyone.

Times were changing. After the devastation of the war, Britain was beginning to get on its feet again, and my daddy took work in the south of England. New factories and new towns were springing up, and he followed the migrating trend. He lived in digs near the factory, waiting for a house in a brand-new housing scheme twenty miles from London, and soon we joined him.

Before our move I took a holiday with a bunch of poor kids from Glasgow in a country-house school by the sea. This was the first time I was away from my parents. I sat in the bus, the mammies and daddies waving at us. Everybody was singing:

Fur am no awau tae bide awau, am no awau tae lee ye
Fur am no awau tae bide awau, I'll aye come back tae see ye . . .
—*Glasgow street song*

We were going to somewhere called Wigtown in the Solway Firth. The school had been a rich man's mansion. It took ten minutes to drive up to the front door from the gate—that's how big. All the kids cheered when we arrived and poured into the dormitories to find their beds.

Half the day was school lessons and the other half we played or went on outings. When the tide receded down the estuary, we walked along to what seemed like the bottom of the ocean. We had to be back by a certain time or the sea would swallow us up, so fast did the tide turn. But on the seafloor we found giant crabs and razor clams, rock pools with huge fishes stranded in forests of seaweed drying in the sun. The girls collected unicorn horns of periwinkle, limpets, and tiny conch shells on the soft blond sand. Then on one field trip we visited the sea cave of the Celtic monk St. Ninian. To the north lay the Great Forest of Caladon, legendary site of a hermitage of Merlin. I was filled with a wonder, and in that glorious summer my boyish heart was full of mermaids, wizards, and warriors.

❖

Back home, Harry and I were in the empty tenement flat. Ma mammy was out. The place was strange without furniture. We poked the wallpaper at the corners of the walls and saw layers going back in time. We opened a golf ball and sprayed the liquid rubber stuff everywhere. Then we tied the wee rubber balloon thing to the water tap and turned it on.

Our eyes widened as the balloon got bigger and bigger, full of water. When will it burst? we wondered. This rubber balloon was *really* strong. Harry and I edged nearer to the front door as the thing got larger and began to look like it would fill the whole room. Just as we opened the hall door to run, it burst! The balloon jumped around jetting water everywhere. We laughed and flew down the stairs.

Three hours later I was gazing out of the train window at a new land. The Flying Scotsman was thundering through the night—great clouds of steam, the clickety-clack of the rails. Sleepy immigrants, we drank scalding tea, ate funny buns, and watched the freezing weather outside.

Full of hope and anticipation ma mammy, ma brother, Gerald, and me held each other as the future drew nearer and nearer. Ma daddy was waiting for us, all the loneliness now behind him. We were going to the green hills and woods of Hertfordshire and the chance of a better life. I never saw Harry again.

Teenage

We lived on a windy hilltop in the new town of Hatfield, Hertfordshire, in the south of England, twenty miles north of London. It was one of the many estates that were part of the rehousing schemes of postwar Britain. Two stories, Wimpey-built—or poorly made—little boxes in lines on a hillside, all looking just the same and just as Pete Seeger would sing.

And yet our family would thrill to the luxury of living in a "new" home, with all the modern conveniences. The year was 1956, and we had never had it so good.

After the gray streets of Glasgow, I was astounded at the colors and sights of my new land, the different varieties of green. Hatfield lay in the lush forested countryside, chirping with birds and bursting with blossom, by ponds filled with fishes, tadpoles, and newts. Sometimes the deep roar of the jet engines could be heard coming up from the plain below. There the factory lay where my father worked for the company that made the first passenger jet plane.

But the new school was a problem for me. I still spoke in a heavy Glaswegian tongue. The other boys made much of this until eventually I transformed my speech into a good " 'Artfodshire 'Edgehog." Mum worked at Nabisco, and I was a latchkey kid for a while, watching TV until she came home.

Then at the age of eleven I went to a secondary coed school. St. Audrey's had lots of glass and concrete with a library, gym, and large playing fields. We boys had a uniform of the usual gray trousers and navy blazer with a tie. The school shield was sewn to the hanky pocket.

In the Phys Ed. periods a couple of years later I was surprised to hear the records of The Shadows being played as I jumped the horse, staggered with the medicine ball, or turned cartwheels. After PE, in the showers, the "Fat Boy" would scream as the wet towels were applied to his clammy exposed skin.

In time I rose to the position of House Captain. The main privilege of this was that it allowed me and my friends to stay indoors in the Common Room at break periods, jiving to records or playing "lap chess" with a girls on my lap, while outdoors the sharp winds froze faces red in the playground.

The records in the charts at the time were "North to Alaska," "One-way Ticket to the Blues," and "Candy Man." I started to buy Buddy Holly records with the money I earned working in the market on Saturdays, selling cakes with my dad.

> I worked a bit on Saturday,
> Pushing cake on a stall,
> Went and bought some Buddy Holly
> And soon I had them all.
> —Donovan Leitch, *untitled*

I couldn't afford albums so I bought Buddy Holly EPs. I collected Buddy in groups of four songs and played them on a Dansette turntable in mono. I learned to be simple from him and to breathe the words. The tracks "Listen to Me," "Rave on," with their clear clean production, are as fresh now as they were when they first rolled onto tape way back then.

By now I was having a better time of it with authority. But one windy day I passed Tania in the central courtyard of the school in view of the headmaster's distant glass office. Tania was a rival House Captain with classical features and long dark hair. We were not that near to each other, but from where he watched, the Head saw her cotton skirt lift in the wind and called me to his room to tell me off for feeling her up and to give me a caning. I was innocent this time, though guilty many times when he had not been looking. Tania was gorgeous, but I was more attracted to her best friend, Gilly. So there I was in class, tipping my seat back to feel up Gilly under the desk. The teacher, hearing sniggers, yelled, "Leitch! Come here immediately!" Not an easy thing to do, crouching and trying to hide my tenting school trousers. "And just what do you think you are playing at, Leitch?" More laughter. "Is this the way you must behave in my class? This is not a biology lesson." By now the class was roaring. I returned to my place where I craftily put my hand to my mouth. The beautiful smell of mermaid juice was still on my fingertips.

The influence of my father's talent for recitation was beginning to show. I would stand at assembly behind the Holy Book and recite to the multitude below. I had no idea what the text meant, but I raised my voice, then lowered it meaningfully.

The Church of England was becoming less and less well attended in those days. Later it would try to increase its flock by introducing pop music into the services. Later still, the reggae songs of Bob Marley would bring many back to God with the Rastafarian Sacrament and the smoking of the "holy herb" marijuana. Christianity's priests had converted the African people while they were enslaved on the Caribbean sugar plantations, but later Bob Marley would influence millions of white people with his pure form of Gnostic Christianity.

On the playing fields I was not excused from games because of my polio. This was, no doubt, good for me, but I was not fast enough on the football field. In the gym I could turn on a penny, though, and my hands were large and talented, so when the PE teacher brought basketball into the school I was in there. Soon I had my own team, wearing American strip and Keds.

My father continued to train me at swimming. I would become a champ at county level. Better than the accolades, I recall the blonde in our relay team. Most nights after school were spent standing in the lane with this girl. "What were you doing all this time?" demanded my mother, dinner cold and homework not done. But the truth was that I was not doing as much as I would have liked. This girl was so beautiful, so perfect that I was a little frightened of her. She was like a goddess, and the words died on my lips.

I had three great pals at school. Mick Sharman, Ron "Dippy" Gale, and David Richards. Dippy had what is nowadays called a nerdish look—round spectacles and a clean shirt and smart tie. But the impression of nerdishness was misleading. His smiling moon face was crowned with a short swatch of black hair, dangerously dashed over one eye, and he was a wicked mimic. Mick had posh parents and was brought up on health food, so he would love to visit my house to eat sugar and white bread. He was a handsome devil, his dark hair and rugged features soon ensuring that he would do all right in any Mecca Ballroom. He was the first in our foursome to become a Mod. David was a Welsh boy, thin, sensitive, with a self-deprecating form of humor. His angular face reminded me of Tom Courtney in the film *Billy Liar*. David was a Celtic immigrant like me and a painter. We four found in each other a gentle gang determined to explore girls, clubs, and dancing.

Up in the local youth club, Downs Farm, boys and girls would jive to records, while the table-tennis balls ticked and the billiard balls clicked in the back room. I remember Dippy, Mick, and I mimed to a single that was out then, "The Monster Mash." I was dressed as Dracula with my two friends in drag as the "Vampirettes." Then we three formed a band, and I played drums. My mother sewed us hoods of black satin, holes cut for the eyes, and the hood motif was painted on the drum. The short-lived Macabres were born: drums, a guitar, a saxophone, and three songs in our repertoire: "Summertime" (from *Porgy and Bess*), "Long Gone Lonesome Blues" (by Hank Williams), and another that I forget. Mick played the guitar and Dippy the sax.

> With a friend I sang Hank Williams
> Wire-brushing a snare
> Became a Mod fast and looking snappy . . .
> —Donovan Leitch, *untitled*

I bought a Grundig "reel to reel" tape recorder and at night I would record secret radio shows in my bedroom in the dark. I used "effects" and spoke the narration to my tales of lonely city streets and solitary heroes. I loved radio serials.

And so I began to chat up the Mod girls and preen and show off the gear I was buying. I had a jacket made in brown cord. No collars. Wow!

On Mick's scooter we followed packs of Mods on the way to Mecca ballrooms to dance with the girls. We danced well to bands like Brian Poole and the Tremeloes, Johnny Kidd and the Pirates, Freddie and the Dreamers, and The High Numbers.

The High Numbers (soon to be called The Who) thrilled the Mods with their mixture of Motown, Beach Boys, and irreverent antics. One night, Roger Daltry leaped from the stage and landed on me, with a bottle of cola mixed—I could smell it—with whisky in his hand. Daltry was laughing as he picked himself up. "Sorry, mate—you all right?" Solid and compact, Daltry was a "likely lad" with attitude and already a youth hero. I smiled at him. "Of course I am; that was fantastic!"

Soon I would be there, with my peers, stage diving into revolution; my mates would be the small fraternity of music stars rising from the squalid tenements and new towns of postwar Britain.

Purple hearts and alcohol were the stimulants that helped pill heads dance all night and into the dawn, chewing gum. Rival gangs in stiff collars and braces prowled the Meccas, their Mod girlfriends in page-boy haircuts.

Now I, too, was actually going out dancing with fully dressed, made-up Mod girls who knew how to smoke cigarettes. When did I lose my virginity, I wonder? There was a Christmas party, and maybe it was young Danny, another school friend, originally from Aberdeen, who was passing round "Johnny Bags" (contraceptives). Was it then I lost it? With a small, younger teenage girl? I do remember the wonder of smooth, silken thighs and her slightly drunken body on the absent parents' double bed, piled high with coats. And afterward this girl stood and cried, softly, then harshly. We were schoolchildren who had lost our virginity together. I can't recall her name, but she appears in a song later, "Rambling Boy."

I was reaching the end of secondary school and the end of my Mod phase, too, because soon I would be introduced to the "Beat girls" and all their jazzy dark and decadent joys.

Rebel

Secondary modern school ended in those days when you were fifteen, and I was accepted by the Welwyn Garden City College of Further Education. The college was a campus of modern buildings in another new town, with an art class that would encourage me to express myself with confidence. It was here that I learned to explore the alternative lifestyle that would help shape my views and form my values.

That summer of 1962 found me lying on the grass by the fountain, with long-haired girls in "sloppy Joes," sandals, and black mascara; talking painting, pottery, and poetry; and debating revolution and banning the Bomb. We loved the songs of Joan Baez, Pete Seeger, and the incomparable Woody Guthrie. And in the common room we kept cool with the sounds of Miles Davis.

Our local youth club leader was all right and gave us "arty types" a small outbuilding on The Farm for a studio. In the barn, Dippy, Sammy, and I smoked, sketched, and talked of Jack Kerouac's book *On the Road,* dreaming of Zen, of a Beat girl and some pot to smoke with her.

Jazz became my bag. On my bedroom wall I pasted up clippings of the great cats of drums from *Downbeat* magazine, Max Roach and Gene Krupa.

I listened to the blue bossa nova sounds of Stan Getz and Carlos Jobin, the bebop of Charlie Parker and Gene Krupa's big band at Carnegie Hall. I discovered the poetry and jazz of the San Francisco scene, the London sounds of the Tony Kinsey Quartet, and the poet Christopher Logue, whose EP record *Red Bird* I played to death.

Photos of the Paris bohemian scene of the 1950s also held a fascination for me. Amazingly, one girl from the photos, Valli, would later dance to my music in the Royal Albert Hall.

I was conjuring my future. I was making plans to be part of the alternative art scene. I felt my way was with the Beats, wherever they were hanging out, so I set my sights on London. Inspired by the young French poet Rimbaud, I was ready to head for city lights.

I was becoming a problem to my parents, dropping school some days, wandering into the great forest park of Hatfield House. Once, wandering on through the old trees to the lakeside, I climbed along a bough to an owl's nest. Removing some material from the lair I rolled it up into a cigarette paper and pretended it was marijuana.

Writing poetry, I felt brave in dropping capital letters and commas, like the poet e. e. cummings.

Patricia was my first deep relationship of those days. This college girl vibrated that special warmth that I was to feel in many North Country females. When it was over, the lines show that the parting was hard:

> 'Cos love is like an ice-cold stream
> From snow-capped mountain high
> And likened unto grapeskin
> Is the touch upon her thigh
> And love is like the savage crows
> In the winter trees . . .
> —Donovan Leitch, *untitled*

The "Beat" poetry of Allen Ginsberg spoke to me, as did the works of T. S. Eliot and Dylan Thomas. Thomas "recited" his poems on record and I eagerly bought them all, but it was the Irish poet William Butler Yeats who became my literary guru. He had searched for the lost Celtic faith and worked toward a rediscovery of pagan myth. Irish culture was fading fast in his day, but he had saved many oral tales. Yeats had also recorded toward the end of his life, and I collected his "song chants."

Books opened up a universe of possibilities. I kept returning to Jack Kerouac's *On the Road*, its celebration of life and search for self reflecting my own longing. And through this writer I was introduced to the term "Zen." Introspection encouraged, I went on to read the works of Alan Watts and Christmas Humphries, Zuzuki and Lao Tsu. This has meaning for me, I thought. I can put this teaching into practice. I can understand this as a way to live. Somewhere inside me I knew that I was part of a universal reality, and that the feeling of separation from all others was an illusion.

And I wanted to know how to stop the flow of thoughts that spontaneously arise in the mind, just as the second aphorism of Patanjali's Yoga Sutras so clearly stated. Not yet knowing how to meditate, I recognized the teaching as true nevertheless. The deeper truths of Oriental religions and the deeper truths of ancient Celtic spirituality were becoming entwined in my mind, and so endless discussions between radicals in college began to sound futile. It began to seem to me that to change a government by political revolution was merely changing the saddle on the same wild horse.

Dad and I had always sat around the kitchen table, heatedly debating the rise of the unions, the child labor laws of the last century, and the insensitivity of the ruling class. I was fired by his passion for justice and equality. But now I pleaded the case of nonaggression. Buddhism is not the cure for the working man, my father insisted. We agreed on the problem, but we agreed to disagree on the solution. All I knew was that the way of direct political action was not for me.

One weekend I visited a car graveyard and found some junk—a smashed speedometer, a sheet of polythene, a piece of plywood, and some nails. I made a sculpture, stretched polythene over it, and lit the bugger up in flames. The speedometer was broken at ninety miles per hour, the plastic burned in the shape of the United States. It was an homage to James Dean.

I painted, too. I remember one painting of a man in a web like Odin on the World Tree. I was happy with the smell of paint and clay. I wanted to study so I could go to art school, but my teacher insisted on other subjects.

What would I need other subjects for, I thought. Why would I need math and science? I was born to be an artist.

I discovered the "New Wave" of British films. Films such as *Room at the*

Top, The Loneliness of the Long-Distance Runner, The L-shaped Room, and *Billy Liar.* Shot in black and white, with melancholy jazz scores, filmed in northern locations (Blackpool, Salford, Bolton, Bradford, Wakefield, Morecambe, Manchester), they were a mirror to the life I had experienced in Glasgow. I also fancied the girl in *Billy Liar,* the character played by Julie Christie. She represented freedom of choice and escape, a liberated Beat girl with no qualms about just sodding off, leaving home and free to take sex where she wants it, without becoming enslaved to a pram.

So I was feeling more and more stifled until, rather than sit the exams needed to get into art school, I dropped out and went to work. My parents were not pleased, but then again, neither was I. I had wanted to go to art school, but because I had been dissuaded from studying art, the exams were now, I felt, out of my reach. I knew the art scene was where it was at: better-looking "chicks" and the freedom to explore reality and unreality equally, the opportunity to challenge the status quo! All this and the smell of paint and the Beat girls' long silky hair—that was what I wanted. But now here I was, heading down to the unemployment office.

"You could be apprenticed to the printing trade," said my father.

"Yeah, I could, but it's typesetting really, not art."

He saw it as a union-protected job. After five years, he said, I would be a real printer, able to fight the factory bosses.

My Mum just slowly shook her head, somewhat bewildered. This was the postwar boom; there were lots of jobs. "Why dae ye not want to work, son, is it coz yer lazy?" she said.

"No, Mum, I just want not to be unhappy every day I go in."

"But you were so good in school at so many things. Look at you now." She returned to silence.

"Well, you will just have to get a laboring job," said my dad, disappointed with me, having expected so much from our new country, the new schools, and the new life he had given my brother and me.

My brother, Gerald, was still only ten so, no doubt, he looked at all this as a game, I guess, though a dangerous one that included raised voices, tears, and the occasional suicide threat.

This came from my mother when she found the telltale signs of puberty on my bedsheets one morning. I found out about it when my father came shouting into my bedroom one afternoon, just after I had returned from Campus.

"See what ye've done now—yer mammy's locked herself in the bathroom and she's going tae cut her wrists!"

This was an astounding situation, and I was terrified. "What have I done this time?" I gasped.

"You've been wanking yourself to exhaustion, and she finds the cum all over the sheets. For chrissake, Donovan, give it a break!"

I was truly horrified as I heard Daddy begin banging on the bathroom door. I was sure this was audible all the way to the next street, so thin were the walls of the new estate houses. Finally, Mum crept out, and I saw the tiny scratch on her wrist.

What could have made Mum feel that my masturbation was so awful? Her own upbringing as a good Catholic girl, perhaps? So there I was, no decent job and wanking my way into hell at an alarming speed.

Mum had been brought up the hard way, and she couldn't "hold" me close. When I was given a polio shot at three and got the disease, Mum might have felt it was, in part, her fault. She was wrong: thousands were infected by the overzealous health department of the war-torn cities of Britain, cities full of broken sewers and bombed-out systems. But maybe she felt guilty and that inhibited her? It was Dad who had always cradled me as I grew up. I was closer to my father. And yet when I was a babe my mother loved me as any mother would.

I am glad for my literary father and all the poetry he read to me. And I am glad, too, that my Mum taught me to speak my mind in the company of paupers, princes, and priests. Thanks, Donald and Wynn. You were good to me.

A series of laboring jobs and factory work followed. The jobs would last a few weeks at most, and I would change again. Cold, damp days on building sites.

Then, one Saturday morning, taking a break from the cake stall in St. Albans market where I worked on weekends, I walked through the crowds to the Old Town Hall for a piss. Down in the dirty, white-tiled chamber I stood up to the china and got it out. To my right was a squad member in uniform who was very, very drunk.

Looking up, I recognized him. "Music Shop Dave" had worked with me in the Welwyn Garden City department store. At the next urinal, trying to piss straight, was his drinking pal, dressed in a duffel coat and also swaying madly.

"Hi, Dave," I said to Music Shop Dave, "how you doing?"

Music Shop Dave, his eyes crossing and his pockets clinking with miniature bottles of spirits, was too pissed to see me. But his pal just about could and said, threateningly, "Are you fucking timing me, mate?"

Scared, I looked again at Music Shop Dave, who recognized me now and calmed his pal down by saying I was a friend of his. "He's OK," he told him.

Feeling relieved, I went back into that Saturday-market afternoon, not realizing that I had just met a wild and crazy guy who would become my constant companion and deepest friend. Music Shop Dave's friend, I would discover, was also called Dave, known around town as "Gypsy Dave," and in the coming months he would help me break free of my small-town world.

In the meantime, I would sometimes just go and stay around older bohemians' pads. The police would inevitably bring me home. It was, in fact, an offense to leave home under the age of sixteen back then. So then I would be locked in my room, only to escape out the window.

Sometimes I lay in the long grass overlooking the open road, dreaming of seeing a sports car stop with a lovely young woman waving to me. She would ask, "Where are you headed?"

I would reply, "Anywhere, honey."

I began to go to the local jazz club at the Cherry Tree Pub in Welwyn Garden City. The New Orleans jazz revival was in full swing, and here the exuberant music was live. We jigged and sweated—full of beer and energy—to the raw sound with long-haired Beat girls in the gloomy rooms.

It was here that I met Gypsy Dave for the second time, and as were talked that night—buoyed up by the great music and the pints—we hatched our plans for escape. We shared a dream and a desire for freedom and the open road.

The road was calling very loudly to me now that I was sixteen. Summer was a-coming in and young Beats were feeling the call of the seaside. So at five-thirty one morning I threw two pairs of socks and some odds and ends of clothing into my rucksack and grabbed my old Scout sleeping bag, feeling exhilarated. To the west and the south lay the beautiful coasts of Devon and Cornwall, and the few who knew planned to hitchhike down to spend the summer in St. Ives. So it was with me and Gyp.

"What are ye doing to me, Son? You cannae be doing this tae me," Mum pleaded. She thought it was all directed at her, but it was all really happening to me.

As the author Colin Wilson said in his book of the same name, the outsider finds his life all unreal, a fake performance by everyone around him. Only one thing can break the feeling of alienation—to leave.

"You're surely breaking your mother's heart," said my father, but I believed he half wanted to go himself. After all, it was he who had read me the rambling poets, encouraged the wandering spirit in me, chanted the verses of Robert Service, the Scottish Woody Guthrie. It was service who told of the "Men that don't fit in," who "break the hearts of kith and kin, / And they roam the would at will." Yes, I had "the curse of the gypsy blood."

Vagabond

Got ma Zen, got ma jeans, got ma duffel, what a scene
Milletts roll-neck sweater and me old Scout doss-bag
Nothin' more for me to say, windy-milling happy day
Ride into the witchy finger on the Cornish hand

When you're ro-whoa-olling Down the Road
When you're ro-whoa-olling Down the Road.
—Donovan Leitch, "Rolling Down the Road," unpublished

The first time I saw St. Ives I was enchanted. I had hitchhiked to Cornwall with Gypsy Dave. With our sleeping bags on our shoulders, we had arrived at the top of the hill. We walked down a road that ran straight for a good length through tall trees, denying us a view of the sea on our right. When we cleared the pines and started to descend we halted, astonished at the beauty of the neat little bay that lay before us.

Since the early twentieth century, St. Ives has been a painter's paradise, a picturesque fishing village cradled in a lovely bay flanked by two white sand beaches. The narrow cobbled streets wind down between the old houses, presenting wonderful entertainment to the eye at every turn: windows, roofs, balconies of wrought iron, and gleaming whitewashed walls. On a clear, sunny day in spring 1963, St. Ives shone brightly.

Gypsy and I wandered through the crooked streets and flopped down on the hot sand. The holiday season had not yet begun, and we were the first beatniks there that year.

A girl came up to us and told us that she met all the Beats. So we met her. She had tangled red hair and green eyes, her Nordic skin speckled with freckles. I am at last in the bohemian world where I belong, I thought.

The gulls hover high in an azure sky, filled with huge puffy clouds. They fly in over "the Island," a round grassy mound, with a small chapel on the summit, connected to the town by a land bridge. The gulls soar over the little harbor front and galleries that sell shells and souvenirs. Over the Ship's Chandler, with thick-glass floats, fishing tackle, and seaboots in the window. On over the restaurant with the trawling net and lobster display. Above the Harbour Bar, Coffee, penny arcade with jukebox. Over the tea shop, plain and very English. Past the pier they fly, screeching and bitching over rotten fish lying in the ooze of low tide. To the lighthouse they sail and on over the second pier, with its lobster pots and crab cages. On up the hill over the tiny railway station and putting green, almost to the bus depot, highest point in the town before the London road begins. Then the gulls catch the down draft and sail into the town again, the sun gleaming on their pure white wings. Such handsome scavengers. I noticed that the Ship's Chandler sold the caps worn by the Breton fishermen who docked in St. Ives, and I decided I would be a handsome scavenger, too.

Gyp and I soon picked up the ways of the scene. After I bought the Breton cap, the money was all gone. To beg was the most direct way, and we made an entertainment for ourselves and our victims, who were usually young girls in pairs, down with families on holiday (one usually pretty, the other wearing glasses).

The approach was simple.

"Hello, love."

Ignored.

"Sweetheart?"

Giggles.

"Give us a tanner [six pence] for a cuppa tea, we're starvin'."

Reaction? Success!

Or Gypsy would dance up to a couple of girls, sidestepping shuffle, waving his outstretched fingers and clucking his tongue, wrap a big rough hand around the sweet girl and proceed to tell her fortune. All this with such speed and agility that he had her seated in no time, pouring out whatever came into his head, holding her hand, stroking her, and staring into her wide eyes. After all, he wore an earring.

"You'll 'ave six kids—two boys—you'll lose one; you've 'ad a disappointment, but you'll soon be surprised by . . . a tall dark man." And so on, while the girl and her friend would giggle and snigger, delight.

Gypsy Dave was brilliant. Dark-haired, earringed, expert at the soft touch, his feigned clumsiness was endearing to all. He stood taller than me and held himself proud, though he dressed sloppier than most Beats—and that was sloppy.

Soon we would persuade the girls to meet us at a café and they would pay. Or they would buy us "snouts," cigarettes, we poor wandering boys.

We would stroll around to the small bakery that sold the sweet bread called "saffron cake," a yellow loaf packed with raisins. The nice lady would give us yesterday's loaves for nothing. We washed it down with stolen milk. I'm just mad about saffron.

We prided ourselves on our ability to exist. We never thought of tomorrow, only of the night.

There were various places we had found in which to sleep—none of them beds. All the "dossers" knew each other and shared the places to bed down. The night was rarely comfortable, but when you are out of the wind, wrapped in your sleeping bag or roll, with cigarettes or a girl, then sleep comes quick. And when you awake, not having slept much, there is always the hot sandy beach to stretch out on and lose the stiffness in your bones; and when the sun rises high in the Cornish sky you feel a happiness unlike any other.

No one could sleep rough in the town itself—the late-night policeman saw to that. He would move any late-nighters from the wall by the harbor. Early in the year there were not so many Beats, and we slept on the sand; but by midsummer the policeman began to move us out of there. He was nice enough about it, even telling us to go to the pillbox down by the railway past The Rowans, a natural woodland. Pillboxes were roughly circular concrete huts situated strategically on hills and cliffs: they had slit windows and were full of tramp shit and old newspapers, yet they kept out the wind.

It was a weary but happy few who straggled up the hill away from the town on our way to a doss, the lamps of the harbor shining on the water like electric moons and the wind off the sea fresh, cigarettes glowing in the dark.

We were "carrying" and were going to make a joint when we bedded down. We showed some caution in those days but not much, as smoking hash was only done by the Beats, and the police were not yet on the lookout for it. Occasionally we even smoked joints in cinemas. Beats were a minority then, dropouts from art schools, campers, trad-jazz enthusiasts, blues singers, folk musicians who listened to obscure jazz records, blind singers, and jug bands. "Hippies" had not yet arrived. Everyone took pills of many sorts and talked their tongues dry as old leather up into the night, and sometimes even past the dawn. Apart from the lack of food, all the kids were healthy then, sleeping out under the stars.

Gypsy and I did not always hang out together. I was often alone, cruising along the edges of the town, looking and seeing. I used to pass the shelter by the lifeboat slope where the "old salts" smoked pipes, their backs to the boards upon which hundreds of names, oaths, promises, and obscenities had been carved. I strolled past and headed out of town to leave the bustle and climb the hill on the island. By now my face was hot from the jeering of the fishermen, because it was common for them to mock our long hair, our rags and tatters. They plainly did not want us to dirty up their nice clean town. Because I had my guitar slung on my back, they would call: "Give us a tune, then! Can ye play Over the Hills and Far Away"?

They never mentioned my limp, but I imagined them thinking that I was a freak. So, flushed from their gaze, I turned at the end of the front and passed through the cobbled streets to the island. I was still conscious of limping when I ascended the first slope.

Later, when I felt a twinge of hunger, I descended and went looking for tea in a café on the harbor front. I bummed a cup from a friend who had just been paid for cigarettes he had stolen. It was a fine, sunny day and after tea I went out onto the beach, lay on the sand, rolled up my jeans, put my Breton cap over my face, and sunbathed. Stars of sunlight filtered through the weave of the cloth when I opened my eyes, the smell of the warm material close to my face.

There were two girls on the beach, Beak and Freckles. Beak was a typical beatnik chick with a pale face, long, straight dark hair, heavily made-up eyes, blue denim shirt, and jeans. She sat on a black duffel coat, barefoot. Her classic Florentine features, beaked nose, tight little mouth, and beady black eyes gave you a bit of a chill. She was nervous and smoked cigarettes in jerks, laughing like a lunatic, very quickly, then stopping just as quick. I could hear her tinkling on a guitar and murdering a song in her nasal Joan Baez voice. " 'Fair young maid all in the garden, da da da . . . ' Oh fuck, what's that line?" She knew that she couldn't play well.

Freckles looked as alive and vibrant as Beak looked ghoulish and dead. She sang in a low sexy voice, " 'Strange young man, passerby . . . ' "

"Oh, 'ere 'e comes now," said Beak.

"He" arrived smiling, and Beak continued: "Look wot the dog brought up."

"Hello, Beak," the fat boy said.

I found out that he wasn't well liked and that his name was Derek. He had an insinuating way and never came up unless he wanted something. He had a job and digs—and perhaps that was his problem. We were proud of our vagrancy.

Derek was about six feet tall and flabby. He dressed in a leather jacket (even in the hot sun) and "real" shoes (unheard of). He grunted as he sat down on the sand, sweating, and pulled out a box of cigarettes. I peeked from under my cap. The sun was blinding.

"Can you smell somethin' dead?" sniffed Beak.

Freckles seemed embarrassed by her friend, her face turning crimson, but Derek just ignored Beak and opened his cigarettes. They were "specials," packed and selected to order, flat and long with Derek's name on them. Turkish Blend from the Burlington Arcade in London's West End.

Children brought cigarette butts up to Beak, while Derek lit up his special and put the box away. I raised myself on my elbows and looked at his cigarette closely. Fat Derek did not, it seemed, hand his cigarettes around; but I nodded to him for one. To spite Beak, I suppose, he gave me one; and I pulled up to him to get a light. He fired me up, half smiling, relishing the great gift of one of his specials, then offered Beak a light for her butt.

She said, "No, thanks," leaning heavily on each word. Then she struck a match on a pebble, breaking the match in the process.

The tobacco was tasty. I felt good—lying on the beach, smoking a Turkish Blend Special.

Beak stormed off in disgust, with Freckles in her wake.

"Do you wanna job, man?" asked Derek.

"Doing what?" It hadn't occurred to me to work.

"Pearl diving at the Harbour Bar—where I work."

To "pearl dive" was to wash dishes in a kitchen.

"I haven't any place to live." I wanted the job.

"If you take the job, man" (pause) "you know" (pause) "you can share a pad with me, man." Derek used the word "man" as every Beat does, but from him it sounded phoney.

"How much does the job pay?" I asked.

"Five pounds a week, and things to eat when you like."

It sounded ideal. Washing dishes was the only job longhairs could get in St. Ives, so I said, "OK, when do I start?"

"I'll ask Mr. Fowler, man, the owner, and let you know." Derek struggled to his feet, sweat now streaming down from under his short, straw-colored hair.

"I'll meet you t'night outside the Ship, I 'ave to go back on." He sniggered. He had been having his afternoon break from service.

Derek is rich, I reminded myself, holding the tobacco smoke in my lungs as if the Turkish Blend Special was a joint.

I stood outside the Ship Inn from opening time onward and waited for Derek. He strolled up in his leather jacket, a clean white shirt, and sandals with socks. Hoping to be invited to meet the boss, I had that afternoon gone up to a hut in the woods where I'd been dossing to pull out my other shirt from my rucksack. So there I posed, my jacket draped over my arm, best check shirt and jeans. Sure enough, in we went.

Sailing prints and *Punch* cartoons covered the walls of the saloon. We elbowed our way up to an old wooden beam by a huge ship's wheel, heavily lacquered. Derek asked me what I wanted to drink.

"Pint of ale?"

He shoved his flab toward the turtlenecked holiday yachtsmen and they parted to let him through. He came back with two pints clutched in his pudgy fingers, three bags of potato chips in his mouth.

"Kg na ga," he mumbled through his potato chips, and I took a pint from him.

The room fairly rattled on. Faces moved, mouths gaped, yet only a few of the more noisy people made clear speech.

"Aaah," gasped Derek, after a long pull at his beer. "That's better—wot a bloody racket in here—let's squeeze outside."

I welcomed the idea. We had just about finished the pints on the first pull, so Derek ordered two more but not before trying to embarrass me by asking if it was my round. Then he laughed with an uncomfortable snort and bought two more beers. We squashed out past the Kensington accents. The air was fresh and clean outside. We walked over to the wall and leaned against it. The night was soft. Folk stood about drinking, enjoying the balmy evening.

"That's so much better," said Derek. "Thought I'd faint in there. Like a bloody railway station—puffin' away and gettin' steamed up."

He brought out some cigarettes, but not his specials. We smoked in silence for a while. I looked at the girls, so airy and light, floating by in their summer frocks.

"An old woman threatened to piss herself in the arcade today, man," he suddenly exclaimed.

"What?"

"Old woman—meths drinker—can't think where from—trying to put metal washers in the machine and—"

"How old?"

"Old, I don't know, man—oldish. I had to throw her out, didn't I, an' she pissed herself right there in the middle of the floor, man—between the bagatelle and the fruit machine."

"That must have excited you, eh, man?" I laughed into my jug.

"Oh yeah, wonderfully, she pissed all down her leg—screaming 'Rape'—I got it on my shirt."

"What?"

"Blood."

"Blood?"

"She cut her hands squeezing the washers, an' I got blood on my shirt."

I looked at his shirt.

"On my other shirt."

"Sounds like a good place to work," I said.

"You've got the job, man," he said casually.

I was sort of pleased yet apprehensive.

"Start tomorrow at eight-thirty sharp—don't let me down." Derek had taken me under his wing, it seemed. Then he told me of the place we could rent on the beach, and that we should go and see it during the break.

I had to make an impression tomorrow. I needed sleep to rise early. I drained my pint and turned to go. As I made to leave, he pushed a bag of potato chips into my hand.

"For supper." He smiled. Perhaps he wasn't a bad chap after all?

A pack of Rockers on motorcycles roared up the hill through the town, the sound reverberating in the narrow streets. I turned left at the pier and walked the dark road up to the secret hut in the woods where I was bedding down. I felt elated as I climbed the rise to the high road above the town. I saw the lights of the harbor below and steadily rose into the dark, passing some French trawlermen singing Breton songs softly by the station wall.

Once on the high road by the coast, I stretched my step and strode gaily along in the dark between the ocean and the forest. It was a road where no cars came. Charcoal blue clouds scudded over the moon, the lights of the town fading behind me. But I felt a little scared as I searched the old stone wall for the gap that led into the woods.

The hut lay about twenty-five feet back in the thick undergrowth. I thought of the fellow who had originally built the hut. Chunky was his name, and he was built like a dwarf, crouching, heavyset, with small hands and feet. He swayed from side to side as he walked, one shoulder forward and lower than the other. But being very handy, he had constructed the hut of stout branches, intertwined with smaller ones, the whole structure heavy with leaves. Gyp had helped Chunky in the construction of the woodland lair. The woods belonged to the Castle Hotel, and we joked about staying in the best hotel in St. Ives.

At last I found a familiar crack in the old, mossy wall and paused before entering. I listened hard in the dark undergrowth, and smelled the dark aroma of the forest night. Far down the slope behind me, the sea sounded on the rocks. An owl hunted over the grasslands beyond the railway line. I listened. No sound within. I pushed softly into the undergrowth, making my way slowly on hands and knees. Twigs snapped and cracked and my breath sounded louder than normal.

The beer had given me a little courage, and I whispered, "Anyone home?"

The silence surged back. I crept along like a mole. It was different in the day, but now what light there was made weird shapes of the leaves above me. At last I felt the outside of the hut. These leaves, being dead, rustled differently.

"Hello—anyone in?" I whispered. I pulled myself in through the small entrance and felt my groundsheet stretched on the floor. Then I got the fright of my life. I touched a leg—and a voice spoke.

"Who's there?"

"Someone," I answered, stupidly.

"John here."

"Don," I said, a little more sure.

It was John Vanstone, an older Beat. I knew him vaguely. I bedded down and looked up at the shapes in the roof.

"Like pigs they are," he said, strangely.

Later I was awakened by his mumbling. I opened my eyes and felt him close to my face. He held a large bowie knife to my throat. But then he just laughed and turned over again. I slept until sunup.

Let me say it again: The only way to sleep well is to sleep in the open. With the smell of the greenery and the feel of the wind sharp in your nostrils. Always the "chorus of the dawn" awakes you and the world is fresh and new. The birds settle down a bit, and you are snug as a bug in a feather down sleeping bag as you roll over for another snooze. But today I had to get up and go to work. John slept on as I left the hut. I didn't know the time so I went straight down into the town to find out.

"A working man," I thought (Gyp would laugh his socks off). I jumped the wall and buttoned my denim jacket against the cold.

The sea was glassy calm in the early morning. Gulls sat on the rocks, cackling and chuckling. I descended into the cobbled streets as the milkman made his rounds. I followed him and stole a bottle from a doorway and put it in my jacket. I had a breakfast of the potato chips that Derek had given me and milk, lovely cold milk; creamy and clean. I lit half a cigarette I had saved from the night before.

The clock tower said twenty to seven. I was way too early and a little cold. A few Beats were about. These ones looked as if they were new to the dossing game and had slept cold or not at all. But they were young like me and happy anyway to be on the road.

I walked to keep warm. After seven the town slowly woke up.

Windows opened. Doors let into small, scrubbed kitchens. Carpets were hung over balconies, and the womenfolk began the day with their smoke signals. I strolled by the bakery to smell the bread and asked for any old saffron cakes. The nice lady gave me three, not old at all.

The boy from the Ship Inn whistled out into the day, rolling an empty barrel down his alley into the courtyard. The gulls hung about on the seawall, expectant. I drifted around until a quarter to eight and watched to see if Derek came.

I met Dominic in the shelter by the water tap. He sat scratching a piece of slate with a small clasp knife. Dominic was a jolly character with a soft, blond curly beard and hair that encircled his face in an untidy fashion. Like so many of the kids in St. Ives that year he had come down from the factory towns of the north, bringing with them that warmth of heart for which they are famous. The girls would always call you "luv."

"Won't you come for a cup of tea and a swim, luv?"

Open-hearted straight talkers with a wealth of humor and imagination, if they liked you they showed it. If they didn't, they told you so, too. I loved those streetwise but warm northern girls, and I remember how, often enough, waking up squeezed into one sleeping bag, two Beats would be surprised to meet each other after a wild night.

Now Dominic sat there in his sloppy beatnik clothes, scratching a design on the little bit of slate that he would hang on a leather bootlace to sell to tourists.

"Mornin', Dominic."

"Hello, man," he returned in his monotone half-serious way.

"Where have you dossed?" I asked.

"That place up the coast."

Some campers had pitched tents on the cliffs, and Beats often shared with climbing-booted, hairy-legged girls and boys who had pots and cans, can openers, and other paraphernalia that they carried around with them.

"I start work today," I told him.

"Good for you. Where?"

"Harbour Bar."

"Washing up?"

"Yeah, man."

"I'll tap ye for a pound at the end of the week," he said, and laughed.

I strolled by the Harbour Bar, trying to give the impression that I was not waiting for anything. Derek suddenly appeared from a passageway in the seafront terrace. "Come on, then, we're late," he said, although we were not.

I started work, and the boss was pleased with me. He was a short man in his middle forties with greasy black hair, thinning on top. He wore one of those synthetic cardigans with piping and cavalry twill trousers. Quite well off.

I got the general idea of the job in a few minutes. Around ten-thirty Derek slipped me a roll and butter with a cup of tea.

I worked behind the snack bar in a small room four-foot by four, out of sight of the customers. I had a sink in which I washed the plates and cups and cutlery used at the counter where Derek served. I liked the job: In came the things, I submerged them, cleaned them, dried them, and there you are, simple. Plenty of time to think about what to do with the money at the end of the week.

I had a little window that opened onto a small yard, the sill level with the cobbles, which led to the front and the harbor. Everything is small scale in St. Ives. From the entrance of the Harbour Bar to the water is no more than thirty paces. If I leaned out of my window I could just see the tourists walk by the alley.

I was in my own little world. On the other side of the thin wall stood the jukebox, which played the Beatles's hit of the month: "Thank You, Girl." The jukebox was in the room with the slot machines, three rows along the walls and another two back-to-back in the center. The sound of the slots was continuous as Derek served hamburgers, coffee, tea, and cakes.

I had a good feeling—I think it was independence. After I had eaten my first square meal in weeks, we took our break and walked around the beach to view the flat that Derek had found.

All the kids were out in the sun now, and music came from the beach, mingled with the laugher and the taunts of Beak. I did not want them to notice who I was with, so I kept to the far side of the promenade. Although Derek evidently liked me, and I him, there was an air of deception about our relationship. He wanted to know my Beat friends, and I wanted to know his contacts with the real world and to get work.

By force of road habit, I set people up to give me something. I always gave of myself in return, but seldom in coin. Derek and I talked as we walked of Hank Williams. I was surprised he had heard of him.

" 'Lo-ong go-one, and no-ow I'm lo-on-some blu-ue,' " he droned in a nasal yodel. He was just saying what Hank records he had when a well-traveled Beat turned the corner, dressed in washed-out blue jeans and jacket, worn Spanish boots, and a small, knitted woollen army hat. His skin was a pale olive and his eyes narrow, almost like slits. As he passed into the sunlight, he pulled at the woollen hat and his jet-black Apache hair fell around his shoulders. The cat's vibe impressed me. I was to meet this stranger later on down the road.

" 'Jambalaya' I like too," I heard Derek say from a distance. I said, "Yeah." He had not noticed the cat who'd flashed by blazing out of the sky.

We turned the corner and walked down a sandy slope to Porthmere Beach, a long, pleasant cove with rocks at both ends to climb on and sit to smoke and watch the sea foam and gurgle in and out of the crevices and crab pools. Here the town came right onto the beach. A long row of warehouses stood close to the waves, old cracked walls with doors and windows that opened onto the sand. Many lived here, artists and writers, potters and their families. At one end where we had started down the slope was a storm-weathered door with two dirty panes of glass set in it. All of the doors in the long row had three-foot-high steps to keep the sand and the winter tides out of the houses.

I jumped up and peered in. It was derelict. Great! A pad on the sand. Derek stood in the sunshine eyeing my appraisal. He was chuffed, proud of his find. He took me around the back to the street, and we entered a dark courtyard onto which all of the dwellings on this block faced. A thirsty old tree stood in the center of the little yard, and a rusty pram and heaps of broken crockery lay shady and cool underneath. We stepped over the junk, and Derek led me to the corner where the flat was. It was dark and dim, but we peered in through the cobwebbed glass at a small, dirty kitchen and were happy.

The place had undoubtedly lain empty for some time, but we would soon have it together. Derek quickly clinched the deal: £2.10s a week. When we moved in we called it Studio 2000.

Wind Catcher

I was happy. I lived in Studio 2000 on a beach.

One day, as I washed my jeans in the Harbour Bar sink, Derek leaned into my little kitchen.

"I've told Greg to get those girls, man."

We had parties every other night in the Studio, and tonight we were having a big one.

"Did you tell Stodge and Gram?" I asked.

"No—are they in town?"

I leaned out of my window and looked up the alley. Julian was diving for coins thrown by tourists. "John's out front—can you ask him if he's seen 'em? They bed down together up at the hut now."

We were getting buckets of beer and large cider bottles from the Ship at seven o'clock. The party was on everyone's mind. We had the Studio together by now and had even painted a driftwood sign with its name outside the beach door, which now served as our front entrance. There was one old single bed, and Derek slept in it. He hung his drip-dry shirts up on wire hangers. I slept on a mattress on the floor in a bag.

Tonight the usual crowd came, but with newcomers. The party was soon in full swing, the beer flowing, the joints blowing, guitars bashing, pill heads freaking, but the real cool Beats were making a whole scene, lying in a corner rolling and smoking, rolling and smoking.

Derek was annoying everyone. "Let's climb the Island, man, and jump off the cliff. . . . Let's say the Lord's Prayer backward in the mirror."

Half-closed eyes of smokers stared at him. He always got more nervous when he was high.

Then a girl at the door said, "The police are asking for someone."

Most hushed, some jeered. None of us were scared. As I say, smoking and the like was still a mystery, especially to the country police; and the inspector was a nice chap who never pushed his way into the room with his lads. Now he excused himself for interrupting and read from a list of runaways.

"Carol Latchingworth, is she here? Your mother is worried. John Frobisher and William Sedgewood?"

Of course, if the runaways were there, no one would let on.

The nice inspector was our object of scorn. He didn't deserve it. Once I made a caricature collage of him. I stuck purple hearts and cigarette papers on it with slogans and mounted the artwork high up on the wall of Studio 2000 for all to see. We all whooped with delight, and I puffed up with pride when the rest of my friends praised my work. What an evil little sod!

The thing was, I had risen in everyone's opinion. The party giver—the beginning of my liking for crowds. Gypsy just smiled. He knew me well.

The summer moved on, with glorious days and star-filled nights. The tide came in and went out, leaving wonderful delights for the beachcomber. I felt the magic and often paddled in the rock pools, gazing into the small submarine lakes of delicate-hued seaweed and translucent creatures there on the shore between the two worlds. I imagined myself swimming there and meanwhile the sea, all-powerful, capable of terrible destruction, would lap and trickle, soft and playful at my feet. Wonderful.

As a child I had read stories of the sea in awe and wonder. I had read of Cousteau and the bicycle trips down to the Red Sea with his new invention, the Aqua-Lung. Later, I watched Hans and Lotte Hass on their TV show. It seemed so easy with an Aqua-Lung and a beard (Lotte looked good in her swimsuit, too). The sea would feature in many of my songs, the seagull, the handsome scavenger with the lovely wing, my totem bird.

One day a fellow came around to the Studio with a proposition. Would I begin a crab and lobster business with him? He said that the restaurants paid high prices for them and all we had to do was dive. Michael was a pearl diver for the Reganna Manor Hotel and he was "together." He had his chick in a bed-and-breakfast place in the council estate high up on the hill.

"We could dive off Crab Rock," he said.

By chance we knew Damian, who had a small room on Crab Rock. Damian had his father's bright red hair but not his stature. The old man would strut around town like a Viking giant, dressed in a long artist's smock, corduroy trousers, and sneakers with no socks. Michael and I tore around to see Damian.

Now, of course, the local fishermen kept the whereabouts of the lobster beds a tight secret. On the way we paused and actually asked one old salt. Maybe we had the romantic notion of him laying his "fishy wisdom" on us two young lads—then we would be on the way to success. The old "kipper" just smiled and kept his toothless mouth clammed shut.

Then, when we reached Damian's yard on Crab Rock, Michael told me he had been promised the loan of a boat from a restaurant owner should we come across any crustacea. So with no idea at all, we plunged into the water, wearing masks and flippers. We floated around for a while until Ben came panting down the rocks, having just run all the way from the harbor.

"Shark! Shark! Shark!" he screamed. "There's a shark in the bay." We left the water faster than any flying fish, scrambling up the rocks and scraping our knees on the way to dry land.

That was the beginning and the end of our crab and lobster business.

Sharks do wander into Cornish bays once in a while, but they are of the basking variety, I later learned. Dull-witted, toothless, and not killers. But when you're in the water, a shark is a shark. We ran around with our friend Ben to see the monster. She was a tiger shark, about sixteen feet long, with a silly looking smile on her face. Crowds had gathered and were peering over the rail. Some of the Beats, quick to make a shilling, offered to dive for coins in the shark-infested bay.

❖

I was with Gypsy on the seawall one summer night when he met Alice. The perfect sunny afternoon had softened as Gypsy and I walked along the front, our hair salty after a swim, just hanging out and looking for chicks to con, making the most of half a fag, when Gyp saw her. We would notice new girls immediately when they arrived, and whoever saw one first had first blag or chat-up.

She sat on the wall in the shadows by the lifeboat slope. She had been watching us, but she pretended she had not. Gyp strolled over to her, full of confidence in his raggy duffel coat, scarf around his neck, and tongue in his cheek. She sat, small and petite, on the wall, ready for him. Her size was deceptive for she quickly showed that she could hold her own in any approach, as most of the lassies from the north can. Dressed in a blue, waisted peacoat and slacks, her short, golden hair was cut close to her face, framing her small features, from out of which shone sparkling gray eyes, flecked with cobalt blue. Her skin was tanned to a subtle shade, and there were delightful patches of pink on her nose where the skin had peeled.

"Hello, love, what's your name?" Gypsy asked.

"Alice, what's yours?"

For once Gyp was speechless. It turned out that she was three years older than us and not a Beat chick. Down on a long vacation from Manchester, where her father owned a gas station, she was living in St. Ives with her gran in the care of her uncle. Attracted by the carefree way of the young beatniks, she had arranged this meeting as only a woman can.

Gypsy and Alice made a strange couple—him so tall and sloppily dressed, and she so delicately small and neat.

That first night I was not so much attracted to her as Gyp was. That was to change.

A few days later, I was first to see another girl. She looked like a tease, and I had a flash of caution as we walked up to her. She was with a plain and prim spotty little girl with glasses, who was dressed in a shapeless anorak and slacks.

Leah was from Nottingham. About five foot ten, she had long dark hair and was about seventeen years old. Hazel eyes were set in her square face. She smoothed back her hair with tiny hands, nails bitten down to the quick. But this girl looked very sure of herself. Gypsy fancied it as soon as he clocked her. She sat, sketching. She screwed up her eyes in the sun, and the breeze lifted her light frock, showing her panties to us. She didn't care.

Although Gypsy was seeing Alice, he made a play for Leah. But since I'd spotted her first, I prepared to chat her up, too. I made some banal remark about her sketches. She was an art student on holiday, she said. I was a folksinger, I replied. Stuff like that. She had nowhere to sleep. I knew of a place along the beach, a little cave. Soon I was carrying Leah's bedroll toward the sexy carpet of long grass on the slope of the hill. It was hot, and I could smell the girl in her.

Walking ahead I flopped down on the grass and waited for her to come up. She sucked a blade of grass and swore. "What a fucking long way."

I liked her coarseness. It turned me on. Down she lay, stretching her long legs out, uninhibited, to sun them. She had fine dark hair on her thighs and calves, and I imagined the dark triangle. I said, perhaps too quickly to hide my eagerness: "You can see the Harbour Bar from here."

"So what?"

Suddenly Leah turned over onto her front, dragging her frock up over her panties, and I felt the pressure in my jeans. I see now that she was teasing me, but then I didn't know it. I had thought sex was the farthest thing from her mind, and that I would have to creep up on her body delicately and have my fingers in her panties before she knew it. With some girls my crafty approach turned them on, but not Leah.

Being close to her face, I now turned my head down and tried to kiss her. She grabbed me through my jeans. I was taken by surprise—it was a first for me. I kissed her full on the mouth, but then she drew her hand away. I was annoyed. This was not the way it should be. She was to be conquered so that I could cradle her after she came. This was altogether different: she was in charge and wasn't willing to be conquered. I got angry with her, then she suddenly pushed herself away and straightened her frock, leaving me shaking on the grass. I was ashamed and angry.

"Do you want to fuck me, little boy?" Leah sneered. "Who do you think you are anyway, Don Juan?"

"You don't know what you're missing," I choked, trying to regain some self-respect.

"Hah, don't make me laugh," she cut in. "Have you got any cigarettes?"

I did, but I didn't want to give them to her. She had become my enemy.

But I lit her a cigarette with trembling hands. She took the packet and laughed in my face.

"No, you don't." I grabbed her wrist.

Leah twisted away with no trouble, got up to go, grabbed her bedroll, and strode down the hill, singing. With my cigarettes!

The fire still burned between my legs. I started rolling like a log, down the hill, toward the beach below. I got dizzier and dizzier, faster and faster. I saw the white clouds and blue sky roll around as I gained momentum. Thump . . . I hit the sand and panted hard. Grabbing a tussock of sea grass to steady myself, I lifted my head and shoulders. The beach spun before my eyes, and I blinked to gain some balance. When the world stopped moving, Leah was nowhere to be seen. Good riddance.

Two children splashed in the waves—with red bathing suits and plastic shovels. The afternoon was growing old, and the few holidaymakers were beginning to pack up their beach junk and make it back to the little boarding-houses for their tea. I fancied a Cornish pastie.

I began the heavy-sand walk to the town. I could still smell Leah on me, so near yet so far. The sun had fallen low and a magic glow touched everything. The golden light brought each part of the scene into a strange and wonderful focus. As I gazed along the deserted beach, my eye caught a glimpse of a couple in the distance. The wind moved over the grasses and lifted a girl's floral print frock. The couple rose and walked up the beach, arm in arm. It was Leah and Gypsy.

I knew that he had succeeded where I had failed. He had taken her how she wanted to be taken.

I had looked for romance where there was none to find. He had simply wanted her, that was all. So they shared a secret that I was denied. As they neared I felt a hatred for Gypsy. I stared as they passed by me. She looked at me without showing any sign of our previous meeting on the hill.

"See ya in the Ship tonight, man," hailed Gyp, as he proudly stomped by with Leah on his arm. He winked at me to let me know that he'd had her.

Leah stayed in town for a while, flirting with everyone. I worked away in the Harbour Bar and soon forgot her. One day on the beach a crowd of us were goofing around making merry, singing and shouting. Gypsy was there, Dominic, Beak, and Freckles. It was very hot, and the beach was packed with tourists and children. I had taken my break and was relaxing after lunch.

"Here comes Bluey," said Dominic, holding yet another piece of slate and scratching a fish design on the soft surface.

"He's back soon," squeaked Sue.

"Hello, Bluey," another called, raising his voice above the barking of two dogs by the wall.

Bluey walked up with this spotty beanpole of a boy who was patting him on the back. "Nice work, nice work, Bluey man," said Spotty, still patting him. Everyone crowded around to hear what the "nice work" was.

Bluey was a short, stocky fellow with longish corn-colored hair. He wore a denim jacket, jeans of a faded–flower blue, and soft suede boots. His whole aura was gentle—yet strong.

"You should 'ave seen 'im do it," went on Spotty, who was very pleased to have had the privilege of seeing Bluey's nice work and then having the story to tell.

"Hello, Bluey," said Dominic.

Bluey smiled and nodded.

"What happened?" shrieked Beak.

All gazes were on Bluey, who flopped down onto the sand, angled his arm under his head, closed his eyes, and spoke in a low tone. "I nearly got a haircut, that's all." Bluey then rolled over onto his back and tuned us out.

So now Spotty had his audience on the edge of their seats. Beak, livid and scorched lobster red in her bikini, stabbed her finger into Spotty's shoulder.

"Tell us then, you 'orrible little squirt."

"Well," began Spotty, pausing to ask for a fag, his only chance this side of the story.

Beak rolled her eyes and said, "Oh, Gawd, anyone got a fag for the freak?"

Pete the Purple Heart lay in the sand snoring with a packet of Embassy beside him. We thought he must have had a cold kip and was now catching up on sleep, so we 'borrowed' one of his cigarettes. Spotty puffed twice and began.

"You know the 'Trip Round the Bay' men, those Cornish blokes who stand in front of them boards with pictures of their boats on them?"

"Yeah."

"Well, Bluey was walking down by their pitch, just come in town, and I was—"

"Don't wanna 'ear about you," spat Beak.

"I," insisted Spotty, "was standing by the wall, and one of the Cornish creeps up behind Bluey with scissors to cut his hair off . . . and all his mates keeping quiet and feeling clever when he jumps on Bluey and clings to his back, and all the Cornish cheer. Then" (pause) "Bluey, neat as you like, threw him in the harbor as if he was pulling off his sweater."

Everybody broke up with laughter—they knew how filthy the harbor was. This was a victory for the Beats against the Cornish, and Bluey was a hero from then on.

Alice stepped onto the beach, and Gypsy called her over. She came and sat down. She wore white jeans and a candy-striped top with no sleeves. Gypsy made a lot out of kissing her hello. Alice mimicked him. She had brought us some food, titbits and leftovers from her gran's table.

"Gran says I eat too mooch."

Gypsy laughed as he munched.

" 'Ullo, Don." She smiled at me. " 'Ere."

I took a cupcake. Her hand felt cool. She went on in a musical way, "What 'appened to Bluey?"

"Oh, a fisherman tried to cut his hair and Bluey threw him in the water," answered Gyp.

"Serves them right." Alice's eyes flashed suddenly. "Serves them bluddy right for being so stewpid."

I had taken more and more notice of her as the summer moved on. Gypsy wrapped his arms around her in a clumsy fashion, crushing her little body in his big hug.

"Geroff, ya bit brute," she protested. I sensed real disapproval in her playful remark.

Pete snored on beside us.

" 'E's deep asleep, that wun," Alice said, peeling a hard-boiled egg for Gypsy. The sounds of the beach droned on, the haze shimmering over the ocean in the exceptionally hot afternoon. From the distance a radio could be heard playing the Beatles' "Please Please Me."

I looked at Pete sprawled out on the beach. The sand had got into his beard. As I stared, he gurgled suddenly as if he was having difficulty breathing. I screwed my eyes up and saw the sand in his mouth. At that moment Alice noticed, too, and she said, "Is 'e all right?"

I crawled over to Pete and put my finger in his open mouth. It was filled with sand. I shook him, but he didn't move. I shook harder. He was unconscious. The sand had been slowly drawn down into his throat, and he had a tiny channel left, through which he drew his gurgling breath. I started digging out the sand with my finger. Gypsy and Alice sensed the emergency faster than the rest, who just continued to laugh at each other and sing.

"Get the ambulance," snapped Alice. Gypsy grew afraid. Bluey unclenched Pete's hand and found an empty box of pills. Overdose. Suicide.

Panic quickly spread, faces fell, someone called the ambulance. I grabbed the empty pillbox and ran to the pier at the far end of the beach. I threw the box into the swirling waters on the windward side of the pier. Why, I don't know.

They took Pete away and pumped him empty. He lived. Everyone felt down—after all, he had been with us, sleeping all afternoon. He came back from the dead and adjusted slowly. He had been a strange enough fellow before his overdose; now, walking around the town with his pale face, he looked frightening. It seemed that he had lost in love. He checked into a hospital. I never saw him again.

Two weeks later, I waited for Alice to bring little "sweet things" from her gran's again. Gypsy had been seeing her less and less, and even though I sort of felt he still held "ownership" over her, I also felt that a relationship was evolving between her and me. Did she know? I never asked her later whether she felt it grow. As I waited I practiced some chords on my guitar.

This, my first guitar, was an old "box." Not much to look at, but to me it was fantastic and it was mine. I had brought it for £3.10s from John Vanstone. It had been a nylon-string Spanish guitar once. John had put on steel strings when he worked in a violin workshop back up north. Now, steel-string guitars usually have geared machine heads to tune with, but John had left the old wooden pegs on. This made it very hard to tune. I worked away at it for hours, the creaking black ebony pegs giving me no end of trouble. Evidently, John had once played classical style and had changed to steel strings to play the blues, and he played well. The fact that he played so well made me surprised when he offered to sell the guitar to me. Apparently he wanted to go up to London and score an ounce to bring back down to Cornwall to blow it and sell it.

I had played some drums back home and had tinkled a few chords on my schoolfriend Mick Sharman's guitar. As soon as this guitar was mine, I had run down to the shore to sit and play. I strummed to myself and was knocked out. I vowed to practice all the time and try to master the finger style. I learned "Working on the Railroad," "Careless Love," and "Cocaine Blues" (well, nearly), all songs that John Vanstone used to sing. When he did return from London he would still play his old box and teach me songs.

Now Alice stepped onto the sand. She looked radiant in a short beach jacket over her swimsuit. She knelt beside me.

"Hiya, kid." She sighed and opened her little basket.

She took out two pages of writing paper, on which she had copied out the words to a song I wanted to learn, "East Virginia," from the Joan Baez record.

"Alice!" I thanked her with a look, but she snatched the lyrics away when I reached for them.

"Not yet," she teased, sticking her tongue out and pressing it against her top lip. "This is a sad song for the evening and this is your break time. Eat this and then we can swim." She handed me an apple, and I crunched into it.

"Let's take a skiff out from Porthcurno Beach," I said.

"How mooch do they cost?"

"Not much. Anyway, I'm paying," I said, indignantly. "I work, you know."

Alice placed her hand on my bare arm and looked at me for a long time. Then, screwing her nose up, she squeezed me and reached for her fags. She always had cigarettes, plenty. Her skin had bronzed in the few days since we'd first met. She unbuttoned her jacket to cool herself. We had not yet kissed.

I never thought there was any gulf between us, despite the age gap. I felt really pleased that Alice, an older girl and very lovely, favored me with her company. I worked; I had a pad. And now, perhaps, I had a girl?

We ran around to Porthcurno Beach. I went over the lifeguard, tanned and muscular, keeper of the skiffs and guardian of the sand. I paid him the deposit for the bit of wood and paddle. Alice and I pushed it out into the bay. We sat on the long strip of coconut matting nailed to the wood and trailed our legs over the side. I paddled us out, singing "A life on the ocean wave." Alice was laughing and shouting "Careful!" as the little waves splashed us.

The sky was cloudless, the sounds of the beach far behind. We were alone, probably for the first time since our original meeting. We felt a calm descend upon us. Far on the horizon a tiny fishing boat could be seen.

"Oh, Don, this is loovly."

We were friends. I paddled slowly. The skiff gently lapped the water. Alice held on behind me and rested her head on my back, perhaps, I thought, more for contact than comfort. Then she placed her tiny feet together in front of me and just squeezed. We had touched. So good was our feeling that we quite forgot where we were. The dark blue of the water drowned any unease. The sun shone bright and yellow. A perfect day.

"Let's paddle all the way around to the harbor," I said, feeling adventurous.

Alice just laughed and splashed her face with water. Her hair shone gold as the sun. She was a brown-skinned girl with eyes now as blue as the sky. Her lips parted, but she said nothing. So I paddled furiously, which broke Alice up into happy, happy laughter. I was free as a bird, silly yet sensitive, and we played as children, floating on a dreamy sea, wishing for nothing.

We turned the point with a "Land ahoy!" and a "Here we come." We had arrived in the town harbor. The tide was out a long way and we beached our skiff by the huge trawlers lying on the rippled sand, their great chains and anchors buried deep down, garlands of green mermaids' hair entwined in the rusty links.

Then we swam and frolicked in the shallow water. Folk looked down from the pier and smiled. We sported and teased, taking more liberties with each other and becoming more intimate in our play. Then, feeling overly confident, I said "Let's go around to Porthmere Beach and call on the kids in the Studio."

Now I paddled out toward the big rocks. It was not until we met the swell that we checked our laughter and took account of what was happening. We had left the pier behind, and the town was out of sight. The sea broke white on the black rocks, and the waves rolled large, washing over the skiff. As much as I tried I could make no headway into the next bay. We were in a current and moving out to sea. We became concerned but not afraid. I think we were beyond fear that day.

"Can you swim?" I joked.

"No," she said. "But I was born with a mask," she went on.

"What's that?"

"Well, if you're born with a thin skin over yer face then you can never drown," she explained, as calm as if she sat on a see-saw in a garden.

"Good," I said, looking down into the depths. We were over the rocks now and huge fronds of sea wrack surged in the swell. I even thought I saw a manta ray swim underneath our little plank of wood. I had no fear of drowning. It was the big fish I feared. Whatever, we were in a fix. The land was some way behind us now, and the breeze had picked up on this open stretch of coastline.

Then salvation chugged up over the trough of a great swell from the open sea. The fisherman we had seen earlier spotted us. We called to him, waving our arms. He picked us up. We sat in his little boat while he secured the skiff with a rope. Under our bare feet the mackerel were twitching and jumping.

"Silly bloody fools," the old man shouted above the spluttering of his outboard motor. "Three-mile-an-'our tide a-goin' out—silly bloody fools, who told you to come this far?"

We took the scolding, holding hands and smelling the fish strong in our nostrils. After asking us from which bay we had come, the fisherman dropped us off in the shallow water. Finishing off his lecture with a disgusted grunt, he was gone.

On the beach the lifeguard stood with his hands on his hips, laughing at us as we splashed up to him, beaching the toy boat.

"Come on, love, let's be going," I said. "I've got to get back to work now." We got into our clothes, grabbed our towels, and I took her hand as we walked along the sand.

I was very excited and proud of our adventure, and I couldn't wait to tell everyone. I could see that Alice, too, felt a special glow in her inner self. We had shared a precious time together.

We ran into town, swishing our towels in the air, and flew down the harbor front. I stopped to compose myself and assume some measure of regret for the inconvenience I had caused my boss by being late. So arranging my face into a suitable expression, I blurted out my awful story to Mr. Fowler.

I was sacked on the spot.

Sacked! I had worked two weeks and four days, a record by my standard. Could he not see how free from guilt I was? Sacked! I picked up the £6.15s owed to me and took Alice for a cup of tea in the Jolly Sailor.

"Do you care?" she asked, really concerned.

"Naw, I was getting fed up anyway." It was true. I slung my jacket over my shoulder and slipped my fingers into Alice's little hand. Her palm was wet. We walked slowly through the passageway. A one-eyed cat strolled elegantly down toward us on the old, worn flagstones.

It was cool in the alleyway, and I felt so good just being with Alice. We turned into Fore Street and there was Gypsy, out of his head on pills and in earnest conversation with a pal named Eddie. They walked fast, stopping every now and again. Gypsy, his arm around Eddie, was listening hard, licking his lips like a lizard and nervously clicking his fingers, waiting for a break in the constant flow of speech to have his say.

Alice and I started. We were both scared that Gyp would find out about us, if the truth were known, but we both pretended not to notice each other's reaction. Gyp was really stuck on Alice. She and I knew this too well. I also felt that curious rift between pals when a serious threat appears in the form of a dazzling girl. Truth was, I was falling for Alice. This might mean Gyp and I would be split apart. Gyp and Eddie had not seen us, but I called out to make us known and cover my fear.

"Hey, man."

"Donno, man." Gypsy turned in a flash, the "speed" in his veins pumping a split-second reaction. Quick as a flash he had forgotten the gist of his conversation with Eddie.

"Alicedarlincomeandmeetthisgreatcateddiejustmethimhe'stoomuch." The words flew from his mouth as if they were knitted and he made low grunts in the back of his throat. Gypsy ground his back teeth, and the muscles in his jaw stood out from his face. The pupils of the two Beats' eyes almost filled the irises, so stoned were they that day. Eddie swallowed again and again, choking softly.

They were in need of liquid, and I thought we would be encumbered for tea. But no, they were moving so fast that they quickly passed by on their way to nowhere in particular, talking in hushed whispers, imparting great revelations to each other about the truth and the way.

Shadows lengthened down the cobbled street. Gulls wheeled in from the harbor and we raised our eyes. We forgot everything and made our way down to Alice's gran's, passing one of the small shops with trays of buttercup yellow clotted cream, hot scones, and jam. Young folk were walking and laughing with cardboard plates full of fish and chips, the smell floating on the early evening air. We hurried on.

"My gran's been on to me again. She knows I hang out with you lot."

"They're all the same, relations, feel like they own you," I said.

We reached the big white house in shadows. I remembered the new song Alice had copied out for me, and I was dying to play it.

"Let's go for a little ramble," I said.

"Where?"

"Anywhere, along the coast."

"But . . ."

"Come around tomorrow to the Studio; we'll just leave."

She looked at me. This was what she was longing for. Adventure. Unexpectancy. No idea of where. "OK," she gasped.

"Goo' night, luv."

"Goo' night, Don."

> I was born and raised in East Virginia
> North Carolina I did go
> And there I met a pretty little woman
> Her name, and age I did not know.
> —*"East Virginia," Lomax IV, 144*

Bright early morning sun shone in through the beach door of the Studio as I awoke in my down-filled commando sleeping bag. I found Alice sitting astride me, very intimate, very nice. She had brought sandwiches for my breakfast. All the dossers had left, and it was peaceful.

Her eyes were made up with mascara, a little pale stick on her lips. Her delicate nails were long and well cared for, a city girl. We both knew we were crossing Gypsy by leaving, but a change of scene was so much on our minds.

We stole up to the bus station through the Sunday streets. Then we sat upstairs in the double decker, watching the twin bays of St. Ives recede and the trees rush past us as we made our getaway.

In the old Victorian seaside resort of Brixham in Devon we got off and walked together through the rain to a small park. Passing strangers stared at us as we laughed and fooled around in the miserable day. Alice shivered. We would have to find somewhere to sleep. We had a little money so we headed for a row of brightly painted terraces built on the steep old streets of the harbor town. It occurred to us that we would be refused by the bed-and-breakfast establishments, so Alice stuffed a jumper under her duffel coat and pretended she was pregnant. As it happened, the lady of the first house was quite easygoing and we took some supper in her kitchen with two swarthy fishermen, who were intrigued by our vagabond life.

That night love came easy and love came slow, as only lovers know.

A few days later, we walked down to the busy little harbor and ran into a friend from St. Ives. He told us that Alice's gran was very upset, and the police were looking for us.

Our wonderful little escape was over, and I took her back. We hitched all the way and were found some miles from the bay by a police car. Inside the car was Alice's "uncle," who turned out to be her fiancé. I narrowly escaped a beating. I was left by the roadside, with a warning never to come back to St. Ives.

I did go into town, but it was not the same. Alice had been taken back to Manchester, and I was not welcome when I called at her gran's house.

I never saw Alice again, and yet now I had a feeling of the kind of woman I was looking for. She would be loving; she would be tender. Soon I would meet such a one.

Folksinger

The summer was over and my life had changed. I headed back to my parents' place. Ten hours, hitching through dark little villages, sleeping in fields on the way and dozing in the seat next to the Geordie, Scotsman, truck driver in the heat of the great engine under the hood. He woke me gruffly to keep him company as he swung the ten-wheeler through the deserted towns, up on "Bennies" and doing a three-day stint to make the extra cash.

Once he let me sleep, but in the middle of the night he swung too wide in a deserted lane and the whole load of cabbages tipped into a ditch. Wide awake by then.

"Ee oop, lad, pay fur yer ride now—get loadin'."

All loaded and back on the old A road, we pulled into Bristol market just after dawn and not even a cup of tea. Then he took pity on me and gave me two shillings.

Dropped by a pub I knew in Bristol to see if any of the crowd from St. Ives were there. Only strangers. Nice middle-class art-school chicks with flawless skin and long hair, but . . .

I walked out to the old road and thumbed a great Tate & Lyle bulk-sugar rig, all black and gold with the best heated cabs in the country. Not supposed to pick up hitchhikers, but he did anyway. He said he had a kid about my age in college, and I told him some lies about being a student myself, having some fun in my summer recess. Best that way. No way to explain what I was looking for. What *was* I looking for anyway?

We stopped at a café on the old A4, and he ordered me up double eggs, french fries, and beans, two rounds of toast, and a steaming mug of thick, brown tea. Lovely. In the dark half of the café, in the shadows, there were great stacks of electric fires, toys, shirts in cellophane, transistor radios, and other stuff that had fallen off the back of a truck.

Eventually he pulled up to the grass verge on the Great North Road to drop me off. Slowly walking the long hill home, I imagined the neighbors peering out from behind their curtains. He's back. Oh, I feel so sorry for his parents.

Mum and Dad weren't expecting me. "Donovan, get right in here and sit down," Mum shouted from the small kitchen.

"Dear God, Donovan, yur awfy thin-lookin', whit hiv ye been eating down there in Cornwall?" Mum screwed up her nose and headed for the kitchen.

"Well, Son, how's the ramblin' life?" Dad was genuinely interested and smiled at the funky boots and Breton fishing cap. But I was subdued and just said something banal about the wayfarer returns.

"Did you get my cards, Dad?"

"Oh, aye, Son, all one of them."

My father was a great letter writer. Those who were privileged to get Donald Leitch letters treasured them forever. But in my early rambles, writing home was difficult. Why should I? I needed to live to write some.

But Mum and Dad were pleased to see me alive, and I was stuffed full of grub until I nearly burst. Though I had become thin in my mother's eyes, I was healthy. I'd been living outdoors under the stars, just like Robert Service, my father's favorite poet. Dad had transferred his own dream of the road to me.

I went up to my bedroom. It was still the same: the cut-out photos of the Paris Beat scene of the 1950s, the plaster sculpture, the candlewick bedspread, and the striped wallpaper. The old Dansette record player, and the Buddy Holly EPs. As I lay down in my schoolboy bed, I gazed up at the Paris photos and saw Val, the Beat-girl dancer. She who would later dance for me in the Royal Albert Hall concert of my London premiere. I slept for twenty hours, waking in the dark and hearing the flapping of a tarpaulin on a parked car like a sail on a St. Ives yacht and dreaming I was still by the sea. I dreamed, too, of flying, being pursued by something I couldn't quite figure out, and a girl, a child with green skin and thick, wiry black hair. I could see her green scalp between the strands.

Next morning I picked up a stolen book, *The Way of Zen*. The words made perfect sense. My ragged little library was filled with longing, and I knew that I was now on the way to fulfilling those longings. It was the week-end and I cadged money from Mum and headed for St. Albans to continue my search. I was on my path, and my close friend Gypsy was on his.

The scene had become vibrant with the new music I loved, the folk and blues sounds imported from the United States. I vowed to learn every bloody song I could and master the mysterious claw-hammer finger style invented by the Carter Family, and the flat-picking of Doc Watson and Ramblin' Jack Elliott.

I drank a pint of mild ale and watched intently as Mick Softley and MacLeod picked their guitars in front of the old stove in the Cock pub. But they both would turn away so I could not see their hands and learn the styles.

Hard to learn from records, but I tried all the same, buying obscure folk and blues disks in the St. Albans record store that catered to the eclectic tastes of the beatniks. I also picked up styles from Mick and Mac when they were too stoned to notice.

My old schoolfriend Mick Sharman was around. We still exchanged the fast funny phrases that we had used in school, but we were not kids anymore. Mick told me of a girlfriend who had a big steel-string guitar with F-holes that I could borrow. I had about exhausted the possibilities of the "Spanish box" that John Vanstone had sold me, so I was pleased.

The beat-up old Zenith guitar was perfect. It even looked like the ones that the blues cats played. The poor girl was never to get it back. I bought new strings and started to learn the songs in earnest. I would put on records and laboriously start the tracks again and again to get the riff, trying to grab as much as I could about the tunings and chord shapes.

But still the main styles eluded me. There were no how-to books, no lessons to take. A sense of mission had been growing and taking shape inside me, though I hadn't yet formulated it in so many words. The direct political action through the trade unions that my father advocated was not for me—I couldn't hold a job down for long enough, for a start!—but I was beginning to see that the working-class values he and I shared could be spread through folk music, both home-grown and American. In a phoney world, folk songs were real and helped assuage my feelings of alienation.

But first I would have to learn my craft.

One day I was in St. Albans and it was summer, when the Beats would all go down to the park and lie around on the grass and play music. A strange fellow arrived in town. He was very tall and had long straggly hair and a beard like Rasputin. Dressed in a long dirty coat, he carried a beat-up old guitar case and played a great-looking Martin Dreadnaught. He knew all the finger styles flawlessly. The only trouble was that he never washed. This handsome young man was avoided by all, and his name was Dirty Phil.

So this was it. I made friends with Dirty Phil. We shared a big English joint, wandered down to the graveyard of the old cobbled town and sat on the tombs, hidden from the patroling policemen. Phil said he would explain the patterns and teach me the fingering, promising that it was dead easy when you knew how. Here at last was my guru of the guitar.

Painstakingly and over three days I followed Phil on my "box," plucking the first part, then the second, then the third, followed by the fourth and fifth conclusion to the complicated pattern. At the third part my brain forgot the fourth and the fifth. Phil explained that the hand needed time to learn the messages from the brain to do what it was told. He also showed me how each picker develops his or her own style and alternates the pattern according to the requirements of each rhythm in the songs. After a long while and slow picking, I got it.

Now I had got it and could never lose it.

Phil's smell was almost unbearable. But one must suffer for one's art, mustn't one?

One afternoon he suddenly said that he was hungry and had to go to work. What work? I thought. I followed him up the hill to a bookshop. We went inside, ding of the bell over the door. It was about three in the afternoon. The little lady sitting behind a desk at the far end raised her head, and

Phil said he was just looking. I followed him as he strolled the lanes of books. He stopped at the art books section and thumbed through the large volumes of Van Gogh, Matisse, Picasso, and Paul Klee, with color plates. I watched as he opened his long coat to reveal four huge "poachers' pockets" sewn into the lining. Into the pockets went the four volumes, and he closed his coat. Turning, he whispered a thank you to the little lady, who looked up from the book she was reading and gave him a nice smile.

We stepped out onto the pavement, and he strode purposefully up the rise of the hill toward the clock tower. Next door, in an old Tudor building, was the Christopher Coffee House. I followed him in with a bemused smile on my face.

Phil sat in the alcove, ordered two coffees and a large wedge of cream cake for us both, although we were both stony broke. Soon the door opened and the place filled with fresh young middle-class art students.

After a while Phil engaged some of these kids in conversation about their studies, chatting them up quite nicely so that they wouldn't be put off by his odor. One student was into Van Gogh, her friend into Picasso. Phil just happened to have a few books, he said and proceeded to awe them with his knowledge of the painters, a few anecdotes thrown in. Soon he had sold them.

So he paid for the coffee and cake with plenty over besides. He had finished his work, he said, and we went back to the graves to top up my finger style as well as ourselves with the bottle of wine he bought.

Dirty Phil left town soon after, and I never saw him again. Thanks, Phil, wherever you are. I will be grateful forever for the gracious gift you gave so freely those long-ago days in the graveyard of St. Albans—and so, as we shall see, would John Lennon.

In this way I began to open the rich vein of ethnic music and experience the wealth of material already created by talented men and women all over the world. Recently I found a list of albums and songs in an old box of papers that my mum had saved. The faded schoolboy script on exercise-book paper shows the seriousness of my folk-blues studies. I am amazed to see the diversity of the music that I was absorbing at the age of sixteen.

Albums from the folk world included:

Artist	Title
Davey Graham	"Angie" / "Davy's Train Blues"
Ramblin' Jack Elliott	"Talkin' Woody Guthrie"
	"Jack Takes the Floor"
	"Jack Elliott & Derroll Adams"
	"The Rambling Boys"
Jessie Fuller	"Workin' on the Railroad"
Woody Guthrie & Will Geer	"Bound for Glory"
Leadbelly	No title
Big Bill Broonzy	"Last sessions"
Cisco Houston	No title

My repertoire was growing:

"Pretty Peggy-O"
"Geordie"
"Gospel Ship"
"Mary Hamilton"
"Lonesome Blues"
"Sporting Life Blues"
"Babe I'm Gonna Leave You"
"House Carpenter"
"Black Is the Colour"
"What Have They Done
   to the Rain?"
"Blowin' in the Wind"
"Don't Think Twice"
"Talkin' Miner"
"Ten Thousand Miles"
"500 Miles"
"900 Miles"
"Trees They Do Grow High"
"Get Back"

"Kevin Barry"
"New York Town"
"Freight Train"
"The Nightingale Song"
"Day We Went to Rothsay-O"
"Hammer Song"
"John Henry"
"Glory of Love"
"Careless Love"
"Good Mornin' Blues"

"Waitin' for the Train"
"Wreck of the No. 9"
"Lonesome"
"When First into This Country"
"Boston Burglar"
"The Craw Killed the Pussie O"
"Coulters Candy"
"The Carlton Weaver"

"New Buryin' Ground"

"Johnny Has Gone for a Soldier"

"San Francisco Bay Blues"

"John Lee Carson"

"Nobody Knows the Trouble
 I've Seen"

"Worried Man Blues"

"Drill, Ye Tarriers, Drill"

"Dark as the Dungeon"

"Delia's Gone"

"Hobo Bill's Last Ride"

"Talkin' Union"

"Hard Rain's a-Gonna Fall"

"Barnyards of Delgate"

"Granny of a Bus?"

"Ella Speed"

"Backwater Blues"

"Lil Maggie"

"Pretty Mary"

"Needle Song"

"Arkansas"

"Blue River Train"

"Two Brothers"

"The Confederate Soldier"

"Brave Engineer"

"Girls of Roedean"

"Ain't Gonna Be Treated
 This Way"

"The Foggy Foggy Dew"

"Cruel War"

"Pretty Mary"

"Alabama Bound"

"Flora"

"House of the Risin' Sun"

"This Land Is Your Land"

"Times Are Gettin' Hard"

"Jesse James"

"CC Rider"

"The Chastity Belt"

"The Women's Prison"

"Nuts in May"

"Pretty Boy Floyd"

"Hard Travellin'"

"Boll Weevil"

"Bed Bugs"

"All My Trials"

"Will Ye Go, Lassie, Go"

"Dead or Alive"

"Mule Skinner Blues"

"Cocaine"

"Take a Whiff"

"Seven Golden Daffodils"

"Where Have All the Flowers
 Gone?"

"A Man of Constant Sorrow"

"The Means Test Man"

"Tom Dooley"

"Stackalee"

"Whip Jamboree"

"Barbara Allen"

"Cooperative Cookie"

"Black Girl"

"Car Car"

"John Hardy"

"Paddy Works on the
 Railroad"

I memorized all of the lyrics and chords the instant I had mastered the intricate finger styles of each performance. As I listen to the surviving archives of my earliest recordings I am surprised to hear I was a virtuoso of all the folk-blues guitar styles by the time I reached seventeen.

The list continues to include important influences of rhythm-and-blues classic artists. The fusion of my later work came from many styles of music.

"Beautiful Delilah"	"Road Runner"
"Love Potion Number Nine"	"My Mojo Workin'"
"Hoochie Coochie Man"	"I'm a Hog for You Baby"
"My Babe"	"Slow Down, Little Jaguar"
"You Better Move On"	"Smokestack Lightnin'"
"Poison Ivy"	"Memphis Tennessee"
"Talkin' About You"	"Johnny B. Goode"
"Baby Please Don't Go"	"I Wanna Make Love to You"

Performed by Muddy Waters, Willie Dixon, Bo Diddley, Chuck Berry, Sonny Boy Williamson and John Lee Hooker, to name but a few.

And the acoustic blues of Robert Johnson, Blind Boy Fuller, Blind Gary Davis, Blind Lemon Jefferson, Sonny Terry, and Brownie McGhee, Lightnin' Hopkins, Snooks Eaglin, Bessie Smith, Big Joe Williams, and of course the great Leadbelly. I later bought a twelve-string guitar because of this giant of folk blues.

And what list could be complete without Her Ladyship—the exquisite Billie Holliday? Her signature song, "Strange Fruit," sends a chill down my spine every time I hear it. Gyp had left St. Ives that autumn and headed north to Manchester, following Alice. Once there, he discovered a new American folk singer and sent me his record, saying this young singer was doing the same as I was and singing Woody Guthrie songs with a cap and harmonica harness.

The new American singer was Bob Dylan. I saw and heard the similarity and was intrigued.

My eagerness to sing and play all of these wonderful songs meant visiting the folk and jazz clubs that were beginning to appear all over the country, in provincial towns and, of course, in the country's capital city, London. Soon the new music would emerge out of these pubs and clubs and change public consciousness.

Cops 'n' Robbers

Let me tell you about the St. Albans scene.

The Cock pub was not overly fashionable, just a wee boozer patronized by the local beatnik set. In the long "snug," were hard wooden benches for the sweet bottoms of the girls who sat with the young dossers and art students, guitar pickers and singers. Young men in peacoats, bleached jeans, and Hush Puppies, cord jackets and check shirts, greatcoats and turtlenecks. The Beat girls were dark-eyed and deathly white, in turtlenecks and tight jeans or black tights and short skirts, long boots or sandals. Bright-eyed and fresh, they rolled their own Golden Virginia tobacco smokes on the benches. The boys held pints of mild and bitter ale, the girls halves in that long rustic room, around the old stove fed with logs. The Cock of St. Albans.

Another pub in town was The Peacock. This larger establishment held a weekly folk club in a room upstairs. It was in rooms such as these all over Britain that the folk revival began. Influential folk stars such as Alex Campbell, Ramblin' Jack Elliott, Derroll Adams, Ewan McColl, and Peggy Seeger toured this circuit. And, of course, a slight figure of a man with birdlike features who stood and played a bell-like sound on guitar, Martin Carthy, the most influential in my opinion. He defined the style we now associate with the Child Ballads, a massive collection of material saved from obscurity by Francis Child. (*The English and Scottish Popular Ballads* as collected by Francis James Child in the 1800s. Five volumes, Cooper Square Publishers, Inc., 1965.)

There in the Peacock folk club, expansive Alex Campbell would move us to tears with his Scottish ballads and rouse us to chorus chants in his gruff, growling voice. Alex is sadly missed now that he is gone.

There too stood Ramblin' Jack Elliott, the first American I heard sing live Woody Guthrie songs, standing flat-picking and finger-picking his Gretsch jumbo guitar in the style of the Carter Family and Doc Watson. I would sit at Jack's feet, with a pint, and try to figure out how it was done. As I said before, the secrets were jealously guarded by some pickers, but the performers mentioned above shared their knowledge with the magnanimity of the true artist.

Other newcomers to the clubs were redefining the Revival in terms of their own virtuosity. My favorite was Bert Jansch, a fellow Scot living in London. Bert was small and laid back, dark shock of hair, languid eyes set in a thin, expressionless face. Bert would write classics like "Running from Home" and "Needle of Death"—songs that would be heard over the water in America by emerging songsmiths like Neil Young, as well as many others. There Bert sat, picking and slapping in his blues-folky way, renditions of traditional material that he would later develop in a jazz-folk fusion group called Pentangle. A superb band of musos and singers gathered around a jazz concert–bass player called Danny Thompson, soon to be known throughout the world.

Bert also sometimes played with another virtuoso on guitar, the bearded John Renbourn. John redefined the classical guitar and lute music of the Renaissance. As a duo they astounded audiences with their guitar exchanges, and all this in small rooms like the one in the Peacock, where a fan could almost touch the pair who sat on the makeshift platform.

I must also mention a very influential tune entitled "Angie," written at the time by Davey Graham. This minor descending chord pattern in A influenced me to compose in the "Bach Descent" style, with blues/jazz phrasing. Davey moved Bert and John Redbourn to experiment, too.

The women of folk began to appear. I saw the young Maddy Prior in St. Albans and watched the rise of this folk star, who later, with Steeleye Span, helped to popularize the new fusion.

Sometimes I ventured farther than St. Albans. I played around the flats of friends or in the London folk clubs, which I visited to hear Derroll Adams or Bert Jansch. Derroll was a direct link to the American Folk Revival—he had known Pete Seeger and Woody Guthrie. Derroll had played duos with Guthrie's disciple Jack Elliott. They had entertained or "busked" in Paris and down on the French Riviera with the giant of the Scottish folk scene, Alex Campbell.

I wanted to know Derroll, and when we met we liked each other fine. In fact we became friends. I learned so much from Derroll even though he played banjo and I guitar. I would sit cross-legged on hotel carpets or in the tiled bathrooms (for the echo) and watch the master. He played in such a delicate "frailing" fashion, brushing the strings very gently and singing soothingly in his low, sonorous voice. He touched each string with such tenderness, then seemed to pause to marvel at the sound that his banjo produced. I fell into altered states, following the one note fading. I was being taught by a master. Instructed with no instruction. Awakened to the knowledge with no awakening. Amazed by his own plucking of one string, he would stop, turn to me, and say, "Donny . . . will ya listen to that, isn't it beautiful?" And it was.

In Zen Buddhism the koan asks: "What is the sound of one hand clapping?"

Derroll was asking: "What is the sound of one note ringing?"

It is the sound of all music. The call to instant enlightenment. The only difference between an enlightened one and an ignorant one is that the enlightened one knows it.

Derroll came from Portland, Oregon, in the American West. A tall, bearded fellow with a cowboy hat and boots, parka jacket, and tattooed hands, he cut an odd figure on the London scene as he performed in the streets or on the folk-club stages. He would beam down on a young girl or boy with his great smiling eyes and tell stories while brushing the strings of his Zen banjo. He was always supportive to the many who fell under his spell. Now and again his story would stop as he made the sound of "chung-chung," nodding his head like an old monk.

Everyone knew and loved Derroll, young and old. His circle of friends were from every walk of life; he made no distinction between them. Gypsy and I loved this guy.

Derroll had a great love for humanity and a true ardor for the life of the spirit within. We cannot forget the many fine songs he wrote, one in particular, "Portland Town," an antiwar song that has been covered by many artists. Unfortunately, this song was generally believed to be traditional, and the artists who recorded it did not credit Derroll as the writer. I tried to get Derroll the royalties in the 1960s but with no result. Later on I recorded some of Derroll's finest songs and made sure that he got paid.

I remember falling asleep and seeing myself from above. While I slept on the little bed, I could plainly see my body below and from a distance. I was aware I was experiencing astral travel, that a fine and subtle spirit form had left the physical body, still attached by the silver cord that attaches us to so-called real life. This direct personal experience of consciousness outside the fleshly body was proof to me that what the mystical books in my small library had taught me was true. The spiritual world *is* more real than the material one. I was immersing myself ever more deeply in my twin obsessions of Buddhism and Celtic spirituality. The Britain I was brought up in—the Britain of the 1950s and early 1960s—appeared stiflingly respectable and ruled by an intellectually bankrupt authority. It was gray, lacking poetry and spiritually sterile.

But in the Beat and bohemian circles in which I was now moving—in places like the Cock and the Peacock—a new spirit was stirring. It was a spirit inspired by old music and new writing, and I, for one, saw how it would break through. I saw the potential to let fly the Bohemian Manifesto on the wings of popular song. In 1964, I felt that spirit move in me, and it inspired me to want to use the new media to sing a program of free music and free thought.

So I continued to learn my craft, but I began to experiment, too.

It is absolutely imperative for a serious young student of music to choose at least six geniuses of the genre that you are wishing to join. As a guitar player or vocalist you must learn all of the repertoire of at least two of your choices. By emulating the masters you will be told how to find your own voice. It is from the roots of the past that future creativity grows. How else would it?

The folk purists groaned when I began to play amalgamated styles. So what? I knew I had something new to say and I was not alone.

The most influential R & B revivalists in Britain were Cyril Davies and Alexis Korner. Cyril Davies's All Stars included in their lineup Long John Baldry. (After Cyril Davies died tragically young—of leukemia—in early 1964, Long John Baldry renamed the band the Hoochie Coochie Men and took on the young Rod Stewart as second singer.) Alexis Korner's band inspired Brian Jones, and Alexis encouraged the young Brian to form a band of his own. Other cats about to emerge on the scene were Graham Bond, Ginger Baker, Danny Thompson, Eric Clapton, Jimmy Page, Jeff Beck, Spencer Davis, Stevie Winwood, Keith Richards, and Mick Jagger.

But Brian Jones, in particular, was way ahead of his time because he realized the potential of the club gig—which would soon become the concert performance—and as a result the British rhythm-and-blues revival was soon in full swing. Cities all over Britain and Ireland produced their own groups. From Glasgow to Belfast, Newcastle to Liverpool, Manchester to London, the news was out and the news was good. Muddy Waters, Chuck Berry, Willie Dixon, Bo Diddley, Howlin' Wolf, and John Lee Hooker were being discovered: the young white R & B groups were copying these great bluesmen and performing their sound in jazz clubs and art-school balls all over the country as were groups like Them, The Animals, The Beatles, The Hollies, The Yardbirds, and, of course, The Rolling Stones.

St. Albans also had its own R & B club and a few friends had formed a band called the Cops 'n' Robbers. I got up and played harmonica a few times. It felt good. I had devised my own workingman's look, partly because work clothes such as jeans, check shirts, and seamen's pea coats were all I could afford and partly in homage to heroes such as Robert Service, Woody Guthrie, and Jack Kerouac, who needed rough-and-ready clothes like those for a life on the open road.

The "Cops" had a couple of managers who got them a gig in Southend-on-Sea. The whole St. Albans crowd went down for the weekend to support the boys, and I tagged along to play in the interval between their sets.

The club was absolutely stuffed with familiar faces when the band kicked off. I got up and did a few wails on the harmonica, and the scene was jumping. Then, in the interval, I got out my guitar and my harp harness and strummed into Jessie Fuller's great song "San Francisco Bay Blues."

Up in the back were the two managers, here to see Cops 'n' Robbers. After I finished I was feeling sick with stage fright and too much beer, so I made my way outside and up to the top of the iron stairwell to get some air. The managers followed me up. They wanted a chat. I turned, looked down the circular stairs, and splattered puke all over them.

They seemed to take it good-naturedly and asked if I was interested in meeting them up in London to record some demos. This is exactly what I want to do, I thought, and arranged to see them. Their names were Geoff Stevens and Peter Edens. Geoff was also a songwriter and he managed Dave Berry. We planned to meet at the Southern Music Publishing Company offices (now Peermusic) in London's Tin Pan Alley.

I returned home and told my mother and father, who were bemused at the news and perhaps a little unbelieving. So I decided to tell my Beat pals, but they only laughed and thought I had finally cracked. I felt I was looked upon with derision by most of the scene, perhaps because I was lame and different, or perhaps too much of a dreamer to be taken seriously.

Songmaker

❖

The day arrived. I hitched up to London and took the tube in from Hendon, carrying my old Zenith guitar.

I was introduced to my first recording studio in the basement of an old building in Denmark Street. I smiled to myself when I saw my pop hero Buddy Holly in a picture frame on the wall. I was in the right place.

I made a set of nine recordings, playing acoustic guitar and harmonica. The tapes have recently been rediscovered, and the songs are now available.

The list includes:

"London Town," written by Mick Taylor (after the Tim Hardin style).

"Dirty Old Town," written by Ewan MacColl.

"Talking Pop Star Blues," written by me in the Woody Guthrie talking-blues style.

"Codeine," written by Buffy St. Marie.

"Freedom Road," written by me.

"Isle of Sadness," written by me.

"The Darkness of My Night," written by me, later called "Breezes of Patchouli."

"Crazy 'bout a Woman," written by Jessie Fuller.

"Celia," written by me (not "Celia of the Seals").

Listening to these cuts now, I am impressed with the quality of my finger styles and flat-picking, as well as that of the vocals. The managing director, Bob Kingston, invited me into his office and offered to sign me to the company as a songwriter. He took me under his wing and began discussions with Geoff and Peter about developing my recording career. My friends remained sceptical when I told them I was signed to management and publishing.

Fuck 'em, I thought.

The owner of the large worldwide publishing concern was Ralph Peer Junior, and when he became aware of the new signing he was pleased. We struck up a relationship that would prove to be a very long and lucrative one for us both. Ralph had inherited a wealth of history and copyrights that spanned generations of songwriting. Ralph Peer Senior had formed the Southern Music Company in the United States in 1928, and the company had its roots in early country music and jazz. Among its first artists had been names such as the Carter Family, Jimmy Rodgers, Count Basie, Fats Waller, Hoagy Carmichael, and Jelly Roll Morton. Good company to keep. So here I was in the pioneering publishing family of early American music.

As I was under twenty-one, my father had to sign me into Southern and to their indie label, Ivor Records. The Southern Music accountant Derek King and my father took a shine to each other and many were the times they took a business lunch, Derek listening to my father's tales of early music hall days. Derek would respond with tales of early escapades in the Southern Music story.

Along the short and narrow Denmark Street (Tin Pan Alley) in another basement, the young Brian Jones and other members of his new band, The Rolling Stones, were recording some demos.

Brian came down to hear a session of mine, and I knew immediately who this cat in the cool gear was—*the* major figure on the new British music scene. Brian had already heard of the new kid: me! He wore a smart, jazz-style jacket with slim lapels and a button-down shirt with a tie. I noticed his short legs and the almost obscenely long slender fingers of a guitar player of genius. His blond helmet of long hair framed a strange and menacing Pan-like smile as he listened to the first demos I ever made. I was being checked out by the most creative and brilliant guitar player to arrive in London—the one who had created the distinctive sound of the Rolling Stones.

But I knew he was a wind-up merchant. I'd heard how he would stand, thrusting his throbbing guitar into the faces of the crowd below, bringing the lads to a frenzy, then spitting in their faces. There were fights wherever he went.

"You sound like Dylan," he snapped. I love Bob Dylan and his music, but he was one of hundreds of influences on me and most of those influences were in Dylan's music, too. "I think I've only one song that's got Dylan in it," I replied guardedly. It was true that my song "Rambling Boy" is in his style.

I did not say it but I thought to myself, for the last year Brian has been successfully trying to sound like the great slide-guitar player Elmore James— so why is he telling me that I sound like Bob Dylan?

As Brian turned to leave, I could not help saying, "I love your stuff, man." He smiled the faintest of smiles, perhaps a little condescendingly. "How's your own session along the street?" I continued.

He turned to me and looked long into my eyes and for a moment I thought he was trying to hypnotize me. "Really good," he said, at last. "We're going on the road soon, and that's what I like the best."

He climbed the narrow stairs up into Denmark Street and somehow, though I didn't know how, I sensed I had just made a karmic connection, made contact with something that would wrench my life around and set it on a course of splendor and misery.

Geoff Stevens and Bob Kingston sent my first tapes around to Associated Rediffusion Television via Bob Bickford, the talent scout for a new kind of television music show that had just come on air that year in October of 1964. Fans would dance in the studio while all the latest names in pop would mime their hits.

The head of the show was Elkan Allen and when we met he said that he saw in me a new kind of poet-minstrel. In an unprecedented move and without a record release as proof of success, he booked me to appear on his innovative music show, the first TV production to reflect the expansive new developments in British youth culture. It was steered by the combined talents of Elkan Allen, director of Michael Lindsay-Hogg, and producer Vicky Wickham. Life would never be the same for me after this. The show was called *Ready Steady Go!*

My first appearance on television was on the evening of 30 January 1965. The other acts that night were: The Animals, The Hollies, Ron and Mel, Elkie

Brooks, Golly and the Gingerbreads, The Who, Rhythm and Blues Inc., and Rick and Sandy.

The floor was crowded with teenagers. Something approaching hysteria swept through them as star after star took to the stage.

I was different from the start. I sang live. I stood on the plinth above the sea of faces, not exactly at ease but happy to be there. I knew something was happening. The young girls and boys in front of me were hearing a new vibration entering the popular music scene from the folk and blues clubs, and I was at the forefront of it.

Of course I knew that the folk scene would not like my commercialization of the tradition. And, sure enough, I received bad "folk" press from the start. Evidently, they felt that the mass youth audience was not intelligent enough for "deep" lyrics.

What kind of socialism were they preaching, I asked myself? An elite kind? My mission was to bring poetic vision to popular music, and as it turned out the young "faces" liked me: that first evening on *Ready Steady Go!* was a resounding success.

My first two appearances on *Ready Steady Go!* were before the release of any record. I would sit there with Cathy McGowan, the young "Mary Quant Look" hostess, playing house minstrel. I even made up humorous little songs about the other artists.

Cathy and I had an easygoing style and our chats were a success. I told her of the "road" and my vagabond life, which I was only months from leaving. Then I got up on the small plinth and sang live to the microphone, songs like "San Francisco Bay Blues" and "Keep on Trucking" by Jessie Fuller. Or I would do a rendition of the children's song "Car Car" composed by Woody Guthrie. And, man, I was gratified when the fab chicks screamed.

The fact that I came across so successfully without the support of a prerecorded, studio-mixed music track to mime to (as the other artists did) showed me that I could project my songs with no added "special" effects.

I wrote to Gypsy Dave, who was in Manchester, and asked him to come down to London, as it was "happening." I wanted my road buddy with me, to look out for me, to share the trip as we had shared the road, and Gypsy duly arrived.

When *Ready Steady Go!* gave me a break from the show, they received a mass of mail demanding my return and a petition from fans resulted in my going back to the show on 5 March. I composed a song for the show in the Guthrie tradition, "Talking Pop Star Blues," about what was happening to me. It was a way of sending myself up. I was trying to hold down my excitement, to play down the success and keep my feet on the ground.

Meanwhile, I continued recording tracks in the publisher's studio and also made my radio debut on 27 February, on *Saturday Club* where I met the first of many DJ friends in the great Brian Mathew. I would also do my second radio spot, *Teen Scene,* on 8 March. I felt at ease on radio, because of the oratory my father had taught me, and I used his deep, orator's voice as I told stories of life on the road. Alan "Fluff " Freeman and Jimmy Savile also invited me on their shows.

My managers secured me a recording contract with Pye Records that guaranteed me £25,000 for the next year and were planning to release a first single to coincide with a fourth *Ready Steady Go!* show set for 12 March. They tried to convince me to record a cover version of a song they had found about a traveling hobo, somewhat like myself. I disagreed, insisting instead that I release one of my own compositions, and there was no question about it—the managers had to follow my lead. One week before the release a reception was held for me in the Pye Studios at Marble Arch, London. Not bad, as I had been a penniless tramp only three months before.

On another appearance on the show the lineup included Adam Faith, Gene Pitney, The Zombies, The Rustics, The Artwoods, and Marianne Faithfull. How odd that I should be rubbing shoulders with all these people while I was still living at home. My mother says I slept late and the limousine had to wait for me to get dressed.

It was at this show that fans pinched the Breton fisherman's cap I had bought from a ship's supplier in St. Ives. I now wore the cap partly in homage to Woody Guthrie, and copied, too, the phrase he had on his guitar: "This machine kills fascists"—except that I dropped the last word, thinking fascism was already dead. My machine would kill greed and delusion.

Woody Guthrie played a harmonica that was slung in a wire harness. My father had made me one on his lathe in the factory, just like the early ones, which were all homemade.

I was proud to call myself the Scottish Woody Guthrie.

Linda Anne

I performed my first single, "Catch the Wind," on TV the evening of 12 March 1965 and a week later fans could actually go out and buy a recording. Amazing, I thought.

The A side was me on my old Zenith guitar and harmonica accompanied by Brian Locking, who had played with The Shadows, on double bass. I also experimented with distant strings on this record, which immediately offended the folk purists. So what? Strings are fiddles, and the big bass fiddle would become my best friend on record. Constant criticism only made me stronger.

As I came off the rostrum and pressed through the crowd of young fans, a young black boy in shades and a suit with thin lapels came in the other direction on his way to the stage and, taking out a harmonica, he said, "Hey, Donovan." Then he played a chorus of "Catch the Wind." It was Little Stevie Wonder. As he disappeared into the crowd, he said, "Dig the tune, man!"

After the broadcast I went for drinks in the Green Room. As I sipped dry white wine standing next to Michael Aldrid, with Cathy McGowan the other "Mod" jock of the show, I noticed a girl across the room and asked him who she was. He said, "She's a friend of mine. I brought her here tonight to cheer her up. Shall I bring her over?" The girl noticed I was looking at her, and I said, "Yeah, I would love to meet her." I wondered why she would need cheering up. Michael wove his way through the Green Room guests and steered his friend back to where I stood.

"Linda, this is Donovan."

I took her hand. "How are you doing?"

She spoke softly and gave me a small smile. "I'm fine, thank you." She spoke in a polite and sensitive voice that thrilled me in a most alarming way. As she stood quietly before me, I was stunned by her radiance and poise, by her long dark hair framing delicate features, and her hazel eyes clouded with sadness. I felt she graced the room with a quiet dignity.

I asked Linda if she wanted to dance. She did and we danced a jazz-jig to "Chain of Fools." The music seemed to be relaxing her, and although she was still a little cool and aloof, the dance was quickly bringing us together as only the bohemian dance can, a Beat girl and a Beat boy, hand in hand, Linda swirling effortlessly in circles as I led her smoothly in a dance that was both formal and free at the same time. It was as if we had danced before, so well did we move together. Everyone else in the room was dancing free-form and now some of them, curious, stopped to watch our moves.

The jazz-jig is a kind of jive, generally thought to have originated in the 1940s Swing era, yet it's actually much older. Dancers touch hands and loop and scoop their feet and swing, turning their partners, with body contact now and again. I could tell from the way Linda danced that she came from a bohemian scene and that she loved jazz and blues. Cool.

Gypsy winked at me as he came up and said, "Let's go on the roof." We three climbed the stairs and stood on the parapet overlooking London. It was cold as Gyp lit the joint. I took a draw and gave it to Linda. I did not know then that it was her first.

Just sitting next to her was electric; I was amazed to be so close to this astonishingly beautiful Beat girl.

Later, as Linda and I climbed down the iron stairwell from the roof of the Television Centre, I asked her back to where I was staying with friends. She seemed to have mixed feelings about whether she should, but then decided to follow me.

When I said I stayed with friends, I meant lots and lots of beatniks in one large room in an enormous Edwardian mansion in Putney. Linda stayed with us, and we sat up all night playing music and talking, though she said little. In the morning, when she was leaving, I suddenly realized how much I wanted to see her again and took her number in Windsor, where she lived with her parents.

I was hoping she liked me enough not to forget me.

A few days later "Catch the Wind" flew into the charts at number four. After nine weeks and five *Ready Steady Go!* programs, one *Thank Your Lucky Stars*, and two radio spots, my name, my face, and my music were now in every home in Britain. I was happening on a major scale.

I called Linda and took her to one of my gigs. I was so excited to see her again, but then she told me she had an eight-month-old son named Julian. She said she was not with the father of her child anymore. She said she was not married. I was stunned. She was so young.

Gradually we began to meet more often, and—though she didn't say much—I slowly began to learn the story of her life. Linda had been fifteen in 1962 when she had met Brian Jones.

She had always loved dancing and was on her way to becoming a ballroom champion when she heard a jazz band in the Ex-Servicemen's Club in her hometown, and she was instantly attracted. Of course it was in the trad jazz clubs that the first rhythm-and-blues bands began to play, and so it was that Linda found herself one night in a pub at the top of the town near Windsor Castle. The advertised jazz band had canceled and a new, unknown band had been hastily booked—The Rolling Stones. That night in the small pub there were very few in the audience as Linda walked in, and the atmosphere was downbeat to begin with; but Linda was overwhelmed by the raw emotion of Brian's slide-blues guitar playing when the music started. Linda had found the music that moved her, and she and Brian fell deeply in love. All the way through 1962, Brian took her to the gigs he was arranging. The band traveled around in an old van, but Linda preferred to journey separately so Brian and Linda went to most of the gigs by themselves in a staid and respectable car, borrowed from Linda's father, Alec.

Andrew Loog Oldham, the Stones' new manager, saw that The Beatles had made it with an original song and invited John and Paul down to meet Brian with a view to asking them to write a single for The Rolling Stones' second release. Linda was at that meeting and told me: "The song John and Paul came up with was 'I Wanna Be Your Man,' which Brian agreed to because it allowed him to show off his incredible slide-guitar technique."

Soon after the record was released, Linda met Celia Hammond, at that time the top model in town. Linda took some modeling classes—encouraged by Brian—and Celia also helped Linda by introducing her to Celia's boyfriend and famous photographer Terence Donovan. Terry took a set of prints of Linda. Brian also encouraged Linda, who was already at The Morris School of Hairdressing in Piccadilly, and so it was that Linda created the distinctive Brian Jones helmet of long blond hair, just as Astrid Kircher had created The Beatles "mop top" hairstyle in Hamburg.

Brian moved in with Linda's family for a while, and Linda conceived Julian in October 1963. Brian heard about this while in America. Though his postcards from this period talk of Linda as the love of his life, it was clear that his career was taking him away from her. The Rolling Stones's success seemed to please and disturb Brian at the same time. Linda *was* the love of his life, but he was already beginning to show the signs of the decline that would make that life such a short one.

Apparently, when the baby started to show, Andrew Oldham had taken Brian aside. The subsequent conversation was like the one that Brian Epstein had had with John Lennon about how fans like their stars to be single, available, and how girlfriends and wives are just not possible if you want the success.

Julian was born on 23 July 1964. His father named him after his jazz-saxophone hero Julian "Cannonball" Adderley. Brian came to see his son, always respectful, loving, and sweet to Linda and their child. In the months ahead, Brian would visit them and would feed Julian with a bottle.

I also learned that Brian had been advised to make a settlement with Linda—on condition that she asked for no more. She signed it because she did not want to make a big fuss as Brian had enough problems. It wasn't really legal because she was underage when she signed. Linda knew this and was still hoping they would be able to work things out. I suspected they were still in touch. I could see that Linda was very fond of me, but I was tortured by the suspicion that she was still in love with Brian. She was achingly beautiful and very sad, and though I took her out again and again, she would not sleep with me.

In early 1965 Brian invited Linda to Morocco to try one more time to work things out. Her mum and dad scraped together all their money to buy Linda some decent clothes and white "fab" boots, as she would be with rich and powerful people who might help her with her modeling career. She was focused on making it on her own, to be independent from Brian, and to earn her own money to bring up their son. Her mum also gave Linda her rings to wear.

In the hedonistic atmosphere of Morocco, with Brian and film people and influential fashion people, she was given *mahjoun* to eat, not knowing it is a blend of honey and hashish. Stoned, yet not realizing it, she tried to swing, but was not able to give herself to anyone. Disillusioned, she walked out of the palace where they were staying and onto the beach of Tangier. She played with the poor children, braiding their hair. Soon she was invited to their little home where they hennaed Linda's hair. She had such an amazing experience. As she left she gave the family her mothers rings. A true gentle soul.

The lyric of my first hit single was all about Linda, although I wrote it before I met her.

> . . . to take her hand along the sand
> ah but I may as well try and catch the wind
> —Donovan Leitch,
> *"Catch the Wind"*

(America Wants
Donovan

AMERICA WANTS DONOVAN.

So read the small clipping in the British musical press in late March of 1965, two short weeks after my first single release in the UK.

The buzz of my arrival on the British scene had been heard over the Atlantic in New York City. My London agent, Aussie Newman, was telephoned by *The Ed Sullivan Show* to fix it for me to make my debut on American TV. Ed Sullivan had, of course, introduced Elvis Presley and The Beatles to the U.S. television audience, exposing them to millions of future fans. I would be next. My first single had been released in America, had entered the Top 100, and would soon rise to No. 3.

My love life was going nowhere, but in my career things were happening fast, and soon the Americans would experience my vibe. Hickory Records rush-released my album *What's Bin Did and What's Bin Hid* on the same day as *The Ed Sullivan Show* on 16 April, changing the title to *Catch the Wind*, the same as the hit single.

It would be mid-May before the British public would see the release of this first album. How fast America turned on to me! The four days I spent in New York for the Sullivan show is a complete blank, though I do remember I refused to come on at the end of the show for the finale. I did not want to be part of the razzmatazz. Among the millions who watched the show was the U.S. manager Allen Klein, who later commented to my father that he had been impressed by my refusal to "cheesecake" with the other performers that night and had made a mental note to contact me.

On my return to London I was distracted from my agonies over Linda as I continued to do loads of press. The phone was literally bouncing "aff the waw," to quote a Glaswegian phrase.

My parents and I were on a much better footing now that I had a job. My father in particular was pleased to see me singing and writing lyrics. Dad had joined me up at *RSG!* Talking to Jimmy Savile one night, Dad told Jimmy that he was worried I might give it all up and just move on to traveling again after a while to see the world. Jimmy replied typically: "Let me tell you, Mr. Leitch, once they get a taste for the small prawn cocktails, there's no going back."

British fans voted me "Brightest Hope" of 1965, and I was invited to play the *New Musical Express* Poll Winners concert at Wembley. My name, with Herman's Hermits, had been added to the list that included, in alphabetical order, The Animals, The Bachelors, The Beatles, Cilla Black, Georgie Fame & The Blue Flames, Wayne Fontana & The Mindbenders, Keith Fordyce, Freddie and the Dreamers, The Ivy League, Tom Jones, The Kinks, The Moody Blues, The Rockin' Berries, The Rolling Stones, Jimmy Savile, The Searchers, The Seekers, Sounds Incorporated, Dusty Springfield, Them, and Twinkle. The whole event was filmed by ABC-TV. (I wonder where the film is now?)

I remember the huge crowd was probably the first large gathering for the new music ever and that we were steered to the stage through droves of fans. There was no serious security in those days. On that Sunday in April 1965, I saw The Beatles over a giant wave of screaming teenagers.

I played electric guitar on this show, five months before Bob Dylan would at the Newport Folk Festival. The UK folk purists were in a rave over me again.

In May I also joined another list of pop stars taking part in the first British Song Festival in Brighton. I continued to do interviews. Again, I was not camera shy, my father having photographed me constantly when I'd been a child. The usual questions asked of pop music figures bounced off me with odd results. The answer to the question "What do you want to be when you grow up?" was simply "A teacher of the way within." I rambled on about the books I was reading, and the journalists would smile and send in their copy, front or center page. I had no respect for the conventions of music and spoke immediately about fusing all styles if it felt good. But there was one subject that the journalists would all raise, of course—the Donovan-Dylan comparison.

Bob Dylan was from Duluth in the United States, an industrial town close to the Canadian border. Since his appearance in 1962, he had only released albums and now Bob would experience his first single release in the UK when he arrived to do his tour in the first week of May 1965. "The Times They Are a-Changing" was the first song from his albums to date that would be available to buy as a 45-rpm disk. It was released two months after my own first hit single "Catch the Wind," when I had a second single recorded and ready to go, a track called "Colours."

My own first tour was set to begin in the middle of May, and Joan Baez was coming over to begin her tour in the same month. Our managers had not planned it this way, but now we three folk singers were on everyone's mind. So the week Bob arrived in town, the music rags were filled with gorgeous pinups of both me and Bob, and Joan Baez featured in all the magazines, too. They were the king and queen of folk; I was the new prince. But I knew what I had. I was no pretender; I was the real thing.

I felt the call to become a bridge to the inner world, a bridge needed in materialistic times. Dylan, the Hebrew shaman with the Celtic name would also sing us within. Hebrew tribes and Celtic tribes, lost tribes indeed.

Dylan did some interviews and asked of me, "Is he good?" Then, when he'd heard me, he said, "He sounds like Jack Elliott."

Jack Elliott had been Woody Guthrie's first disciple before Dylan. Dylan was right. I had really studied Jack's style of Guthrie interpretation. Anyone who knew, knew.

"A 'This Machine Kills' slogan on Donovan's guitar smacks of some cynical work behind the scenes. If Donovan sincerely wanted to carry on the Guthrie tradition he would be singing in the pubs of North Kensington and the East End." So read one letter to the editor from a Michael Moorcock, London W.11.

Oh, really? Well, the audiences who watch television are the North Kensingtonians and East Enders. Guthrie sang to the working class (that's me) and wanted to spread the news of change as broadside balladeers had done for centuries (that's me again). My father and his father before him had made great strides for freedom by helping to make trade unions strong. I was from the tradition in all respects. There was no "cynical work behind the scenes," I was not invented by a manager. I created my own sound and image from the heart and from the start.

As I have said, polio had hardened me to ridicule. I was ready for them with their snide and uninformed opinions.

To quote Guthrie: "It has been my hard luck many times to choose between what I thought was the truth and a good pay check."

Pop music lyrics had carried no message before the folk invasion of the charts. All the invaders felt a camaraderie, no matter what the press said to the contrary.

It is strange that Guthrie, Dylan, and Donovan are all Celtic names, but maybe not so strange when we remind ourselves just how much music and poetry from the Celtic lands has influenced the world.

I decided I would have to meet the Hebrew shaman with the Celtic name.

My string of *RSG!* television appearances came to a close on 2 April. Gypsy and I had a few chuckles about the craziness of it all, saying we could always leave when it got boring.

Love, Love, Love

✦

When I was in London, Linda and I would go clubbing in her little DKW car to drink Scotch and Coke and dance to soul music with other ravers on the scene. We danced all night and into the London dawn. It was certainly "swinging," much more so than the books tell of.

The class barriers were breaking down. London was a magnet that attracted all who were fed up with the separation that kept rich and poor apart. No longer could upbringing prevent anyone from joining the quest to discover the new and innovative things that were happening almost hourly in the capital. In one of the cool new hairdressing salons on three adjoining chairs you could find a young builder's laborer in cement-smeared jeans and boots, an heiress with Mary Quant bangs, and a bright, young pop star, yawning after a night of clubbing. And doing their hair? A savvy young man with an art-school flair. It was everything and anything goes. And, of course, the very streets were rocking with the sound of the new pop music.

Youth culture was exploding with cheap 45-rpm records and affordable fab gear. No longer could state school or the Church herd everyone through the narrow gate. The bohemian manifesto was finally turning the capital on.

"All right, darling?"

"Who does yer hair?"

"Where did you get that miniskirt? More like a hanky, love."

"Fab gear."

Pills for thrills.

The wine's just fine.

Nineteen sixty-five and great to be alive.

Too bad if you missed it.

My first single, "Catch the Wind," was still at number four in the UK charts when I released "Colours." Dylan's own first single entered the charts the first two weeks of May. Joan Baez would release her first single, "There But for Fortune," that year.

"Colours" was a little number with me on acoustic guitar and a double bass. I had bought a fine White Lady banjo on Cambridge Circus and accompanied myself in the style of Derroll Adams. The harmonica was there again, though this time I sucked blues-style in contrast to the Guthrie "blow method."

"Colours" was hitting the top of the charts as my first tour began. The king and queen of American folk were out on tour also. I was delighted. Folk was popularizing conscious lyrics, and I was part of the movement.

I left London to do my first gigs for money. I would headline my own tour with Unit-Two + Four, and Wayne Fontana and the Mindbenders as support. We opened in Glasgow, my hometown, at the Odeon. Newcastle and Leicester followed. The Pretty Things would join me in Sheffield, Bournemouth, and Portsmouth. At the last minute a night at the Fairfield Hall in Croydon was added.

The Pretty Things were not pretty at all, their name coming from the title of a Bo Diddley song. (They had a hit with another Bo Diddley composition, "Mona.") Phil May, the singer of The Pretty Things, had created some of the first white R & B music that Britain was to hear and had been considered for the singer of The Stones at a time when Mick Jagger had not been a contender. I hung out with the band, and we spent many a crazy night blowing joints and generally carrying on. Viv Prince, the drummer, was particularly out of order, but then again so were we all that spring.

Two hit singles and an album rising in the charts all over the world made for a very strong beginning to my concert career, and it was clear to me from my first performance that it would be my live concerts that would endear me to my fans, much more than my records. I enjoyed singing live.

During this first UK tour, Derroll Adams traveled up the country with me. I also played at the Anglo-American Folk Concert in Newcastle Town Hall with Derroll. He introduced me to the queen of the American Folk Revival, the raven-haired beauty Joan Baez. I had all of Joan's records—she had begun in 1960 at the age of nineteen.

I was in awe of Joaney when I met her. She was exotic. Her tawny brown skin shone like a creature of the jungle. I fancied her like crazy. As she played for me, I gazed at her slender fingers, a tangerine ring gliding over the strings of her small Martin guitar. She had amazing eyes, concerned and pleading, I felt, for sanity and compassion in a mad, greedy, violent world.

Back in London, I entered Joaney's room in the Savoy one spring afternoon and lay on the silken spread with her. I wondered where all this was leading. Soon this goddess and I were folded into each other's arms. I commented on the soft quality of the afternoon light filtering into the darkened suite. We kissed tenderly, but then my reverie was broken as she told me of her recent love affair with Dylan, of intimate poetic times with her former lover, how he had made her laugh in his quick-witted, lyrical way. My desire for her began to fall away. She spoke of a time when they had lain in a yellow afterglow of love, and he had chimed, "It's like waking up inside a banana." Joaney read the papers with amusement on the Donovan-Dylan controversy. She had spoken to "Bobbie" and he wanted to meet me. She said she would introduce us when we all returned to London. I think she was still a bit in love with him.

It was Joaney's habit, I now realized, to swear. She swore freely and naturally in a way I hadn't heard from a woman before, and I thought, as we lay, "Here is a classic beauty who sings like an angel and curses like a market girl." She continued, "I want to meet John [Lennon] while I am here."

Suddenly the phone by the bed rang violently. She turned to grab the phone, revealing a lithe brown body. I could hear a panicky voice loud and strident down the line. Forty wild and unruly fans had found Joaney's hotel suite number and were making their way up to it.

She was a little scared. "What should we do, Don?" she asked.

"That's easy," I said. "Leave it to Gyp."

"Forty mad fans?" she exclaimed.

"Yes, leave forty mad fans to Gyp. He's used to it, knows exactly what to do."

Joaney and I hightailed it out of the suite with the sounds of eighty feet pounding down the corridor. Joaney looked back at Gyp as if she never expected to lay eyes on him again in this world. I turned, too, and there he was, standing legs apart, hands on hips, waiting for the stampede that was heading his way.

Later, when Joaney saw Gyp alive and uninjured, she asked, "How did you handle it, Gyp?"

"Inspiration," said Gyp. "I just held up my hand like a traffic cop and pointed to an imaginary line on the carpet. 'See that line?' I said. 'Anyone who crosses it, I will flatten! So just stay where you are!' They immediately stopped in their tracks. Two minutes later I turned and walked slowly down the same corridor you and Donno escaped from."

Gentle Joaney asked, "You wouldn't really have flattened them, would you, Gyp?"

"No my angel, they most probably would have flattened me." Gypsy laughed.

As we three parted that day, Joaney hugged Gyp, looked into his eyes, and stroked his "third eye" with one slim brown finger. I, too, hugged Joaney, held her svelte body again. We were not lovers; we were friends. She then slipped a ring from her finger and gave it to me as a token of our friendship. I wore it as a symbol of the hope for freedom Joan sings for everyone.

John Lennon and I would have a connection through Joan. I do not know whether Joaney and John lay in the afterglow together, but a song I wrote for Joaney would be a song that John included on his recently discovered custom-made jukebox of 1965. It is titled "Turquoise":

> Your smile beams like sunlight on a gull's wing
> And the birds cease to sing when you rise.
> Ride easy your fairy stallion you have mounted,
> Take care how you fly, my precious, you might fall down.

In the pastel skies of sunset I have wandered
With my ears and ears and heart strained to the full.
I know I tasted the essence in those few days
Take care who you love, he might not know.

—Donovan Leitch,
"Turquoise," Donovan Music London

Bobbie

To all outward views I was immersed in folk music, but from inside came an urge to fuse my new lyrics with my old love of jazz. As I write this memoir, I listen to Miles Davis from his *Seven Steps to Heaven* album of 1963, and I am reminded of the far-off summer when I scuffled around St. Ives beginning to learn to play the guitar.

Where would popular music be without jazz? In the world of the trumpet the seven steps to Miles began with Buddy Bolden and King Oliver, then through Louis Armstrong, Bix Beiderbecke, Red Allen, Roy Eldridge, Dizzy Gillespie, and on up to Miles Davis himself.

The pure line that opens the first track of Miles's album *Seven Steps to Heaven* had been a call to me in 1963 in St. Ives, a herald announcing a new consciousness in music. We all heard it. Now, a year or so later, at eighteen years of age, I wanted to project a new meaning into music—"Love and Compassion." I began a song in the jazz feel that spring of 1965, called "Sunny Goodge Street."

> In doll house rooms with the coloured light swinging,
> Strange music boxes so sadly tinkling,

You drink in the sun
Shining all around you
Listening to sounds of Mingus mellow fantastic.
My-my, they sigh,
My-my, they sigh.
The magician he sparkles in satin and velvet,
You gaze at his splendour with eyes you've not used yet.
I tell you his name is Love-Love-Love.
My-my, they sigh,
My-my, they sigh.

—Donovan Leitch,
"Sunny Goodge Street"

I had begun in earnest to introduce the Bohemian Manifesto into my work and the practice of compassion, two years before the bloom of "Flower Power" and "All You Need Is Love." This denim-clad beatnik from Scotland with a limp and an attitude was becoming a shaman.

This song would not be recorded until the summer, and in the meantime I was keen to meet the "Moonshine Zimmerman" (Bob Dylan) in all his glory.

I strolled nonchalantly into the Savoy and called Joaney's suite. On the newsstands the papers were full of outrage that The Beatles were on the Honours List. They were to be awarded the Order of the British Empire. Others who had been awarded the same Order would be returning their medals in protest, in "protest," mind you, at being associated with such "vulgar nincompoops." Another headline told of an American astronaut who was scheduled to go for a stroll in space. Springtime in Looney Land, I thought.

The hotel staff stared in amazement as I strode to the elevator in my rags and tatters on my way to meet your man. When I entered her suite, it seemed Joaney was furious with Dylan. Her mother was listening sympathetically as she ranted, "Bobbie is being a complete idiot!" while storming around the room. "Bobbie is being a complete idiot—he won't come down with me."

Joaney's manager, Manny Greenhill, said "Calm down, Joan." I watched all this open-mouthed, then ventured, "I'll come with you, Joaney." The three Americans turned to me.

Bobbie was in another suite. It seemed that he had refused to take an active part in any street protest with Joaney over the American involvement in

Vietnam. Having "arrived" in 1963 with "Blowing in the Wind," he had seemingly abandoned protest songs.

Meanwhile, there was a growing protest in Europe in the streets and legislatures. There were a number of violent demo clashes in Paris, condemning foreign involvement in Vietnam, and Joaney was infuriated with Dylan because he had previously advertised his radical views in song, but in Joaney's eyes had now become "vague" and would not follow her into the streets to protest.

Joaney took me to Dylan's suite. Dressed all in black, he wore a pair of black Anello & Davide boots worthy of any gypsy. He was quite small and slight of frame, a very pretty young man with bad teeth and curiously solid hands. His slim features were widened at the jawline with powerful muscles. Definitely the thinking girl's dreamboat.

My impression was that he was delighted to be in England as his music was more appreciated here at this time than it was in the United States. His manner was very "up." His close friend, Bobbie Newirth, spoke just like him, a lilting slow drawl to his speech and a half smile. Dylan's manager Albert Grossman, was big, gray-templed, and altogether the éminence grise.

Although Joaney said that Grossman and Dylan had been a little worried about my arrival on the scene, I think the truth is that the press controversy served us both in projecting our music out there. Bobbie evidently liked me, and I visited him many times in the days that followed.

"Dylan Digs Donovan" ran the headline in the *Melody Maker* on 8 May. "He's a nice guy, I like him," the strapline read. The reporter went on, "And so one of the biggest controversies that has ever split the British music scene ended when Donovan met Dylan."

Or so it seemed. Thousands of Dylan fans voiced their anger at me at his shows. Dylan mentioned me in his song "Talking World War Three Blues," and his audience jeered my name. Backstage Dylan told reporters: "I didn't mean to put the guy down in my songs. I just did it for a joke." In their turn my fans were just as vocal in championing me. It had obviously got out of hand.

On another occasion I visited the Dylan suite and was pleased to meet Allen Ginsberg there. I had at last connected with the American Beat scene. Ginsberg suggested we all write out the lyrics of the song "Subterranean

Homesick Blues," which Dylan intended to film out the back of the hotel. On the deep pile of the carpet we sat and started to do lines of the lyric on big cards. Bobbie saw my pen style and told me to do more. We swapped songs, and he particularly liked my number "To Sing for You."

One time when I visited, Bobbie was sick with the flu. I sat by his bed and sang him "To Sing for You." I sang it soft in the gloom of the heavily draped bedroom.

The party scene in the film *Don't Look Back* speaks for itself, and much that was said was powered by the tension from the "drunk" berating Bob. The film was edited by its director, D. A. Pennebaker, to reflect the discords and not the harmonies. It was, after all, a PR piece for Dylan's tour.

In the film, as I remember it, I sit with Bob in his suite. Derroll Adams is there, gently drunk, and there is another guy who followed Derroll in with me, a belligerent drunk who is chiding Bob about his song "With God on Our Side."

"It's Dominic Behan's tune, not yours," the drunk slurs at Bob.

"I don't like drunks," Bob says. He scans the room as the camera focuses on him. I decide to sing a song and ask to play his guitar, a Martin, I think. The drunk continues to harass him but Dylan settles himself, crosses his legs, a cigarette in his hand, long fingernails, black, tight-fitting trousers, with Anello & Davide boots pointing to the ceiling as I move into the first verse. Bob listens closely and does not take one drag of the cigarette, hard for any-one who is on "uppers," yet he pays me the respect of keeping absolutely as still as possible as I sing to him. After I finish, he asks: "You wrote that?" He is impressed.

I smile a little and say, "Yeah."

"You play like Jack Elliott, not me." Bob throws an aside.

"Play 'It Ain't Me, Babe,' " I request of Bob.

"You want that?" Bob takes his guitar from me and plays me his song.

I am so pleased. The world missed the traditional exchange of songs. I sang for Bob and he for me. This is the way folk singers passed on songs down the millenia.

Later we are in the suite with company again, and Alan Price, keyboard man of The Animals group, is there with a bottle of vodka in one hand and a bottle of something else in the other. He takes alternate swigs from both. His

Newcastle accent comes across the room. He comments directly to Bob on the Donovan-Dylan comparison. "He's not a fake [Donovan], and he plays better guitar than you."

Alan is right. My guess is Bobbie would accept that.

Our tours came to a close and we had all played to sell-out halls. The future of popular music would be very much influenced by this arrival of folk music on the scene. I was buzzed with meeting Joaney and Bob, and they both encouraged me to develop my songs in any direction I felt was positive, no matter the opinions of others.

That June I marched with Joaney to the protest rally in Trafalgar Square, linking arms with Vanessa Redgrave (British actress), Tom Paxton (U.S. folksinger), Olive Gibbs (chairperson of the CND), and a very young, very small Marc Bolan. I gave my support that day, and yet I felt that protest in the streets would not be as successful in spreading the message as would the singing of songs.

Subjects then considered radical would soon be on the agenda of all media of the free world, and it would be songs that would take them there.

Meanwhile, in the States, the great father figure of American folk music, Pete Seeger, was introduced to my music by Joaney, and he invited me to play at the next Newport Folk Festival that year of 1965. Joaney had introduced Dylan at this festival in 1963, so I was knocked out to be asked. The greatest folk festival in the world would include me. With this acceptance by Pete, my credibility would be established. I will always be grateful to Pete and Joaney.

I visited Bobbie again just before he was returning to New York. The excitement of the previous weeks had settled down, and it was another quiet night in for the man in black. I arrived at the Savoy and passed through the polished brass-and-hardwood swing doors, the doorman checking out the "Celt in Rags" again. I traipsed across the Persian-patterned hall to the house phone and called Bob up in his aerie overlooking the Thames. Bobbie Newirth said, "Come on up, man."

Door open, stillness inside. "Hey, Don," said Newirth, and led the way through the silent apartments to a door that opened into a small room.

"Bob's in there." I went into what I saw was the TV room. A television was on, no lights except the tube. "Hey, Don, come in. Siddown."

On the floor I sat, beatnik fashion, little Bob in a big soft chair. On the screen, ice-skating. It's late and British TV is nearly in its pyjamas. I was a little stoned on hash, and we said nothing. We viewed the chick sketching the ice in her mini-miniskirt. As my eyes slowly became accustomed to the dark, I became aware that we were not alone.

Shapes appear, on a sofa, on chairs. Four figures emerge from the still corners. The one nearest speaks. "Hullo, Donovan, hawareya?" The accent is unmistakable, the nasal drawl. It's John and the rest of the band. Bob stands and switches on the light. "Have you met these guys yet?" asks Bob.

It was the four Beatles and they stood also, smiling and nodding to me, amused at my surprise. The four were dressed in identical blue jeans, powder blue, soft and bohemian. I smiled back. There was very little to say. After a smoke of the herb, silence *is* the best way to communicate.

Here I was with five of the most influential musicians and songwriters on the planet, accepted into the inner circle without fuss, no pop celebrity bullshit. They were all a few years older than me, and I felt like a younger brother.

George Harrison was to say later, "You felt out of your depth, but you weren't, you know." I did feel awestruck for a bit. For Christ's sake, it was only a few months earlier that I was sleeping in a pillbox in St. Ives and washing dishes a cardboard wall away from a jukebox jumping with Beatles's hits.

I also remembered an even earlier time back from St. Ives when I had been alone in my parents' house in Hatfield, both parents at work, and I had wandered around my schoolboy bedroom with its cut-out photos of the Paris bohemian scene, the sculpture I had made, and my small library, the candlewick bedspread and the striped wallpaper. Downstairs the radio had been on in the kitchen, a 1950s Bakelite job, black and white with a grille like an American automobile. A record was playing, two acoustic guitars, drums, bass, harmonica, and two strange aeolian vocal harmonies. The effect on me was instant. I had to sit down on the Axminster stair carpet. I went into some altered state for a spell as a chord was struck deep inside me.

Then I heard a voice that I *think* was me saying, "I want to do that!" The song on the radio ended, and the DJ said, "That was 'Love Me Do' by the fabulous Beatles!" This combination of Celtic harmonies and acoustic guitar, harmonica, and pop sensibility had, I realized now in the Savoy, gifted me with the desire to make my own fusion.

As we made to leave the small TV room of Bob's suite, George said, "Do you wanna lift?"

Bob and I said good night, and he invited me around again before he returned to the States. He and I were seeing a lot of each other. George, John, Ringo, Paul, and I went down the hotel stairs, hoping to avoid any possible fan or media mania, and walked across the Savoy foyer to the parking lot where I was amazed to see four identical custom Mini-Cooper cars ready for "The Boys." I guessed it was Peter Sellers who had turned the Beatles on to these little cars. The four young blades in blue stood by their four minichariots, and John said to me, "See ya, Donovan. Let's get together again and play a few songs." I got into George's mini, furnished inside with leather seats and a fab hi-fi. I did a double take and thought, What a flash bloke. George saw me judge him and understood. He revved up his sporty mini and the natural driver in him zoomed us through the graveyard streets of London to my pad. George and I would become dear friends on the path.

The Trip

❖

With the release of my second single, "Colours," I had begun to weave a world of my own into which thousands of fans would enter. I wanted to share a visionary world and found that millions of younger and older fans wanted this, too. My music would be more than pop music, more than a dance record, more than a love song.

I thought to myself, it is storytelling, man, and a soundtrack to your changes.

If I thought that my first spring in the music business was busy, it was nothing compared to the summer of 1965. It seems I was always in two places at the same time, which doesn't surprise me in the least, considering all the flying Gypsy and I were doing.

A hectic four-day visit to New York back in April was a blank experience for me. I had no time to meet the American musos who were about to make their first impression on us Brits and the whole world, reversing the "invasion." Of course I speak of the invasion by British music that had taken over the airwaves in the States during the previous twelve months. Groups like The Animals, The Beatles, Chad and Jeremy, The Dave Clark Five, Gerry and The Pacemakers, Herman's Hermits, The Kinks, Billy J. Kramer and the Dakotas,

Manfred Mann, Peter and Gordon, The Rolling Stones, The Searchers, The Who, and The Zombies. And, of course, the solo female performers Petula Clark and Dusty Springfield. I was part of the invasion, too.

Then, waiting in the wings and about to fly in the opposite direction, were the young Americans, Roger (Jim) McGuinn, Neil Young, Steven Stills, David Crosby, Joni Mitchell, John Sebastian, and the San Francisco Bay area groups Jefferson Airplane and The Grateful Dead. Up in Canada, Leonard Cohen set his sights on becoming a "recording poet."

All of these new artists from the coffeehouses and campuses would fuse into a sound called "folk rock." The initial reaction to Dylan's first move into fusion was such a shock as to cause an audience in Forest Hills, New York, to boo Bobbie off the stage. I would have dubbed Dylan's fusion "folk blues." The British fusions to come would take a different turn, and I would originate a particular blend that came to be known as "Celtic rock."

During The Byrds's first trip to London, I visited them in their hotel and smoked a good few of the herb, chatting with McGuinn and hitting it off brilliantly. The Byrds were the first band to make the folk rock sound, following Dylan's lead. Barry McGuire had a hit, "Eve of Destruction," but The Byrds achieved permanent cult status overnight. Roger McGuinn was a great exponent of the folk sound. He knew many old sea ballads and would soon compose fine songs in the tradition with his experimental talents. I love the music of McGuinn. He is one of the finest and has influenced my music with gusto. My song "Breezes of Patchouli" is dedicated to him.

In late June I found myself on the plane again, bound for Hollywood, California, to do a string of TV shows, crazy, surreal shows like *9th Street West, Hollywood a Go Go,* and *Shindig.*

Out on Sunset Boulevard the teen girl fans were still in ponytails and bobby socks. They stared in wonder at our long hair and rags, realizing we were from another planet entirely. Then the girls threw their suntanned bodies at Gypsy and me when we tried to reach our limo. The police looked on, perhaps worried about the weird new musicians so welcomed by their daughters.

We turned around again and headed back to Britain to top the bill in a summer season of concerts at the North Pier, Blackpool.

Gypsy and I were accompanied on our train journey north by a young music reporter. Once inside the old-style compartment (two doors and no corridor), Gyp took out his tobacco tin and papers to roll up a large English joint. The reporter, thinking that we poor boys could not afford "real" ciga-rettes, offered one of his own. Gypsy gave one of his big-hearted laughs and finished rolling the joint. Passing it to our reporter, he said, "Try this." Gyp lit him up. The young man puffed and blew the smoke out immediately. "No, man," Gyp said. "Hold it down."

Gyp tips back his head when he laughs, and in short, loud barks his laugh fills the space around him. Green eyes flashing, he raises his hands, palms up, to mime "Life is good" and the golden earring trembles silently. We are all in-stantly embraced by Gyp's exuberance and all is well with the world. A strange expression began to appear on the face of our guest as slowly the herb released its pungent power.

"What d'ya think?" asked Gyp, grinning.

The cub reporter said nothing. What was there to say?

Life would never be the same after this for the writer, and aren't we glad of that? The reporter would tell of the strange world of Donovan and Gypsy Dave in his article that followed.

When the old English train with the seaside prints in its carriages pulled into the station, Gypsy and I took a taxi to the hotel, bay window overlook-ing the promenade, lace curtains and cucumber sandwiches, a drunk porter, and no TV. After a fish supper and a turn around the amusement arcade, it was down to the pier for the show.

The taxi pulled up at a pier absolutely stuffed with young girl fans screaming at the arrival of The Walker Brothers. We sat in the cab in amaze-ment as two pier attendants, in rubberized long coats and caps with the pier's name on the hatband, pushed a large box on rollers up to The Walker Broth-ers's car. The hysterical girls crowded around. The attendants told them off in a fatherly fashion, calling some of them by name.

"Now, Veronica, I'll tell yer mam on ye if ye keep that oop."

Around the top of the wooden box, holes to breathe had been drilled at regular intervals. Right up to the car door went the box. The pier police opened first the box doors, then the car doors, thus preventing the girls from touching the stars, and the boys jumped in. Once they were inside the box its doors were closed. Down the pier the box was pushed by the attendants.

The girls followed, banging and clawing the box, screaming at the top of their lungs, and poking their schoolgirl fingers through the holes in vain. Gypsy and I were in tears, laughing at the scene.

Then it was our turn. Into the box we went and out went the lights, except for the small amount that came from the holes filled with waggling fingers. Once inside the venue, we went to our dressing room and lit one up. Down the corridor, The Hollies frowned at the aroma. What happens next can only be described as refreshing. . . .

The old theater at the end of the pier had seen many music-hall stars of the past bring the house down, and the gilt plasterwork and red velvet had seen better days. Now it was crammed full of a very different audience, the teenage daughters of the industrial north, all of them in a state of hysteria about the new musical stars that they were to experience.

As I took the stage and tried to play "Catch the Wind," the screams rose. A little way into the song I felt a drop of water hit my eye. I paused, then continued, even though no one could hear anything over the row of the fans. Some seconds later, another drop of water, this time landing on me quite hard. I stared up at the proscenium arch to see if the roof was leaking. A third blast of water, this time a definite high-powered stream, made me look down into the orchestra pit. There, grinning all over their faces, were Roger Daltrey and trickster Keith Moon, two large spacegun-style water pistols in their cheeky paws. Laugh? I only just managed to finish the song.

After the show we were on our own, with no pier police to box us up; they were, " 'avin' their tay," no doubt. So Gypsy planned the escape. Simple. We would burst out through the backstage throng and run like blazes down the pier. We flew past the girls, Gyp giving a few of them a squeeze as they pursued us, some with scissors for a lock of hair. The plan was to leap over the side of the pier when the sand was near enough. Over the side we went. The girls ran round to the promenade to continue the chase. Then Gyp discovered that he had dropped the hash. He insisted on staying to search on the dark sands, as I continued running to the hotel.

As I left the sound of the fans behind I became aware of another runner by my side. He panted along in the dark with me. Turning to me, he said, "I've done this before quick, in here." Into a street urinal, that meant, and, once in there, nature called. As we watered the porcelain I realized that my fellow fugitive was Peter Noone of Herman's Hermits, on the run from his own show. He then led me to Billy Fury's hotel.

There was a very British Norman Wisdom kind of madness about this early pop world, I thought as I sat there with Billy Fury, having an English

cup of tea in a B&B. 'Likely Lad' Peter Noone looked every bit the pier comedian with his jaunty manner; Billy was the cool, well-groomed star in cardi-
gan and quiff from the Larry Parnes stable of pop hunks; and I was the
denim-clad bohemian waif. We were three upstarts from 1950s Britain, riding the wave of the 1960s.

Somehow Gyp arrived. He winked at me to show that he had found the
block of hashish and we said goodbye, strolling in the dark along the promenade to our own B & B, the sounds of the sea surging on the pebbles. Distant
tunes from the dodgems and the neon lights of cafés led us to our separate
bedrooms and the good-night joint.

In the middle of an eleven-week season in Blackpool I flew to the States
again to be presented at the Newport Folk Festival by Joan Baez and to do
more television in Hollywood.

When I arrived at the New York airport I was dressed in a slightly better
set of rags than usual, including a suede jacket I had swapped with a friend
in England. At Customs I was stopped and taken off to be frisked for you-
know-what. I was relaxed as I knew I was clean. The officer was a large black
guy, friendly and considerate as he asked me to strip down. Very thorough,
he slowly went through everything. Finding nothing in either my luggage or
on my person, he asked me to get dressed. But as I was about to put on the
suede jacket he said, "Just a minute," and gave the top pockets another feel.
This time he slipped his two fingers into the pockets down to the seams. A
smile broke out on his face as he slowly withdrew a tiny African pot seed,
held between his fingertips.

"What's this?" he asked.

I gazed in wonder at the little thing and explained that I had just swapped
the jacket. When he heard I was headed for the festival he became even more
friendly. He said, "I will let it go this time, but watch out next time, ma man."

On parting company, he said the strangest thing: "I'm the guy who busts
Ray Charles." (Not "busted" but *busts*.) "When he needs busting they call me."

How nice for Ray.

I continued on to Rhode Island and the Newport Folk Festival. I was welcomed at the festival backstage by Pete Seeger and presented as the new voice
of the folk revival. I played my own concert but also sang in Joaney's set. I

joined Joaney on stage where we sang my song "Colours." I hung out a bit with Bobbie, too. I sat and caught his two folk performances, but he was also planning to do a set with the Paul Butterfield Blues Band. The preparations and rehearsal for this went on with only Peter Yarrow of Peter, Paul and Mary showing any concern as Bob plugged in an Electric Fender and ran through a rehearsal of a tune with Al Kooper on keyboards. The sound level bothered Peter and he said, "It's too loud, man. You'll have to turn it down when you do the set." But Bob just ignored him.

When the show started and the Paul Butterfield Blues Band kicked into the first number, a hush fell over the huge crowd. Then the booing began as Bob slurred out his songs to the rhythm-and-blues backing. The combination of Bob's fast, poetic delivery and the edgy electric instruments was odd at first, then I started to like it. This was Bob's new direction, and he was obviously excited about it.

There was so much booing that Pete Seeger went to the sound booth and actually pulled the plug on Bob, or so I heard. The music died. The boos continued as Bob left the stage.

Bob's experiment that August of 1965 would be hailed as the first "folk-rock" fusion, but I went electric on stage back in the spring of that year.

That week the first Joan Baez single ("There but for Fortune") entered the British Top Thirty, I was called by the papers. I said I was delighted for Joaney and the folk revival in general. She was doing so much for the emerging consciousness.

The papers were full of love-tryst rumors about us, but I said we were just good friends. When I spoke to her on the phone from Tinseltown she apologized for America.

As for my first impressions of Hollywood, I thought it like a gigantic advert. The television shows were very showbiz and frightened me. I was announced as "the fabulous Donovan from Britain." I strolled on, took off my sunglasses, and by the time the DJ had slung three impossible questions, I had slowed the whole thing down.

I was staying in the Tropicana, a famous musicians' motel on Santa Monica Boulevard. The rooms were cardboard boxes with a TV and toy beds, very "pop art" in a washed-out and colorful way. Musicians were considered trash, so we were all housed in these motels, but I liked the seedy confection of the place.

Back in the UK I was in the studio again, recording a set of songs for an EP (which was an extended-play, seven-inch, 45rpm record with four songs on it). I recorded the protest song "Universal Soldier," composed by another great lady of folk, Buffy Sainte-Marie. I "compressed" the sound of the guitar, and it jumped right out of the speakers when I heard it back. I was a one-take kid then—and still am, really.

"Ballad of a Crystal Man" was a new composition of my own, a protest song with harmonica and a very slick finger-style picking, which fairly flew along compressed to the max.

I also recorded another cover version, the anti–Vietnam War song by Mick Softley, "The War Drags On." This was played in the drop-D tuning that Mick had learned from Buffy Sainte-Marie's song "Codeine," strummed with a flat pick, driving it into the modal D bass. The lyrics spoke of the plight of the Vietnamese, who had been torn to shreds by French colonial expansionism even before the United States had joined in. Since then France had seen their folly. America would have to learn.

The fourth song was a classic by Scottish folk-blues legend Bert Jansch, "Do You Hear Me Now?" Of course, Bert had long been my guitar hero and had graciously taught me the styles he played so that I would develop my own versions. His influence over the whole music world is now appreciated by all serious guitar aces. This track was a simple vocal and acoustic guitar with a not-so-simple finger style. I began to get the knack of the recording art.

I had bought a new guitar in Hollywood, a cherry-red J45 Gibson acoustic, and I was in heaven. I adopted the same strings that Joan Baez was using, La Bella Silk & Steel. Now I was composing a very different kind of song as I developed my guitar picking to a fine degree with the soft strings, using the longer nails I grew.

One night, off we went to Westbourne Grove to score some African Bush. In an empty old house we sat cross-legged with the Rastas, smoking the chillum, a water pipe. One Rasta blew out a huge cloud of smoke, pulling off his woolen beret. His hair fell about his shoulders. I recognized the hip cat I had seen in St. Ives that long ago summer's day.

When the press heard the news that I would release an antiwar song and feature it on my new EP, they all thought it a gamble. My managers advised me not to do any TV for the promotion, suggesting instead that I do a short film, an early "video."

So off we went to the beaches of Normandy in France with the *Top of the Pops* television producer Johnny Stewart to make the video. There on the wide beaches were the rusting tanks and a few landing craft, relics of the Second World War. Shot in black and white, it showed me walking along the beach and miming to the tinny sound coming from a Nagra tape recorder. The cover of the EP was a photograph of toy soldiers, marching in front of a sketch of First World War trenches. The "Universal Soldier" EP jumped into the Top Thirty, becoming the best-selling EP ever.

It was only July and five months since my first TV appearance. Things were moving fast.

A DJ slammed me for having a go at the hard-working soldiers "only doing their job." I replied to the DJ that I was, in fact, interpreting Buffy's lyrics to mean that the common foot soldier has always been cannon fodder.

Upon meeting me, a journalist described my "shy, almost withdrawn" nature. I must have had a joint before that interview!

There were other folksingers happening in new folk-rock groups such as John Sebastian (in The Lovin' Spoonful) and Jerry Garcia (in The Grateful Dead). I was the only other big solo success apart from Dylan. His lyrics are without equal in all of popular music, but I think that musically I am more creative and influential. I was dynamic, obsessed with developing pop style, creating new combinations, mantras for a questing youth.

The way I use double bass and acoustic guitar on my first recordings was like early Elvis Presley tracks such as "That's All Right" and "Mystery Train." The folk element had always been there on Presley's first sessions. The traditional roots of Tennessee reach back—through immigration—to the folk music of Ireland. Presley is an Irish-Celtic name. I think he was part Native American, too. Today I still feel a raw excitement in my first recordings, an echo of those early Sun label sessions recorded by Sam Phillips. I was beginning to feel at home in America.

In between the promotional spots for the new EP, I continued to hang out in the folk clubs of London. One night in Les Cousins, I met an American singer/songwriter from Texas named Shawn Phillips. Shawn played a cherry-red Gibson twelve-string guitar. Now, Gibson cherry-red was what I played. I was intrigued and wanted to know this young Texan. We struck up a relationship and hung out together. Shawn had a pad just off the Edgware Road, and we broke out the guitars and started to jam. Our interests were similar, and in between the songs we raved on about everything we could. We also rehearsed a bunch of my new songs.

Shawn's manager at the time was Ashley Kozak, a string-bass player and employee of the music agency NEMS Enterprises. This company was run by Vic Lewis under the auspices of Brian Epstein, manager of The Beatles. One night around Shawn's flat, another young singer songwriter from America dropped by. He was quite straight really, no long hair or rags. He said very little as Shawn and I ranted and raved. Then Shawn introduced me. He looked pretty preppy to me. His hair was on the short side, as was his stature. He wore a *real* jacket and *actual* shoes. Little did I know he was over in England to suss out the scene, find inspiration. There was plenty of that in London for Paul Simon.

We did not speak as Shawn and I dominated the cross-legged group on the floor of the flat. Paul never got out his guitar. Most folkies are not shy of breaking out their instrument and jamming along with whatever is happening, but I did not get to know his work that night. Later I would hear that he had recorded "Scarborough Fair," and I guessed he had heard Martin Carthy play this very strange and esoteric ballad. Paul was to say in the press that his biggest influences were me and Bert Jansch.

Shawn had penned a masterpiece called "The Little Tin Soldier." This song drew on the tale collected by Hans Christian Andersen. I immediately warmed to this song. I see now I identified with the two characters in the tale. A delicate ballerina and a tin soldier with only one leg. That is Linda and me. Me with my polio leg, and she with her Libran dancer's form. "The Little Tin Soldier" became part of my music. I sing it in concerts to this day.

I was sleeping at a house in Putney when I first took an LSD trip. The large Edwardian drawing room was filled with young beatniks and a few older ravers, rolling joints and swigging cheap wine in the gloom of red lampshades. I became aware of a slow change in my perception of visual events. A diffused pool of glowing red lamplight in a corner of the room appeared to become a cave, the figures inside it sitting cross-legged on the floor. Suddenly a brilliant beam of crystal light flashed into the room.

Someone had lit up a spliff. Colors began to vibrate intensely. A Ravi Shankar record, newly arrived in London, was on the turntable, and I closed my eyes. The vibrant colors were inside me also, in circular, pulsing patterns, flowers of light and energy. The inner mandalas vibrated and changed through incandescent hues of living light. I opened my eyes because the fast passages Ravi was playing moved the "visions" too quickly for me.

I stared at the carpet and became transfixed with the interlaced patterns moving to the slower raga that Ravi now played. As this slow raga continued, Ravi gently caressed the "sympathetic" drone strings, and my breathing became deeper and slower. His musical mantra moved the flowering mandalas. I became centered. Exquisite sounds from another world and glowing patterns led me into a realization of great meaning. I became Awareness. Descriptions of the Divine Vision that I had read of in Buddhist books were now my own.

Of course I am writing here about the expanded consciousness experienced by those ingesting or smoking the holy plants, opening the eyes to a new level of "seeing" both the outer and inner worlds.

The mild euphoria of marijuana or hashish relaxes most smokers or eaters of this plant. They become laid back and able to absorb the experience of art, music, and nature without the usual analyzing logical brain logging in visual and aural experiences like a scientist. In this way a deeper level of experience may be found below the ordinary everyday mechanical processing of data that we need to walk about on two legs and protect the vehicle from damage. Giggles and uncontrolled laughter are often signs of the natural relief that comes from letting go of the conditioning society forces on us.

Now, for me and many others at that time, magic mushrooms, mescaline, and the synthetic LSD opened what Blake calls "the doors of perception." Aldous Huxley wrote of his mescaline experience in his books *The Doors of Perception and Heaven and Hell.*

The experience usually involves seeing "the matrix," the interconnectedness of all living things, an actual web of light that can create the dawning of a new compassion because it leads to a new realization that we are all one.

How brave we all were to enter the matrix is clear when I remember that it required us to leave all conditioning behind and face the challenge of confronting fears and doubts as we plunged into the unknown.

Although my first LSD experience was one of revelation, many would follow that were disturbing. The circumstances for a voyage to the inner reality are to be chosen carefully. I do not recommend any reader taking any preparation today as the street drugs of unscrupulous dealers are concocted with no thought other than to turn a profit. No one knows what is in them anymore. The 1960s was a naive period and therefore a safer time. The commercial exploitation of early experiments with altered states of consciousness would come soon. LSD was actually legal to make and buy in 1965. It was banned the following year.

It was at Shawn's pad that I met his manager, Ashley, and as a result I changed management from Geoff Stevens and Peter Eden to Ashley Kozac.

Ashley's lovely Greek wife, Anita, was a vivacious dark beauty who sang Billie Holiday songs. Anita took to Linda immediately, sensing her great heartache and seeing clearly how much I was in love. She believed, too, that Linda was in love with me, yet holding back after all she had gone through. Anita also had had her hard knocks early.

That August "Colours" hit the U.S. shops, and I flew over again to do the crazy little TV shows: *Shindig, Lloyd Thaxton, Hollywood A Go Go, American Bandstand, 9th Street West, Shivaree, Where the Action Is,* and *Shebang.*

It was on one of these shows that I met Sonny and Cher. We struck up a friendship, and the duo became my LA hosts for a while. Each time I hit Hollywood we would hang out, driving down Sunset Boulevard in their convertible Mustang with KRLA radio turned up full volume, Cher's long black hair blowing in the breeze. We were young and happening everywhere. I liked their attitude and their penchant for designing their own stage gear, which was their day gear, too.

The U.S. trade magazine *Billboard,* in its issue of 14 August 1965, headlined "A hit over here, Donovan, England's newest sensation, sings 'Colours.' " They spelled the song title in the British way and the B side was "Josie" from the first album.

My songwriting was being commented on, and I gained more support from the music community there for my melody and innovative vocal phrasing. I was on the Hickory label out of Nashville, Tennessee. The U.S. booking agency Acuff-Rose Artists Corporation also worked out of Nashville. This country music connection had begun with my original signing with *Southern Music Publishing Company,* who were pioneers in the field. There would be many "covers" of my songs by the so-called C and W artists from that music city: Jim Reeves, Glen Campbell, Chet Atkins, Flatt and Scruggs, Buck Owens, Dottie West, Willie Bobo, and—a teenage favorite of mine—Duane Eddy, better known for his rock-and-roll "twangy" guitar but also an accomplished acoustic player of traditional American music.

The recordings of my work by other artists would be so far-ranging as to include Jeff Beck, Joan Baez, Eartha Kitt, The Platters, Cher, Sammy Hagar, Van Dyke Parks, The Kingston Trio, Nana Mouskouri, Jefferson Airplane, Marianne Faithfull, Mary Hopkin, Ken Dodd (yes, even Ken), Butthole Surfers (ouch), Nigel Kennedy (such an animal), Steve Hillage, Neil Young, Trini Lopez, Deep Purple, Ronnie Scott, Harold McNair, Kate Bush, James Last, Georgie Fame, Herbie Mann, Jasper Carrott, Julie Felix, Herman's Hermits, Helen Reddy, Sandie Shaw, Noel Harrison, Brian Auger and Julie Driscoll, Lou Rawls, Mike Bloomfield with Al Kooper, Al Kooper with Steven Stills, Vanilla Fudge, Cleo Lane, Judy Collins, Big Jim Sullivan, the Allman Brothers, Richie Havens (yes!), New Christie Minstrels, Dana Gillespie, The Lettermen, Johnny Rivers, The Animals, Theo Bikel, Joel Gray (yes, even Joel), Jim Horn, Jack Nitzche, David McCallum, Lionel Hampton, and another teenage favorite of mine, the instrumental drum artist Sandy Nelson.

This list goes on and it pleases me to see so many of my heroes in there, so glad to have turned them on to my tunes. From country to folk, jazz to classic, rockers to poppers, and balladeers, funky to soul, riff rock to trash rock, I certainly am "covered"! I believe all music is one music.

The summer of 1965 blazed on. The formidable figure of American manager Alan Klein had been ruminating over that first *Ed Sullivan Show* of mine, watching my progress into the charts all over the world. He set his sights on managing me, The Rolling Stones, and The Beatles.

I was with Pye Records in England, who licensed my records to Hickory in the States, set up through my first managers, Steven and Eden. Alan Klein made plans to attack my business.

Pandemonium

Ashley and Anita's flat was on the ground floor of Alexandria Court, Edgware Road, a stone's throw from the canals of Little Venice. Anita had decorated the place in soft, fine furnishings—velvet, lace, and beautiful prints on the walls. She would cook lovely dinners, and Gypsy, Ashley, Linda, and myself would thrill to her exuberant laughter rising above the guitar, congas, and bass music that Ash, Gyp, and I would jam into the night. Anita sang Billie Holiday songs and Ashley played double bass. In the loving vibes of Anita and Ashley's home, Linda seemed relaxed for the first time since I had known her.

That late spring of 1965, I wondered if she was finally forgetting about Brian. But she still said very little and often I understood her silence to mean that she did not care, nor had any feeling for me.

And yet, I said to myself, here she was with me.

Linda would not be with me always, and I knew that she visited the London clubs and would occasionally see Brian there. Brian had a close friend, Ronnie Money, the wife of Zoot Money, the British singer and keyboard player. I learned later that it was to Ronnie that Brian bared his soul, crying over the breakup with Linda. He wanted to be with Linda, but the other members of the band were persecuting him for being so nice to her, a great taboo in the world of music back then. Brian was also doing more bad drugs, and I also learned that he told Linda that she should not marry me as it would just be more of the same madness.

But when I had free time, Linda and I ran around town in her little DKW toy car, dancing in the clubs—The Ad Lib, The Bag O' Nails, and many others. I gave Linda her first Chinese dinner across from Edgware Road. She giggled at the chopsticks, smiled at the tiny teacups. It was good to see her smile and to show off that I was a man of the world, a traveler to foreign lands.

The atmosphere was right for love, and we lay together that night in my single bed.

> You know I want only you,
> I long for you to want only me.
> You feel me enter
> And our bodies become as one.
> There between the worlds,
> You let me love you.
>
> —Donovan Leitch, *untitled*

The next morning I was elated to be in love, but also worried that I would lose Linda back to Brian or someone else.

I asked her to come and meet my parents. I wanted to marry her. I thought I might catch her with my ring!

The drive down in Linda's little car was strained, and when my mother met Linda she treated her coldly. Then she took me aside and my own mother called Linda "secondhand goods." That she had a child, unwed, with another man was disgusting to my mother.

I was devastated. We left quickly, and I vowed never to return home again. I had come back from my vagabond life to show my parents my success—and now this. I would stay away for good now. I'm sure my father liked Linda, but he was curiously silent in the face of my mother's rejection of her.

Linda told me later that my offer of marriage had excited her, but that she still felt that Brian had left her because she had not been independent. This experience had shaped her expectations in love. She wanted to be an equal, and my offer of marriage had not come at the right time. I sensed this reticence in her and thought it was a rejection of my love.

Linda also told me more about the darker side of Brian Jones. He had been back to Morocco to record "The Pipes of Pan." He had been introduced to the Master Musicians of Jajouka through the bohemian painter Brion Gysin, friend of Paul Bowles and mentor to William Burroughs. Brian learned from Gysin that the musicians of Jajouka continued seven-hundred-year-old traditions, the ancient rites of Pan.

Powerful, hypnotic piping is played on black wooden oboelike pipes with an otherworldly wailing sound. All through the night, by firelight, night after night they play, then suddenly—from out of the shadows and into the firelight—leaps Bou Jeloud. The smell of he-goat is strong. The strange and twitching dancer seems to have cloven feet, so nimble and truly frightening are his steps. His face is hidden in the cowl of skins, and he holds two long wands of oleander branches in each hand. Shock! A second Bou Jeloud leaps from behind a tree. The two Pans dance away from the fire and suddenly curve alarmingly toward the screaming girls, chasing them and whipping them. Those touched by the wands would be fertile in their marriages.

This, I saw, was where the spirit of pandemonium of the Rolling Stones came from—and it would inspire the whole of rock and roll. But I knew, too, that my own tutelary deity was an entirely different member of the pantheon.

On Sunday I took Linda down to the Portobello Road market and bought her an antique lace gown, velvet costumes, and Victorian baubles. I wanted to dress her in the style of the Pre-Raphaelite paintings that I loved. I saw Linda as a Burne-Jones maiden—my maiden, my love. We wandered through the market with its hundreds of stalls, jewelery, antique rags, clocks and watches, china and silverware, old books and magazines, Edwardian writing-cases, delicate porcelain and papier-mâché dolls, music boxes, cigarette cards, military uniforms, brass ornaments, old furniture, regimental medals, oil paintings and old prints, 78-rpm records and fantastic record players with wind-up handles and large horns.

The long street teemed with people, smiling and calling to each other, buskers and street entertainers playing guitars, and the aroma of African weed wafting out of the Blue-Beat record store, scenting the soft summer air. Finally, I bought Linda a bloodstone ring.

I was in love and making music for the fun of it. My love and I were just eighteen, and I could see our love glowing. We were young and we were running against the wind.

The British hit parade saw the arrival of a new American male singer in 1965, the heartthrob P. J. Proby. He was tall and spoke in a slow Texas drawl. Very handsome, with features curiously similar to Elvis's. He quickly became a huge live performer, causing fan mania on a major scale, particularly with the young girls. Then he became a front-page sensation when one night on stage he split his tight pants and the audience went wild.

Needless to say he made sure that he split his pants each night thereafter.

P. J. Proby and I struck up a friendship at the many TV shows we were doing. He had a kind of a roadie called Bongo Wolf, who was dressed in early hippie outdoorsy-type togs and carried a large bowie knife in a sheath in his belt.

I hung out at P. J.'s Chelsea house off the King's Road, filled with the chic and the raggedy all that summer. It was at one of his many parties that I met Paul Bernath, a young guy from the States, over here checking it out. We became friends as we sat and watched the circus of party goers file in and out of the Chelsea terrace.

One night Proby had just returned from Scandinavia and brought back two young blondes to live with him. He danced with them both in the living room as Paul and I waited for the trip to come on. Once again Ravi Shankar was on the turntable. At one point I found myself in the bedroom that Bongo Wolf had secured as his lair. The small space was filled with those dolls that fans gave us in those days, weird Scandinavian Gonks, troll-like figures with long hair and ancient, wrinkled skin. Bongo sat in the midst of the Gonks, smiling like a clown. I sat with Paul on the other side of the room, flashing on how Bongo was really a Gonk. This got to him. All around him the other Gonks began to talk to him and climb all over his flabby form. He took his bowie knife and began to stab at the Gonks. This made us all convulse with laughter, so odd did he look as he leaped around killing his Gonk friends.

Laughter changed to dread as I realized he was headed our way. What if he saw me as a Gonk? I quickly grabbed Paul, and we left Bongo Wolf to his tripping in the little bedroom and the poor wee Gonks.

In the early dawn I walked through the silent house, passing the open door to Proby's bedroom. He lay sound asleep with the two nubile maidens draped around him. From his long dark hair, which he wore in a tail, to the tips of his slender fingers he was a most beautiful young man, like a raven-haired Brian Jones.

Fairytale

A second album was called for, so I went back into the studio and continued recording new songs.

Down below the streets of London, I opened my guitar case and the session for the second album, *Fairytale*, began. Shawn and I had had a few joints, of course, but concentration was not impaired. Fine tracks were placed on tape. Shawn played his twelve-string on two songs—"Summer Day Reflection Song" and "Jersey Thursday," both my own. The first was a very painterly lyric, the second a gaze into a crystal and a weekend on the Isle of Jersey. Shawn's raga-style picking complemented the moods perfectly.

I also recorded an autobiographical song of mine, "To Try for the Sun." This lyric told of the life I had recently lived on the road with Gypsy Dave. My melodic airs were improving, and I wrote chorus sections easily. The piercing harmonica flew above the complex finger-style guitar I was developing.

"Belated Forgiveness Plea": when I hear it now I see a girl called Tristy whom I'd loved in Welwyn, but left behind for the life on the road. The seagull, my "totem" bird always represents freedom in my songs.

"Circus of Sour" was written by my friend Paul Bernath. His song is a great little parody of real life seen as a circus.

I also recorded "The Little Tin Soldier," Shawn Phillip's classic retelling of the Andersen tale.

Another "cover" I recorded for this second album was the country blues classic by Blind Gary Davis "Candy Man." I had picked it up from Bert Jansch and given it my own rendering. I was to meet The Reverend Gary Davis when I guested on Pete Seeger's TV show in the States the following year.

The "Ballad of Geraldine" I wrote for a friend. I sang it as if she were telling her sad tale.

This album would include two self-penned songs already recorded and released, "Colours" and "Ballad of a Crystal Man." The latter was an antiwar song but suggested New Age interests to come. The track had been previously released on the "Universal Soldier" EP that month of August 1965.

I was still learning from the folk blues master guitarist, Bert Jansch. He had written a beautiful song called "Oh Deed I Do." His use of language to convey a traditional mood with a modern experience absolutely blew my mind. I wanted to record this one, and he consented. Now that I hear it all these years later, I know that I sang the lyric for my Linda: "I got a jealous dream of losing you, Oh deed I have."

All of this music could be described as coming from the folk-blues tradition, with the exception of a dimension you might call a "new way of seeing" that I was developing. The track that definitely moved me into another space entirely was the jazz fusion "Sunny Goodge Street." The coproducer, Terry Kennedy, came up with a fine arrangement around my descending waltz-time finger style. I was learning major seventh- and ninth-chord structures from the flying fingers of Bert Jansch.

But it was the lyric that was the most different way of seeing that I had written so far. I was describing the subculture emerging from the underground and the elusive search for the self.

Two years before the beginning of flower power, I was singing:

> The magician he sparkles in satin and velvet,
> You gaze at his splendour with eyes you've not used yet,
> I tell you his name is
> Love, Love, Love.
>
> —Donovan Leitch,
> *"Sunny Goodge Street"*

I felt the urge to introduce key spiritual ideas. Astrologers will tell you my stars confirm this. The term "mellow" also makes its first appearance in this song, describing the music of the great jazz bassist Charlie Mingus.

The Buddhist virtue of compassion had also entered a song of mine before "Sunny Goodge Street," one that was never released until the 1990s; it was "Darkness of My Night" (later titled "Breezes of Patchouli"). One couplet sings of:

> Riding feathered wings to make like I'm a dove
> Often have I heard the world as it cries out for some love,
> Cries out for some warmth, a little compassionate light,
> They're feeling so alone, love, in the Darkness of their Night
> —Donovan Leitch,
> *"Darkness of My Night"*

The message from the Buddhist teachings I had been studying was clear. Compassion for all sentient beings was a lesson no government cared to teach. The realization of the Oneness of all life was definitely not being encouraged by Church or State. As far as the unenlightened world was concerned, God was in his heaven and his priests in tanks.

The songs are also full of Celtic imagery. I was continuing to explore the connections between Celtic and Buddhist writings. Celtic nature poems are sometimes as short as Japanese Haiku. The direct experience of the Celtic poet or artist, which he weaves into interrelated patterns of scrolls and interlacing lines of energy, reminded me of the Daoist flow of energy in the yin and the yang.

Scholars have recently confirmed that an ancient connection between India and the Celtic world shows up in place names and deities. In India a "dun" is a fort just as it was in ancient Ireland. "Taras" are Tibetan goddesses, and the sacred temple complex in ancient Ireland is called "The Hill of Tara." Small world, large spiritual reality. But to my mind, the most important connection between Celtic magic and the Indian subcontinent is the music. When The Beatles released their first record, "Love Me Do," it was clear that the aeolian cadences they had harmonized with their vocals were chants of an ancient order. Since the 1960s the whole earth has been harmonized by Celtic musicians.

On the back sleeve of the *Fairytale* album I put a second title, "Songs for

Sunshine People," and from my art studies I brought to this a Celtic sense of design, selecting a Gothic typeface to convey a romantic mood.

Up to this time most album covers were happy mugshots of artists. I chose a black-and-white shot by Jack Pia, a photographer from the town of St. Albans where I had spent my early beatnik years. I wore a jeans jacket and, rather than smile into the camera, I gazed down at the floor. In the background were four of my campus friends, artists and musicians. On the front cover I printed the chorus of the song "Sunny Goodge Street."

This second album, *Fairytale,* set the scene for my arrival as a bard who would present a way of seeing the wonder of the natural world. I was mocked as a simpleton, when I sang of birds and bees and flowers like a child. Indeed, I was keeping the "wonder eye" open—just like a child.

I was also showing concern for the future of the world's ecosystem. My early "Green" philosophy would later be called flower power by the press, but it would take two decades for the world at large to realize the danger to our Mother Earth. The hallucinogenic shamanism of the Celts finds the supreme spiritual forces in the natural world. This is why, for the Celts, Mother Earth is the Goddess.

The *Fairytale* album was completed and scheduled for release in Britain in October 1965. That September I went to the Savoy Hotel once again, this time to attend the awards ceremony for songwriting initiated by Ivor Novello. I received the Ivor Novello Award for my song "Catch The Wind". It was the first time such an award had been given for a first song. I gave it to my mum. She treasured it like a film Oscar, which it resembles, and it sat on her mantelshelf.

The EP record "Universal Soldier" had entered the British charts and featured high in all the other countries too.

My life as a beatnik had attracted the attention of a television documentary director, Charles Squire. The London television company Associated Rediffusion hired Squire to make a film, which he envisaged as a film of my life as a vagabond, leading to discovery and subsequent rise to fame at eighteen years of age. The documentary would trace my scuffling days in London to the beaches of Cornwall and on to my success. In October 1965 we commenced filming. Scenes would include Gypsy and myself hitching down the road to the coasts of Cornwall, sleeping in ruins on the way and washing in streams. This was near to the truth, but obviously lacking in authenticity in many respects. But yes, Gyp and I did sleep almost anywhere we could when we traveled, and we did eventually arrive on the beaches and sang songs and lived the life of the wayfarer in search of our fortunes. Sometimes we even washed! Unfortunately it was late in the year when we filmed, so that the summer splendor of St. Ives was missing. The film shows a gray cast to the sky that matched my mood at the time.

Because despite all the good times, Linda and I were slipping away from each other. She said she needed space, but this only made me more desperate to hold on to her. I invited her to St. Ives during the filming. She kept out of most shots, but sat on an old pillbox while I sang "Ballad of Geraldine." At the end of the song she blows a candle out, and the look on my face as I sing the last stanza shows whole worlds of feeling.

The filming rarely went on past sunset and one night I took Linda to the pictures to see the new Anthony Quinn and Alan Bates film, *Zorba the Greek*. This story of a British writer who moves to Greece impressed me. I sat holding hands with Linda in the little St. Ives cinema, dreaming of taking her to the Greek Isles. But for all the love I was feeling for Linda, we did not make love during our time in St. Ives.

The film crew moved to London to re-create the first *Ready Steady Go!* and the mad life of the new star, buying clothes and stuff for the flat in Maida Vale. I draped a Union Jack over my bed. "Up in the morning early" shots were taken of Gypsy and me eating cornflakes and yawning.

To complete the film the director suggested a beatnik party in one of my painter friends' studios. So we set the date for a party to take place in Meadow Studios near Watford. I arrived late, and by then the whole party was already completely pissed on the gallons of free wine that the TV chaps had thoughtfully brought along. My friends were reeling and jigging to the music and generally behaving with complete abandon, so much so that the hash smokers had rolled up in front of the cameras and were blowing away regardless. "Charlie," I protested, "What gave you this great idea to bring twenty gallons of wine for my friends"? "Well, it's a beatnik party, is it not?" he replied. I was concerned that the cameras were catching all this. This was the first time such a party was shown to the British television audience when it was broadcast some months later on 19 January 1966.

The film was titled *A Boy Called Donovan*, and it is a record of a way of life that was very common in many provincial bohemian communities all over Britain in the first five years of the 1960s.

After the film I continued recording and released another single, "Turquoise," with "Hey Gyp (Dig the Slowness)" on the B side. I blew my first strong blues harp on this B side. This was followed the same month with a second EP and the single record "To Sing for You." Both went into the charts.

The World Is
Beautiful

Meanwhile, Linda was busy being independent. It was in the clubs one night that she met an American, Alan Pariser, heir to the Dixie Cup fortune in Illinois. Alan was in London to meet and swing with the new upcoming 1960s in-crowd. He asked Linda if she wanted to try her luck as a model in the States, and she liked the idea. When he offered her a ticket to fly over, Linda refused because she did not want to owe anything to anyone, so she sold her little car and bought her own ticket. She left her son with her mother while she journeyed away from her home to seek work to support him.

In New York she met Barry Feinstein, Alan's friend and a photographer who was married to Mary Travers of the folk group Peter, Paul and Mary. Linda was asked to be nanny to their children. Her friend, Celia Hammond, was also in New York for a modeling job and they had met at a club, when Brian Jones walked in with Dylan. Once again Linda felt the pain as they looked at each other across the dark room. They did not speak. Dylan had Brian in the corner, deep in conversation.

Linda flew on to Los Angeles and moved in with Billy, a young actress and friend of Alan's. Linda was glad to be away from the "paparazzi" of England, who hounded her as she was the first celebrated girlfriend of the most charismatic British Rock Star, Brian Jones. The actress took Linda down to the film set where she was working; it was a beach movie. Although Linda was offered work there she did not take to the beach-movie scene. And she did not want to play the game. She quickly realized, too, that modeling was considered a very different vocation in America. *Playboy* was the magazine to be seen in, not *Vogue, Harper's,* or *Queen.* Although she needed the work, she decided to pass.

Linda was also offered a boutique in Hollywood by Phil Specter, whom she had met at a Stones session. Vidal Sassoon offered her a job too, but again she was wary.

When I flew to the States to begin my tour, I hoped to see Linda in Hollywood, and I was hoping against hope that she would agree to marry me. The Californian sun was shining when Gypsy, Ashley, Anita, and I arrived in the City of Angels. We would stay in the Southern Music Spanish Rococo mansion in the hills as guests of Mrs. Monica Peer and her son, Ralph Peer Junior. We pulled in through the gates in a classic 1950s Cadillac limo. There was a wonderful garden with rare flowers and exotic trees.

I was ecstatic when Linda agreed to see me. The plan was that I would stay with her in the main house, while Ash, Anita, and Gyp would stay in the cottages below the jungle-style pool, like in a Tarzan movie with a waterfall and dense greenery hanging over the cool waters, blossoms floating on the surface.

Linda arrived, looking radiant, slender, and tanned from lying by the pool at her friend's house. The sun had done her good.

My heart leapt when I saw that she was still wearing the ring I had given her. We started to have fun the minute we met, and I quickly began to wonder if Linda really would commit.

On the street I was recognized from the TV shows I had done. The fans were still very "straight"—no style—the boys with short hair, the girls still in bobby socks and ponytails. I was a freak from another planet called England. On the airwaves was a British DJ named John Peel, who had captured his audience with the very distinct Liverpool intonation, and so fans would ask me to speak just to hear my accent.

Sometimes Linda dressed in the lace costume I had bought her from the antique stalls of the Portobello Road back in London, then I bought her Mexican blouses and swirling skirts that we found down on Alvero Street, the original village of Los Angeles, as we explored the city. We ate Mexican food, raced round the fairground on the pier, and drove down Sunset Boulevard in the limo to the beach to walk on the sand and to see the magnificent sunsets over the ocean. Then we returned to our painted room to make love on the cool silk sheets.

> I bought you lace and velvet
> And Victoriana trinket,
> Dressed you up in Art Nouveau
> When nobody else kink it.
>
> Dark-eyed blue-jean angel,
> Red Egyptian hair,
> Dark-eyed blue-jean angel,
> Watch the people stare.
> —Donovan Leitch,
> *"Dark-eyed Blue Jean Angel"*

One star-filled night I gave Linda her first LSD trip. On the walls of the bedroom, there were framed prints of cherubs. She gazed into my eyes, and when I looked at her I could only see her as a frightened young fawn. I did not know that she saw these babies as a warning that she was in danger of going through with me the same terrible cycle she had been through with Brian. It was all too much. She leapt from our silken bed and ran upstairs to where Anita and Ashley slept. She told Anita that she had seen that our relationship could not go on if it meant another child so soon, and to be torn apart again by fame.

I was confused and did not know then what had happened. The next day all seemed to be fine again at first, but then she would not make love to me. So we kissed awkwardly at the airport. I returned to London after the tour ended. Linda remained in Hollywood, promising to write to me every day.

The cold gray skies of England did not cool my ardor for the girl in the sun. I waited desperately for her return.

I had not seen George Harrison for a while and missed him. The Beatles had released another album, and I eagerly bought it. The dawning consciousness of my spiritual quest appeared on the new album *Rubber Soul*, released in December 1965, two months after *Fairytale*.

Apart from the obvious reference to "soul" in the album title, no fewer than seven of the songs were a "new way of seeing." Lennon's "Norwegian Wood" and "Nowhere Man" contained folk elements and revealingly truthful lyrics. George Harrison spoke his mind on "Think for Yourself." "Love" takes on a different meaning in the song "The Word."

The opening chords of George's "If I Needed Someone" had a strong modal feel, the guitar-picking sounding a little like the sitar that he had amused himself with on the set of the film *Help*. Echoes of things to come. And although this amazing quartet would not take LSD until the following year of 1966, they had heard me and other friends talk about the experience and their song "I'm Looking Through You" was not about the Invisible Man.

John Lennon sang a dolorous farewell to his past, the introspective ballad "In My Life." The plaintive melody only just covers the distress he felt inside, but perhaps the best word to describe what these four young men from Liverpool were feeling *was* "Help." They were experiencing the dark side of fame.

Over in the States, spiritual-quest lyrics had always been sung by the great gospel groups like the Staple Singers. The soul singers who came from the gospel background were enthusing audiences with spiritual excitement and secular lyrics. Definitely inspirational.

Bob Dylan's songs on his three debut albums *Bob Dylan, The Freewheelin' Bob Dylan,* and *The Times They Are A-Changin'* chronicled Guthrie-Kerouac-style travels around America, a drifter's tale through the ruins of the American Dream. Here was a sharp and incisive poet railing sardonically against the military-industrial complex. He was also an occasional humorist and he, too, sang songs of Love, Life, and Death, such as outside the "Gates of Eden." Although no mention was directly made of Eastern spiritual schools that were part of the beatnik scene, Dylan's dedication in the collection *Bob Dylan Writings & Drawings,* reads:

> . . . and to the great wondrous melodious spirit
> which covereth the oneness of us all.

The search to find an answer to the great questions of life and death had begun for all of us. Conscious lyrics had reemerged from the folk tradition—gospel was an influence, too—and then a certain holy plant was opening the eyes of many of us to "see."

Over in the States, Roger McGuinn of The Byrds had pioneered the magnificent twelve-string guitar sound on Pete Seeger's song "Turn, Turn, Turn" (lyrics from the Book of Ecclesiastes). That December my little flat in Maida Vale was constantly filled with the sound of The Beatles and The Byrds as I waited for Linda.

In every life there comes along a song or an album that comes to us when life is tearing our heart apart. The Byrds' album *Mr. Tambourine Man* was that for me. The songs "Here Without You" (Clark) and "You Won't Have to Cry" (Clark/McGuinn) were, it seemed, written for Linda and me.

But two months after I had returned, I finally came to terms with the reality that Linda would not be joining me. On the other end of the phone she would fall into silence as I pleaded for her to come and be my wife. So I did the work set out for me—and to be involved with my music would help for a while—then night would fall over the city and my heart would pound. Gypsy watched as I collapsed into a deep depression.

There was only one thing for it: I must fly over to Hollywood and carry her away on my shining charger. And so, dressed in the heavy gear of a London winter—peacoat, Norwegian turtleneck sweater, and boots—I boarded the airliner and headed west to see my love. I arrived in California with high hopes and in a great sweat. I checked into the Tropicana on Santa Monica Boulevard and called Linda at the motel where she was renting an apartment, hanging out with her American friend Cathy Cozy, a lovely girl of sixteen, long blonde hair, and a tan. Linda identified with Cathy, as she also had been drawn to music very young. They palled up and went to all the best parties. Linda's rock-and-roll pedigree opened many doors. Everyone wanted to know her.

But acceptable offers of work had not materialized, and Linda was spending the days by the pool in the motel, opposite the Body Shop strip joint on Sunset Boulevard.

I arrived and walked into the cool air of the darkened room. An Indian bedspread and scarves over the lamps gave the apartment an Oriental air. Linda lay on the bed and said nothing.

You had one eye on the TV and one eye on me,
You just sat there saying nothing while I made my plea
—Donovan Leitch,
"Motel Plea"

Then she told me she wanted me to stay with her in California. I said I could not do that.

Cathy took me to the coffee shop next door, and I sat dazed as she explained that Linda was looking for independence to grow. But, stupidly, I could not see why she could not return to England to marry me. What was I to do? I was the male. She should follow me, I reasoned.

I boarded the jet back to London, a heavy lead weight in my chest.

Nineteen sixty-six opened with great expectations and so many positive vibes from Gypsy, Anita, and Ashley, but I remained heartbroken.

Anita would take me aside and hug me, saying, "She really does love you, Don. I know she does; she is an amazing young woman and needs time."

I thank you, Anita, for your sympathetic love. And although you have passed over to the other side, I feel your love still, in waves behind my eyes. As the Greeks Say, *Sag a por puli? Aga Pi moo?* Oh, 'Nita, we did have such good times in the two little flats on the Edgware Road, you, Ash, Gyp, and me. Nights full of music and joy. Only your good-hearted humor saw me through that winter.

Slowly, I recovered. It is said that the music business loves an artist in heartache, for then the songs ring with a longing that sells records. Soon a first song was forged from my sorrow. I guess that deep inside me I knew we were loving each other. The song was called "Sunshine Superman."

The quality as well as the quantity of my songwriting was increasing dramatically after my break up with Linda Lawrence. I penned a song or two every day. Although I would not admit it then, she appears in most of them.

And so in January of 1966 I began to hear in my head the songs for an album that would not be released until September in the United States and early 1967 in Britain. Into the night and through many a London dawn I would work, writing and drawing. From out of the page would come sketches of Linda as a dancer, delicately turning in her leotard, with my ring suspended in the air before her, the old gold ring with the bloodstone that I had bought Linda down the Portobello Road so long ago last summer, a ring I pictured her still wearing over there in LA.

In my room over the street, I sat on the tatami mats, cross-legged, cradling my cherry red Gibson J45 guitar, the little darling box that I had bought with Linda in Hollywood with the first money from my first record deal. Towering majestically over me was the huge brass bed with the lace spread. Such an odd combination, this metal bed on the Japanese mats, but I was young. My tastes swung from Victorian to Oriental, together with much else I had adopted earlier on from nineteenth-century Paris. I had studied the Japanese paintings of Van Gogh and Gaugin. I was reading Tennyson and Lewis Carroll, and buying silk prints of the Art Nouveau artist Alphonse Mucha. But above all, I drowned in "memories" of Montmartre, as if I had been there. I continued to collect books with photographs of the cafés and studios of Montparnasse, too, looking for another life for myself. I could smell the paint and taste the garlic. Looking now at press cuttings from the time, I see that I was considered a very odd sort of creature. I readily used the word "beautiful" to describe music, art, an event, or the fellow musicians of the time who shared my enthusiasms. In bold, two-inch type the music press came up with a phrase: "Donovan thinks the world is 'Beautiful.' " It would come up again and again, every time I was mentioned.

Strange, too, to see from the press articles at that time that I was considered "gay." Well, not really, I suppose. The feminine side of the male had not emerged from its chrysalis, due, no doubt, to the patriarchal Christian culture of the previous two thousand years. All things female were considered weaker, sillier, of very little consequence. So feminine feelings from males were seen as worthy of scorn. Yes, witch hunts had successfully overpowered the old religion that honored women as goddesses. She, who is the Mother Earth, She who gives us birth, She who raises us to life and heals us with Her herbs.

> Women were dying to be free—
> Isis, Astarte, Diane, Hegati, Demitra, Kali, Inarna.
> —C. Murphy,
> *"Burning Times," Bal Music Ltd.*

When I sang of the feminine nature of the male I was ridiculed, but I was in good company. Perhaps my songs appealed to so many millions of young girls for this reason?

I love women and, although I longed for another night with Linda (as Gypsy would always say, with a wink and a laugh) "there are many other fish in the sea."

> But I was having none of it, I still had my toys,
> Playing snakes and ladders with my business boys,
> Strutting like some rocking rolling hipster of the slums,
> Waiting in the dreamtime for a love that never comes.
>
> —Donovan Leitch,
> *"Motel Plea"*

Sunshine Supergirl

❖

In December of 1965, I arrived back in London and went straight into the EMI Recording Studios on Abbey Road to complete the remaining few tracks for my experimental album *Sunshine Superman*.

Mickie Most, my new record producer, had an instinctive ear for a good song and for the simplicity that represents the best arrangement. I was obsessed with my mission to present bohemian ideas in a pop music frame, and I was happy to be with the top pop music producer of the era to help me do this.

Mickie introduced me to John Cameron, a new whizz-kid arranger with classical training and a love of jazz. John had come down from Cambridge with a group of bright young men, who included Peter Cook and Dudley Moore.

To prepare, I sat with Mickie and John and played them the new songs. I knew we three had a creative bond. Mickie asked me what I heard in the songs and listened sensitively to every crazy idea. He realized I was hearing sounds that came from many sources: classical, jazz, ethnic, medieval minstrelsy, and he saw the potential for a veritable new fusion of music, a "world music" sound, before this term was thought of. I consciously intended to frame my meaningful and poetic lyrics in popular musical forms.

John saw my songs as minimovies and began composing sound effects around the melodies I had created.

In the London studios at this time, records were made with "session men," hired musicians who were booked to play for artists who had no band of their own. I fit into this category. I was a solo artist. The musical parts for such sessions were "arranged" for the musicians to play.

John and Mickie had heard my jazz track "Sunny Goodge Street" from the previous year and knew the direction to take on the first song I played them, "Bert's Blues." John surpassed himself on the arrangement, creating the first of many jazz suites. The jazz musos and classical cats and kittens were overjoyed to be able to play such music, and I made solid friendships with master players Danny Thompson and Spike Healey (concert bassists), Tony Carr (drums and percussion), Harold McNair (flute and sax) and, of course, John Cameron (keyboards). Danny Thompson would become my favorite bass player and close friend over the long years ahead. He would also become the premier player on his instrument, courted by hosts of top artists to play on their records.

Mickie booked us into Abbey Road Studios where, a year later, the Beatles' *Sergeant Pepper's Lonely Hearts Club Band* was to be recorded.

I sat with John and went through more arrangements. There would be parts for classical rock, blues, jazz, and my own acoustic guitars, all woven in and out of the lyrical stories.

> I've been looking, oh yeah, I say I've been looking
> For a good girl, you better believe it baby, yeah!
> I've been looking for a good girl, you better,
> Ain't kiddin' you, ain't kiddin' you,
> Ain't kiddin' you, yes.
>
> —Donovan Leitch,
> *"Bert's Blues"*

It's a song for Linda yet, I denied it to myself.

It was a treat to watch Cameron conduct, and the next track we cut showed off his talents perfectly. "Legend of a Girl-Child Linda" was arranged as a purely classical piece. I played live in the orchestra on finger-style acoustic guitar. John conducted me; and the orchestra, with a sensitive touch, expressed my deepest longings with this 6.50-minute track. We certainly broke the mold of pop music—and folk music, for that matter.

Strange to say, I had dreamt the writing of this song, waking Gypsy up one night and playing it to him in a hotel in Sweden. I had seen and heard myself composing in the dream. I have done this many times since, actually waking up to write down the words and play the tune on my guitar.

Gypsy always listened to my new songs and gave me support when I needed it. There were no songs like mine to compare with. It was all new directions, uncharted seas. Yet Gyp felt the waves and was always there on the shore to urge me onward. Thanks, Gyp, more than I can say.

In those days it was considered normal to record three tracks in three hours, an album in a week, and my sessions were no exception. After the initial rehearsal for parts and sound tests, I usually got the vocal in one take or two. Multitracking was yet to come. All the music was recorded on four-track machines. The sound engineers were wizards at separating the instruments. All of the recordings were in glorious monaural sound.

I recorded a song called "Museum." This was the first time the flute became important to my music. The late, great Harold McNair played his silver flute on this one. We continued with the same musical lineup, plus the addition of lead guitarists Eric Ford and Jimmy Page. This track was not included on the final album, but it can be found on the *Troubadour* box set.

Jimmy was a session man then. He was in demand for his skill in so many styles, and my fusion of jazz, folk, and Latin rock gave him an interesting lick to play. Quiet and withdrawn, he was one of the three major British guitarists of the time, alongside Eric Clapton and Jeff Beck. Elfin features, slim body, and the dark clothes of a bohemian drifter showed me he was from the same scene as me. Later, Jimmy would develop an image that came out of his interest in the occult, the Western path of magic. This was later misunderstood as dark and evil, just as his hero Aleister Crowley's image had been misunderstood in the 1920s.

"Sunshine Superman" was a three-chord Latin rocker, scored for two basses, one acoustic and one electric. The drummer was Bobby Orr and the percussionist Tony "the Maltese Falcon" Carr. The electric guitars were Jimmy and Eric again. The new sound of rock harpsichord was played by

John Cameron—Baroque & Roll! I, of course, played the acoustic Gibson J45, and as soon as the unusual array of sounds leapt out of the speakers in the control room, Mickie's face lit up with delight. He knew this was a hit single. He just knew.

> Sunshine came softly through my window today
> Could've tripped out easy but I've changed ma way.
> It'll take time, I know it, but in a while
> You're gonna be mine, I know it.
> We'll do it in style
> 'Cause I've made ma mind up you're going to be mine
> Any trick in the book now, baby, that I can find.
>
> —Donovan Leitch,
> *"Sunshine Superman" 1966*

The term "sunshine" was a slang term for LSD then. I would soon be dubbed the first British "psychedelic singer," I guess a reference to "trippy" lyrics. I knew then that I should create music to "trip" by, musical journeys into the hinterland of the soul. Over the years many fans have told me that my music settled the terrors of bad "trips" on acid.

I also felt that my "superstrength" as a man should be gentle and penetrating, the power of Love and Will combined. All this for a girl I believed was out of my life forever.

What was going on?

Despite the business machinations that were beginning to threaten any release of my ambitious new work. I carried on regardless, designing the covers with my artist friends Mick and Sheena McCall, in their apartment at Fifteen Cromwell Road, London. We wanted to "design" the record sleeve to reflect the images in the songs. This was a breakthrough. The art schools of Britain had given many British musicians a grounding in the visual arts, and—following my example—many of the bands from art schools adopted a "look" from the particular visual styles they liked. The Who were "Pop Art," The Stones were "jazz-cool." At that time I was pre-Raphaelite.

But actually my image was just then changing. I went down to the tailor to the stars, "Granny Takes a Trip" on the King's Road in London. I bought a double-breasted, brown-striped suit in the style of the 1940s and picked up a pair of two-tone shoes I had ordered from the bootmaker John Lobb, of St. James.

Although the European label had frozen my career in the courts, the single "Sunshine Superman" was set for a U.S. release in July 1966. I flew into New York City to have some pictures taken in my new gear and meet my new record company, Epic Records. The president of the label was Clive Davis. We posed in his office signing the deal.

The photo shoot for the album was with hot photographer Barry Feinstein, then husband of Mary Travers (of Peter, Paul and Mary) and, of course, a friend of Linda's. He knew the New York Woodstock scene and had also photographed Dylan around the same time.

Barry set me up with a cane chair and a cane walking stick, capturing a set of classic images in black and white and color, me in my double-breasted suit and tie, posing like a posh Chaplin. These images would grace the cover of the new album *Sunshine Superman*.

While in New York, Gypsy and I went down to Andy Warhol's studio, The Factory. Maybe Barry took us down, or Ginsberg, I can't remember. Andy was a difficult person to talk to. In fact, more than difficult: he didn't say a word. He was in his "Silver Pillows" period and the plastic pillows were floating high on the ceiling of his workplace.

Andy's second in command, Gerard, had set up a Super-8 Film Camera to document guests. I sat in front of the lens on my own, staring blankly. Lots of young chicks were also filming anything that went on in the old warehouse.

Andy's band, The Velvet Underground, were around, too; and I remember a vague gig with strobe lights, Lou Reed and Nico droning lyrics to a loud electric cacophony of sound.

One night I followed some of Andy's filmmakers into a cab and down to a psychiatrists' convention. Upon arrival at the event, these girls stood on the pavement awaiting the psychiatrists who were about to leave. The chicks had been given questions for impromptu interviews.

One girl raised her microphone and said, "We are from the studio of Andy Warhol, and we would like your comment."

The psychiatrists began to warm to the beautiful young lady. Then she asked, "Do you still masturbate?"

The answers from the various psychiatrists were filmed, some embarrassed, some intrigued.

Andy Warhol was definitely a blond. I like to recall the story that the British pop artist David Hockney told his North Country mother when he returned from his first trip to California. She was obviously surprised to see that David was now quite blond. Hockney explained, "It's all the chlorine in the swimming pools, Ma'am."

Pop Art images would soon be part of popular culture as 1966 raced on. Of course I had written a song with a pop comic title, "Sunshine Superman" and the "collage" method of layering popular images had influenced my writing. Soon Andy Warhol would create a record cover for his band, The Velvet Underground, that depicted a banana. It would seem that Andy had not missed the phrase "electrical banana" in "Mellow Yellow," my number-one song earlier that year.

Before we left New York we were surprised to see at my press reception a strange figure crouched and creeping through the crowd toward us. He leapt up in front of us with wild hair and hypnotic, staring eyes. It was Salvador Dalì. I flew back to London and did my first interviews in ages with the British press. I was keen to tell of my adventures in the States and announce the new record. The *Melody Maker* ran a story on 4 June 1966 by Bob Dawbarn, titled "Donovan, now for the comeback."

Interesting to note, I had only dropped out of Britain for a few months and was already having to make a comeback. The British press are eager to dismiss an artist if she or he is not featured high in the charts. This is a put down of the thousands of artists who are serious about their work yet do not have hit records. Shame on music writers who should be encouraging *music,* not fame.

He was the curly haired lad who used to have records released and they went straight into the top 50. He went to America three months ago—since when news of him has been scarce. Now he's back, tanned, brimming with confidence, full of new plans and wearing spectacles that have apparently been made out of red bicycle reflectors. Was it, we wondered, possible that he had been off the British scene too long?

"I'm not worried by it," said Donovan. "I look on it as a stop in all the dramas of contractual battles. It's the end of one scene and the beginning of another. I'm coming back a bit cleaner and freer to write what I want to write."

My impressions of America in 1966 continued in the article:

"Music is changing fast. It's taken a long time but beautiful things always take a long time and there are a lot of beautiful things happening right now."

The British press had slammed a Dylan song while I had been away.

"I hear Bob Dylan has been given a hard time here. His 'Rainy Day Women' will become a college song in the States. It's like the national anthem over there."

The article closed with:

Donovan's act was billed in the US as the Now Music.

Now? Yes, and in just one night I would become the stuff of reporters' dreams.

Magician

❖

On 19 January 1966, the documentary *A Boy Called Donovan* was shown on television in Britain. This film of my early life would attract very heavy changes in my life in the months to come.

February came around, and I set out once again for the States. The *Fairytale* album had been released in the United States in December and was doing well.

On 19 February 1966, I made my debut in Carnegie Hall, New York City. I had arrived as a concert performer. The package tours were behind me, and I was recognized as an artist by the toughest audiences in the world.

The company executives of Hickory Records were ecstatic at the reception I received. They were actually surprised that I could hold the audience for two hours with only one guitar and a small simple voice. Deceptively simple, I might add. Shawn Phillips had also accompanied me on the Carnegie Hall concert, playing his twelve-string and sitar. This was the first time a Western pop audience had seen and heard the sitar on stage.

We went down to Greenwich Village to dig the scene, man. I met John Sebastian of The Lovin' Spoonful, who were playing in a small club called The Bitter End. He was handsome and affable and set folks at their ease quite effortlessly. John would become a life-long friend. He and I shared a love of country blues and jug band music. John is one of the great guitar pickers of this style, and his harmonica playing is second to none. Later he would marry Linda's best friend, Cathy Cozy.

John Sebastian and Paul Butterfield had the harp sound down that year. The Village was really happening as we stood and talked on the corner of Bleeker and McDougal that they sang about.

One night as I walked past a small club below the village streets I heard a dark, sonorous voice coming up from the basement. It was Richie Havens, a tall African-American singer/songwriter, who sang out of a mouth with no teeth. He astounded me, forming his chords on the guitar by curving his thumb over the neck in a most unorthodox manner. He also tuned the strings to his own particular tuning, and the music was wonderful. Richie and I struck up a friendship that has lasted the course. Richie adopted my song "Wear Your Love Like Heaven" so it became part of his own music. He now has a very good set of teeth, so he must have had dental work done to replace his lost ones.

I visited the studio where John Sebastian was recording with the rest of The Lovin' Spoonful. Sebastian's songs are superlative. He was the composer of a little masterpiece called "Summer in the City," a big hit that year. He would also write another huge hit, "Daydream." The Lovin' Spoonful were to have a third hit that year of 1966 with "Did You Ever Have to Make Up Your Mind?" This last song describes the dilemma we young musos were faced with, so many girls attracting our attention.

Gypsy and I ran into Allen Ginsberg. Dressed in a conventional suit without beads or bells he looked like an eccentric, long-haired professor. He took me down to see a new and quirky artist in a small underground venue. I sat in the funky little room and watched Tiny Tim do his show. Tiny Tim played Music Hall standards on a small ukulele in a high-pitched, wistful way. The audience gaped at his ill-fitting clothes and long straggly hair falling over his shoulders. I had never seen anything like him and marveled at his arrival on the scene.

Incredibly, it turned out that Tim had stayed in Linda's mum's guest house in Windsor, and had actually learned some of his repertoire from her mother, Violet, who is a fine singer, songs like "Tiptoe Through the Tulips" and "The White Cliffs of Dover."

Also on the bill that evening in the Village were The Fugs, a collection of "performance artists" who shouted outrageous lyrics to a rock backing. The singer, Ed Sanders, drew blood as he smashed the microphone into his mouth. This was early punk for sure.

After the show Ginsberg took Gypsy Shawn and me to a party in a brownstone town house. We smoked some DMT, and the fleshy paintings on the ceiling began to writhe. Allen held my hand and gently came on to me. I declined. He smiled a cool OK and withdrew.

During that trip to New York, Gyp and I were staying in a hotel called The Hampshire House. Up in the dark rooms overlooking the park, I sat up late with Shawn and a young girl singer. Her hair was cropped, an unusual style then. She explained that her hair had been caught in a Ferris wheel. A near-death situation. There in the dark gloom of The Hampshire House apartment I felt a chill, like a pall, descending on my journey. Was it the ghost of my love for Linda? Was fame a trap? Was it taking me away from the love of my life, as it had Brian Jones? Was my freedom slipping away?

Gypsy saw what we were losing sooner than I. Out of love for me, he kept close. He continued to protect me in so many dangerous valleys and on so many perilous heights. Thanks, Gyp!

The next morning I packed and headed west for California.

I arrived in Hollywood to do ten nights at the hip club on Sunset Strip called The Trip. I stayed in the Peer mansion again, this time without Linda. She was somewhere in the city, but I did not try to find her. I felt hurt and was trying to overcome my desire for her. I thought, Why should I bother trying? All that stuff.

Elmer Valentine, the co-owner of The Trip, and another club called Whiskey A Go Go! was like a big soft bear with heavy-lidded eyes and a laid-back attitude to all the excitement of "The Strip." He booked soul artists and the new up-and-coming U.S. bands arriving that year. Mario was the business; Elmer the entertainment.

There were plenty of young girls who crowded the night with their eager dance moves and roving eyes. Gyp, Shawn, and I were receptive to casual come-ons from the uninhibited American chicks. After a wild night in the Whiskey we three and my manager, Ashley, piled into the limo to go back to the mansion and continue the party there. Outside the club were a group of girls who had been dancing with us and they jumped into the long black car.

One chick had gathered a few girls for the British bands to party with when they were in town, and she fancied Shawn. In the limo I was crushed next to another chick with a winning smile and a friendly way about her. Her name was Enid. She was sexy and funny. Soon the company pulled into the court-yard up in the hills.

I dropped some acid, grabbed the young dancer, and headed for the bed-room. The young woman and I found each other's lips in the painted room where I slept. Shawn was with his date in the bathroom on the Spanish tiles.

Other partygoers had followed us up to the mansion and then Ashley told me that Linda was in the house. The trip was now coming on, and I felt Linda's vibes below in the large drawing room. I heard later that Linda was also tripping that night, playing DJ, putting on records, and vibing me. When Linda gave Dylan's "Rainy Day Women No. 12 & 35" a spin downstairs and the sounds reached me, I connected with her on our internal airwaves. She knew I was with someone else and left the party.

I dated Enid for some days after the party. She couldn't know what was go-ing down between Linda and me. She was gorgeous and wonderful company.

I was lonely, missing Linda terribly, but unable to overcome my pride to go and find her and talk it out. I was physically attracted to Enid, and I found I wanted to see this American girl again and again. I was convinced I could love another after Linda.

Such are the lies we tell ourselves when in pain.

At other times I was alone and visiting the party pads in the hills. One night the host opened his giant fridge and there lay a huge quantity and va-riety of trips on ice, the likes of which I never saw again. I chose mescaline.

I had met some twins, Bernie and Lennie. So identical were they that their girlfriends thought them to be veritable supermen in bed, poor confused chicks. That night Bernie and I found we shared a sense of humor as the trip came on. We both felt like seeing the lights of the city and walked into the dark courtyard. Our host followed with his dogs. I gazed at the iridescent sheen glowing on the silky coats of two silent black Great Danes. The host said their names were Acid and Mescaline.

Bernie and I stood for hours by the car, it seemed, then our bodies moved of their own volition. We watched ourselves drive off down the hill to The Strip. Flashing on Sunset Boulevard was a sign I read as "Trip-Trip-Trip."

Bernie turned to me and said, "Welcome back." Then he smiled and said, "Beep-beep."

> We was a-d-d-drivin a downtown LA
> About the midnight hour.
> An' it almost a-b-b-blew ma mind,
> Ah got caught in a coloured shower.
> The lights they were a-twinklin' on Sunset,
> Ah saw a sign in the sky.
> It said t-t-t-trip, a-trip a-trip,
> Ah couldn't keep up if I tried.
> We stopped at a reality company,
> To get some instant sleep,
> And the driver turned, he said a-welcome back,
> He smiled and he said, 'Beep-beep'.
> What goes on, chick chick?
> What goes on, Ah really wanna know?
>
> —Donovan Leitch,
> *"The Trip"*

We had booked the CBS Studios, and I was excited to continue recording. The new record would be a fusion of the many styles I was discovering. "Candy" John Carr flew in to play percussion. Shawn Phillips was already with me. We wanted a rock-combo sound on some tracks and picked up two young guys in the clubs; Lenny Maitlin on keyboards and Don Brown on electric lead guitar. The Mamas and the Papas had been recording with Fast Eddie, a drummer from Chicago, and he came down to play, too. Bobbie Ray from LA was on electric bass.

The LA sessions would eventually include Cyrus Faryar (bouzouki) of The Modern Folk Quartet. Peter Pilafian was on electric violin—the first time this instrument was plugged into a pickup. The purist folk fiddlers would be up in arms, of course, decrying any modernization of the acoustic sound on either side of the Atlantic.

With the addition of "Candy" John's hand drums and Shawn's sitar I had a truly "world music" line-up that spring of 1966.

I kicked off with the rock-combo songs "The Trip" and "Season of the Witch."

Mickie and I were amazed to find the recording engineers in the CBS Studio wearing white coats, as if they were in a clinic. When Mickie asked the engineers to raise the level of the electric bass guitar on tape for "Season of the Witch," they refused and went into a conference upstairs.

They were concerned that the four-track tape machines could not take such levels. The needle on the dial was going into the red. After much wrangling they were convinced by Mickie: "The president of the company gave me a million dollars. I'm sure he'll give me more bass." The bass was duly turned up, and Bobbie Ray's great bass line entered rock history. Led Zeppelin often played "Season of the Witch," and loads of groups found it a great little jam. The tune was seminal.

I played a white Fender Telecaster Electric Guitar on "Witch," chunking down on the chord pattern, wailing a chilling chorus. A major seventh with an open G, to D 9th with a G-flat bass (Bert Jansch chord). The riff is pure feel. My early practice on drums found its way into the "groove." The song would be recorded by Al Kooper and Steven Stills. Julie Driscoll, and Brian Auger would also make it a must in their music.

The lyric of "Season of the Witch" proved to be prophetic in the months to come. There is a line in it that goes "Some other cat looking over his shoulder at me," and there certainly were cats looking over their shoulder at me. Soon these bad cats would come calling at my door.

I also recorded an acoustic song, "Guinevere." Shawn played the sitar with Peter Pilafian on electric violin. "Candy" tapped the skins on his bongos. My ancestors arose out of their caves to attend me on this one. The lyric spoke of magical ways of seeing, and I was not surprised when girls at my concerts gave me gifts of crystals, flowers, and velvet pouches sewn by themselves. To many I was the embodiment of the New Age movement, Mystic Studies, Alternative Healing, Self-development, and Yoga.

"Guinevere" in the story is "The Lady of the Land of Faery," the Celtic otherworld, an aspect of the Triple Goddess. My fascination with all things Celtic would help bring many to its mysteries.

I took a break from the studio sessions and prepared to open a string of performances at The Trip. This venue sat below the Playboy Club next to a vacant lot across The Strip from the Ben Frank's restaurant, which never closed.

I liked the look of the room at The Trip, low ceiling, long and dark with a small stage and a bar in the shadows, and the seating at tables. The Trip was apparently visited by many Hollywood celebs.

The neon sign above the club flashed "The Now Music of Donovan." By now I had become a "romantic" dresser and wore crystal spectacles and velvet rags from the antique markets and hung a mirror ball around my neck.

As well as playing the songs I was known for at the time, I debuted the new work with the little band from the sessions.

The opening nights were filled with an audience of the latest happening bands and solo performers in town at the time. The Mamas and the Papas, Jackie De Shannon, Noel Harrison, The Byrds, Phil Spector, Barry McGuire, Anthony Newley (a teen favorite of mine), Sonny and Cher, Van Dyke Parks, The Modern Folk Quartet, Ian Witcomb, The Young Rascals, Peter, Paul and Mary, P. F. Sloane, John Peel, and Tim Hardin.

There may have been others in the shadows with their hats pulled over their eyes or their shades on. Gyp spotted Dylan in disguise and said hello. Bob then sought out a darker corner where he would not be noticed. Suffice it to say it was an interesting and a curious audience of known and unknown faces out there when I took to the stage and kicked into the new set of songs. Shawn sat cross-legged on the stage, playing the sitar. I heard later that Linda was also there with Cathy, listening to the lyrics and hearing herself in most of the songs.

I was keeping up a distant rapport with Linda in my writing all that year. I still avoided her, though. Still hurt.

After each night's performance I would meet with my new friends. I got on really well with John Phillips and Cass Elliott of The Mamas and the Papas. John had had a previous career in the folk group The Journeymen. We both appreciated a wide range of folk classics and guitar styles.

As I write in a secluded cove in the west of Ireland, a squall of rain falls, chasing the old billy goats to seek shelter. Looking out on the winter sea, my memory moves over those early days. And you, Cass, now singing in heaven no doubt, how you made this "Celtic Cutie" welcome with your large heart. You know I wrote "The Fat Angel" for you before you went "over the top." It is with fond memories that I recall your dulcet tones, charming us all with your songs.

Where in heaven's name is that drawing I made of you, Cass, as a fat angel with wings, reclining in the long grass? I guess your man at the time of your passing gathered up a few things in the house before the sharks arrived. Hey, if anyone has it, let's see it again to remind me of Cass Elliott, a lady indeed. The San Francisco band, The Jefferson Airplane, appear in this song. They also recorded this song and called it "Trans-Love Airways."

Well do I remember sitting with the lady of the canyon herself, Joni Mitchell, watching the animated film *The Wind in the Willows* with Cass cheering along with Toad in his new car, his bug eyes rolling at the thought of driving down the highways, not a care in the world. Cass pointed out that Toad was us musos.

"Only wanted to see what was on the other side of the hill, m'lud. Honest, I didn't mean any harm, and the keys were in the car."

Oh, Cass, how right you were.

Back in the studio I recorded "The Fat Angel" with me on acoustic guitar, Shawn on sitar, "Candy" on bongos, and Bobbie Ray on bass. I followed this with "Three Kingfishers." This mysterious song was another offering to Linda, a dream of her in my magic kingdom. Ah, the strange Arabic flavor of the melody that came to me.

I also recorded "Celeste," a classical fusion of sitar, bouzouki, electric violin, celeste, harpsichord, drums, bass, and me on acoustic guitar. The ringing tones of the harpsichord were an homage to the wonderful sound of Roger McGuinn's Rickenbacker twelve-string guitar. The low strings of the sitar from Shawn are particularly effective, too, a tamboura drone that would reappear later on "The Hurdy Gurdy Man."

My producer, Mickie Most, outdid himself and gave a large orchestral ambience to "Celeste" as I sang an aching lyric that said I was disillusioned with everything. The line "I intend to come right through them all with you" was on one level about the changes my generation was going through, but on a deeper level I sang to Linda.

There were no so-called protest songs on the *Superman* album. My quest now was to engender a feeling of love and compassion.

This was the spring of 1966, and the new music scene was learning how to break free from previous constraints. Mickie Most has said I was ahead of the scene. I was singing about flower power on this album at least a year before its "official" arrival.

This much I knew then: I was making the music and writing the songs that reflected the emerging consciousness of my generation. I was here to do this. Knew instinctively I should present the Bohemian Manifesto to the world.

I awoke in a Californian dawn with no more than a mild hangover and went down to Canter's restaurant on Fairfax Boulevard to have lox and bagels, washed down with strong coffee. My sessions for the new album continued.

The last track to record was "Ferris Wheel" (the story of the girl who had lost her hair), an acoustic arrangement with Shawn on sitar, "Candy" on bongos, and Bobbie Ray on electric bass.

I felt the spirit move within me. I knew that the album I was recording was my masterpiece.

So the seven LA tracks for the album were finished. Back home in England, Pye released two more singles and one EP from the two albums of 1965. The single "Josie," with "Little Tin Soldier" on the B side, hit the shops in February 1966. The EP with "Sunny Goodge Street," "Jersey Thursday," "Deed I Do," and "Hey, Gyp (Dig the Slowness)" was released in March. Another single, "Remember the Alamo" with "Ballad of a Crystal Man" on the B side, was released in April.

But now the legal hassles began. Alan Klein suggested to me that I leave Pye Records. Ashley would share management with Klein now.

Klein placed me where I could be best presented, Epic Records in the Columbia Record empire, but the price I had to pay was the loss of future record royalties from my first two albums and the singles and EPs to date.

The new album would also have to await release due to these heavy business problems. High-financial hassles would prevent my breakthrough album *Sunshine Superman* from reaching the European scene until long after it hit the States. The wait was filled with Pye releasing more singles and EPs from the old albums that they now owned outright. Nevertheless, all of the releases went into the charts.

I wanted to take a holiday. I had met a friend in Hollywood who suggested I go down to Mexico. Ben Shapiro was involved with Indian music, bringing

over Ravi Shankar to do U.S. concerts on the West Coast. Up in his house behind the Imperial Gardens restaurant on Sunset Boulevard, he introduced
me to Ali Akba Kahn, a fellow musician of Shankar. My appreciation of Indian philosophy and music was growing and bringing me toward a closer
bond with George Harrison.

Ben and his wife, Mickey, had a few tropical acres on the Pacific Coast of
Mexico in a village called Yelapa. The tiny seaside hamlet was not served by a
road at this time and the only approach was by water, out of the resort town
of Puerto Vallarta. Ben's instructions were simple: "Fly down to Puerto Vallarta and go to Rosa's Cantina. She will be expecting you, and a speedboat
will take you down the coast to Yelapa."

Soon we white boys were sunning ourselves on the hardwood deck as we
sped down a gorgeous green coastline, the flying fish leaping high in shimmering arcs of sea spray.

We approached the bay of the village and came to a slow, curving pause
some way off the beach. There was no dock and native boys in canoes made
of tree trunks ferried us to the shore. It was a happy band of travelers who
landed that day—Anita, Ashley, Shawn, Gypsy, and me. We were greeted by a
friend of Ben's who ran the little straw-hut cottage hotel that skirted the sand
at the northern end of the beach. We checked into what would be our rooms
for the next few weeks.

Gypsy and I were to share a spacious room with a tall grass roof, the bam-
boo walls open to the air, woven mats on rollers to close the windows. Up in
the main cottage was the bar and a small restaurant. We visited a bohemian
home high on the hill. A long-haired woman of indeterminate age welcomed
us with quiet hospitality. Dressed in a loose shift, the Amazon glided around
the open terraces in bare feet. Gyp raised his eyes in appreciation of her
beauty. Silent children stared. We ate in the restaurant and drank long, cool
grenadines and the occasional mescal. In the evening we walked a well-worn
path under tropical trees to a hillside with panoramic views over the ocean.

The next day opened gently, cocks crowing in the jungle. The ocean bed
fell steep and deep just off the strand. A little group of native boys watched the
big crazy man called Gypsy leap and dive into the waves, laughing and
whooping at the top of his lungs.

Now, Gypsy had a false front tooth that was held in place with a small
dental plate, not too secure. As the sun set, he lost the tooth. He tried to

recover the plate from the deep waters. We all left him there diving again and again in his search. Then the boys burst into the little bar. "Yipsy, Yipsy," they cried. "Yipsy is drowned."

We all ran down to the sand in the last light of the day. There on the beach lay Gypsy's clothes scattered by the tide. The sea was empty. We ran along the coast and called his name. If he had left the beach, then why did he not take his clothes? Anita became alarmed. I walked along the fringe of bushes toward our hut thinking, this can't be true. Gyp's not drowned. Then I heard the slow sound of distorted snoring. There, in the undergrowth, lay the prone figure of Gypsy Dave, collapsed from exhaustion. More than exhausted, he was unconscious. I turned him over and pumped him. Anita arrived, saw what I was doing, and screamed.

"It's OK; he's OK," I gasped, as I pumped harder. Water poured out of his mouth in short jets. Gyp groaned and returned to the world. I had saved his life.

Later we all sat in the hut, looking at the dejected Gyp. He had not found his tooth and the ladies' man in him knew his smile for the chicks would not be there.

The sky blazed in magnificent gold and purple. A black-eyed native girl came in to light the lamp. We smoked the holy herb and lay down to sleep under the countless stars.

A river came down from the mountain interior through a jungle where jaguars prowled—we would hear them at night—and flowed over the beach and into the sea. We had not been there for many days when we scored a large bag of highland marijuana to smoke. We had no papers to roll the herb, so Gypsy made a pipe by breaking an aerial from a portable radio, and half an oyster shell. Cleverly inserting the small tin tube into the shell he filled the pipe and lit up. We saw the mother-of-pearl colors glowing in the light of the smouldering grass. Cool, man.

Smoking herb invariably brought on an attack of the "munchies," and we craved sweet things. In the center of the hut hung a large stalk of bananas. But we soon got sick of them. One day, on a trip to the village, Gyp saw a pastry pie in the window of a small, dusty shop. He immediately bought it and came running back to the beach. We made a great ceremony of the pie, a new sweet. With anticipation we watched as the pie was slowly sliced open. Our mouths fell open with astonishment. It was—banana pie!

That evening there was a party in the fisherman's bar across the bay in the village proper, where the locals came to have a night of music, drinking, and dancing. Anita washed her hair, and we all dressed up to go over and check out the scene. We were met on the sand of our beach by teenage boys and one old man who would ferry us over the bay to the dance. The sun was almost gone as we climbed into the log canoes. The sea was black and calm as the oars swiftly moved us off the beach in the dark. I gazed at the rippling wake behind us and was amazed to see glowing light sparkling in the water. The sea was rich in phosphorus, and we all marveled at the sight.

Upon arrival in a small, dark cove, bordered by trees, we stepped out of the canoes and onto the shore; in the distance we could hear music and see the glow of lamps. Anita screamed. She had stepped into a family of piglets who were rooting around. Convulsed with laughter, we made our way up to the brightly lit concrete circle that was the open dance floor.

We walked into the midst of tables at which only men were sitting. On each table stood a tall bottle of tequila and bowls of lemon and salt. We sat on the side and watched the scene while a waiter brought drinks. All along one wall the young girls and some older women sat placidly, waiting to be asked for a dance, dressed in cotton skirts and blouses, their hair tied back with bands. Another wall was painted with psychedelic images. A visiting American artist had made the mural, it seemed. Yelapa was a haven for "heads" from the States. Later, loud Mexican music blared out of small speakers hanging from wooden poles, and half a dozen silent men danced roughly with the expressionless peasant girls. A man would unceremoniously grab a partner from the line and drag her onto the floor. (The scene looked like those line drawings by Woody Guthrie of working-class bars in the 1940s.)

Anita attracted attention with her dark features and long raven hair. One large man approached our table and asked her to dance. Ashley said nothing and it seemed that a refusal might offend, so Anita was whisked by and twirled around the floor to the energetic music. After a while Anita disengaged herself from her partner and returned to our table, a little disheveled but none the worse for wear.

We shot our tequilas with lemon and salt, dug the action for a spell, then wandered home, happy and tired from the long, lazy day, to our beds by the lulling sea.

One cool and cloudy day, Shawn announced that someone had brought crystal mescaline from Los Angeles. He and I swallowed a strong dose and went rock climbing. The trip with mescaline is softer than LSD. Ever so slowly the Paradise appeared before me. I was in the Garden of Eden—no, I *was* the Garden. We sat for hours, gazing into the crevices of the incredible rocks, where tiny plants softly breathed in living color, encrusted with gems. Shawn cautioned me about the large Mexican ants that sting, but I sat and marveled as they walked across my feet.

I felt the Earth breathe, "breathing without returns to a starting point, with no recurrent ebbs but only a repeated flow from beauty to heightened beauty from deeper to ever deeper meaning" as Aldous Huxley wrote. I was experiencing *SAT-CHIT-AMANDA*, i.e., Truth-Knowledge-Supreme Bliss.

Down by the edge of the sea, where the rocks entered the water, I stared into the translucence and saw-heard-felt

> Symphonies of seaweed dance and swoon,
> God's celestial shore beneath the moon.
> —Donovan Leitch,
> *"Voyage into the Golden Screen"*

I wrote the song "Sand and Foam," which summed up all that we had experienced in Mexico.

> The sun was going down behind a tattooed tree
> The simple act of an oar stroke put diamonds in the sea
> And all because of the phosphorous there in quantity
> As I dug yon diggin' me in Mexico
> —Donovan Leitch,
> *"Sand and Foam"*

Anita, Ashley, Gypsy, Shawn, and I flew out of Puerto Vallarta to Los Angeles and took a flight back home to London. Somewhere in Hollywood, Linda was thinking of me, sending me her thoughts, but I blocked them out of my mind. I was blind, lost in the spin of the dance of dreams.

I learned that things weren't going very well for her. Brian Jones had not provided for their son, Julian. She had been struggling to get enough money to bring the boy over to America, and he stayed at her Windsor home in the meantime. She did eventually get some work as an extra in the Barry Feinstein film *You Are What You Eat*. This was not the work Linda needed, though, so she would dance away her blues in the clubs.

I also heard that Brian had turned up one night, but that they were both too locked into their own pain to speak to each other. Things were beginning to go very badly for Brian. He was being frozen out of his own group.

I hoped Linda still thought of me. I wrote letters that were not answered. Then I couldn't stop myself from trying to speak to her on the phone. Down the phone a silence would fall, and I wondered if I was in trouble.

Yes, I was.

Busted

The documentary *A Boy Called Donovan* had been shown on 19 January 1966 on nationwide television in Britain. Beatniks smoking pot had not gone unnoticed by the London Drug Squad.

This was the first time a British television audience had caught a glimpse of the lifestyle of beatniks, and many were shocked. So I was now the youth demon, and I had to be punished. The Drug Squad (newly formed) would make an example of me. I would be the first sensational "bust" of the 1960s. Little did I know that the British newspapers and the London Ding Squad were planning to systematically bust all important music stars of the time.

By the time the squad staked out where I lived on the Edgware Road in Maida Vale, I had left for America and had rented the apartment to two young girls who had had a few parties, as young girls do. The squad watched the goings-on as a stream of beatnik types moved in and out of the flat, including one they identified as a junkie. I did not know any of the girls' friends, hardly knew the girls, but, of course, the squad awaited my return with growing anticipation. The head of the squad prepared his men to raid my flat as soon as I was back home.

When Gyp and I returned to London, the girls left the flat. The "Superman" sessions were complete, and I lazed around London writing songs. I was seeing a young girl. And Gypsy had just split from a difficult affair with a chick from the north called Sammy. Sammy was a tough bird to handle.

One night Gyp lay in his room reading. I was turning in after a joint with my girlfriend. I had a tiny piece of hash and smoked it all. I turned out the light then heard a ring at the door. Gyp went to see who it was. He was wearing only his shirt.

"Who is it?" I heard Gyp ask.

"It's me," replied a girl's voice.

Gyp pulled aside the curtain of the door window to see who was calling so late. A beautiful young woman stood looking at him, saying nothing. He drew back the curtain farther and wondered to himself, "Who could it be?" He decided to open the door. The policewoman stepped aside and nine burly coppers crashed into the hall.

I heard Gyp shout, "Don! Lock your door!"

Naked, I leapt to the bedroom door, but they were already in.

All the coppers wore suits. It was a special occasion, this. One big fella stomped across the Japanese-mat floor in his boots and tore the lace spread from the brass bed. He dragged the naked girl into the circle of men who were busy smashing up the place looking for drugs. The poor chick sat on the floor petrified, her arms crossed, trying to cover herself.

I stood in my birthday suit, astonished as they ripped up my pad. My antique ivory pagoda in its glass dome sat on a tiny Moroccan side table—until a policeman lifted the dome and crushed the Chinese carving, saying to me, "Is it in 'ere, lad?"

Gypsy had tried to stop them, but he was roughly manhandled and restrained as the raid continued. I was furious and jumped onto the back of one cop only to be laughed at, as I was quickly grabbed around the throat in an arm-lock. What a sight, thin little me, dangling naked from the arm of a bloody great policeman. He dropped me onto the floor. I stumbled into the kitchen to get a drink of milk, coughing from the throttling. I opened the fridge, but the milk was snatched away. "Quick, men, the LSD's in the milk!" the cop screamed.

Things quieted down, and we were allowed to dress. The raid was over. I saw my manager and his wife appear downstairs in the hallway. It seemed that Ashley and Anita had been busted, too. Ashley said the police had found a huge lump of hashish in his place, and that they'd also found a huge piece

Winifred Leitch, my mother, as a
young woman *(Donovan Collection)*

With my parents and brother, Gerald
(Donovan Collection)

Donald Leitch, my father, as a
young man *(Donovan Collection)*

Me in my bedroom about
to flee into Bohemia
*(Donovan Collection/
Donald Leitch)*

The "Posh Chaplin" photo
session, New York, 1966.
This photographer truly
presented me to the world.
(Barry Feinstein)

In 1965, the Scottish Woody
Guthrie is in the charts!
(Rex Features)

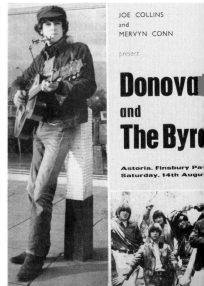

JOE COLLINS
and
MERVYN CONN

present

Donova
and
The Byr

Astoria, Finsbury Pa
Saturday, 14th Augu

I meet the Byrds on the stage and we all become
friends in 1965. *(Donovan Collection/Donovan Music)*

I meet Dylan in the Savoy Hotel, May 1965. (Don't Look Back, *D. A. Pennebacker*)

Gypsy Dave and I, self-exiled on Paros Isle, Greece, 1966
(Donovan Collection)

Jimi visits my record launch for *Barabajagal* album in Hollywood, 1969.
(Donovan Collection/Sandford Schor)

I sing to Linda in St. Ives during the filming of *A Boy Called Donovan,* 1966.
(Donovan Collection/Charles Squire)

At a record launch of the Apple group Grapefruit. Brian Jones and I both with mustaches. Ringo Starr and John Lennon listen to my chat, 1968.
(Mirrorpix)

In India to study meditation with Maharishi Mahesh Yogi and to swap musical styles with the Beatles
(Donovan Collection)

Hostess Mama Cass and host Kirk Douglas at the record launch party for *Barabajagal* album, 1969
(Donovan Collection/Sandford Schor)

Linda and Julian
on their way to Brian
Jones's funeral, 1969
(TOPFOTO)

I teach Julian guitar in Ireland, 1970.
(Stewart Lawrence)

My son Donovan Junior and I
in Greece, 1970 *(Donovan Collection)*

Linda and I on honeymoon
in St. Lucia, Caribbean Islands,
1970 *(Sid Maurer)*

Linda with our daughter
Astrella inside, 1970
(Donovan Collection/Norbert Jobst)

George Harrison plays me his new song
on my twelve-string at Castle Martin,
Ireland, 1971. Patty Harrison
is in the background.
(Stewart Lawrence)

My American son,
Donovan Junior, and
daughter, Ione, are reunited.
(Donovan Collection/Linda Leitch)

My three lovely
daughters (left to right)
Oriole, Ione, and Astrella,
and in Ione's arms my first
grandchild, Sebastian, by Oriole.
(Donovan Collection/Linda Leitch)

Donovan and Linda, 2003 *(Beth Hannant)*

in my flat. I knew I had no drugs in my flat, having smoked the last little piece of hashish before the bust. A Sergeant Pilcher introduced himself. There was definitely something fishy going on.

We were taken down to the Marylebone Police Station, booked, finger-printed, and given a cup of tea, almost civilized like. Then at four a.m. on a cold London dawn, we were let out onto the streets of London. As we left, Sergeant Pilcher took me aside and said, "I am sorry about all this, Don; it's only me job, you know; can I 'ave your autograph for my daughter?"

We went back to the flat and tried to sleep. The next morning the papers were full of it. At 9:30 a.m. the phone rang. It was George Harrison. He asked me how I was. He knew I had been victimized. "You can have £10,000 by noon, Don, if it helps."

No small sum in those days. The equivalent would be around £100,000 today. I felt better now that George had called and replied, "Thanks, George, that's really so good of you to call. I'm OK with money."

The word of our bust had spread like wildfire. Gyp and I were instantly shunned by the music-business community and most of the artists we had thought were our friends. They were all scared shitless that they would be next. So this call from George was brave and brotherly. "They're trying to make an example of you and Gyp, Don. What'll you do now?"

"Gyp and I have to split, leave town for a bit."

"Where will you go?"

"A deserted island, maybe, to get away from the press." I laughed. "Me and Gyp will go to a little island off the west of Scotland, called Islay, for a few days."

"Well, Don, you can come and stay with me if you want."

George was aware of what all this might do to Gyp and me, having been so hounded by the media himself. He also knew I was being targeted because I sang of freedom and equality. A poet under fire.

"Thanks, mate," I replied sincerely. "I'll call you when we get back from Scotland. Gyp and I will take you up on it. When all this blows over."

"It'll never blow over, Don. We'll be next."

After I hung up, George's last words echoed in my head. Perhaps he was seeing the future?

The next call was from a gossip columnist of the *Daily Mirror*. He also wanted to know if I was OK, but for very different reasons. I refused to give my story. This wasn't about a little bit of hashish. This was bigger than the little joint I'd smoked that night. I represented the beatniks and their evil scheme to turn the whole world on. I wanted to turn the world onto self-transformation, not drugs. I was only using hashish, not selling it.

No doubt the British public smiled at the incident where I leapt naked onto the back of the cops, screaming obscenities. The story had all the elements of a scandal—sex, drugs, and rock 'n' roll. My face was on every newsstand. A taxi driver waved at me in the street, shouting, "Hey, Don, got any of them funny cigarettes?"

And when I got in the cab he refused to take any money. Most of the public saw me as victimized.

My father, Donald, called my lawyers and employed the top barrister David Jacobs to represent me. He took control.

Every paper in London turned up at Marylebone Court. The press jostled for a picture as I was hustled into the building through the crowds.

Once inside Gyp and I took our seats before the three judges, two old men and one younger woman. Hear ye, hear ye.

The evidence having been recorded, the barrister pleaded my case and sentence was pronounced. I was admonished and castigated for being a bad example to the youth of Britain. I was advized to be more of a positive influence. We were fined £250. In the early 1970s Sgt. Norman Pilcher was charged and convicted in connection with planting illegal drugs and sentenced to four years in prison.

Outside Marylebone Court the press posed Gypsy and me on the steps. Every paper carried the story, the *News of the World* choosing the meanest pictures possible to show us as degenerate drug addicts. Gypsy and I were the first sensational "bust" of the sixties. A worldwide story.

Cannabis sativa has never been found to be addictive by any government studies, in stark contrast to the heavily addictive and life-threatening legal drugs, alcohol and tobacco. *Cannabis sativa* was the herb of choice for Queen Victoria when she was on her period, so the story goes.

To this day, Gypsy and I are labeled "criminals" on our U.S. visa application forms and we need "waivers" to enter America.

Anyway, with all the press coverage, everyone knew that I had made a comeback.

But we still wanted to get away for a few days, so Gypsy and I flew to Glasgow, Scotland, and on over to the Isle of Islay. The four-seater propeller craft

The Daily Mirror 15th November 1973 4

Three police jailed for perjury

FREED

The detective who puts fear into the big drug-pedlars

Kelaher . . . "Happy to continue my career."

TOP detective Victor Kelaher, the man most feared by Britain's drug-traffickers, was acquitted last night of plotting to rig a drugs trial.

As he stepped from the dock at the Old Bailey after a 38-day trial, the 43-year-old Scotland-Yard man said: "I am delighted.

"The strain on my wife over the past year has now been lifted.

"I would be happy to continue my career, if that is possible, now that my innocence has been established."

Detective Chief Inspector Kelaher—at one time operational head of the Yard's drug squad—was suspended from his job a year ago.

Plot

He was due for promotion after a spectacular crime-busting career in which his teams pounced on drugs worth £20,000,000.

Over the years, Chief Inspector Kelaher had collected twenty-three commendations.

Then his world crashed . . . when he and five other detectives were accused of a plot to get three people convicted on drugs charges.

Two of the five were also

By GEORGE GLENTON

acquitted yesterday—woman Constable Morag McGibbon, 33, and Constable Adam Acworth, 30.

But the jury found the other three guilty of perjury.

They were ex-Sergeant Norman Pilcher, 37; Constable George Pritchard, 30, and Constable Nigel Lilley, 31.

Pilcher was sentenced to four years' jail. The judge, Mr. Justice Melford Stevenson, told him:

❝ You poisoned the wells of criminal justice and set about it deliberately. What is equally bad, you betrayed your comrades in the Metropolitan Police Force, which enjoys respect in the civilised world—what is left of it.

Not the least grave aspect is that you provided material for the cranks, crooks and do-gooders who

Pilcher . . . jailed

attack the police whenever opportunity offers.

Pritchard and Lilley were jailed for eighteen months.

The judge commented: " I do not doubt that you were overborne by dishonest superiors."

The jury had heard that the detectives were arrested when drug-trafficking sentences on Mohammed, John and Kathleen Salah were quashed.

Singer accused after drugs raid

FOLK SINGER Donovan appeared in court yesterday, hours after a police raid on his London flat. With him were 20-year-old Doreen Fabienne Samuel, his friend David John Mills, aged 19, and his manager, Ashley Kozac, aged 26.

They were accused of possessing cannabis (Indian hemp) at Donovan's flat in Alexandra Court, Maida Vale—a block of flats where all four live.

Contested

Mr. David Jacobs, representing the four, told the court: "This case has already received wide publicity because one of the accused is a very well-known young man, and I am bound to say at this stage that the case will be strongly contested."

The four were remanded on £50 bail until July 28.

Donovan (right) and David Mills yesterday

made two approaches over the tiny airstrip to shoo the sheep away, and then we landed. The peace and tranquillity of the beautiful island soothed our stress away. The shocking violation of our privacy became a fading memory.

We took rooms in the only hotel in town and were left to ourselves.

The islanders are respectful people. It was summer and we swam in the sea, shivering a bit in the cool northern ocean, and the island gifted me this song:

> How high the gulls fly o'er Islay.
> How sad the farm lad deep in play.
> Felt like a tide left me here.
> —Donovan Leitch,
> *"Isle of Islay"*

After our return from Scotland, we stayed with George for ten days. This was so needed at the time. Gyp went back to the Maida Vale flat just to see what was going on. He ate in our favorite goulash restaurant around the corner, then—as he walked along Edgware Road—he passed a film camera pointed up at our flat. Gyp asked, "What's going on, mate?"

An anchorman walked in front of the camera with a microphone in his hand and replied in a heavy Glaswegian accent, "Weer heer tae try and catch some foootage of the sex, drugs, and rock-and-roll life of Donovan and Gypsy Dave."

Gyp phoned me at George's home and said, "This is fucking ridiculous, man; we gotta split from the flat for good now."

So we vacated Alexandria Court that week and looked for new digs.

As much as we wished it would all go away, our bust kept coming back to haunt us. The *News of the World* got hold of an ex-girlfriend of Gyp who was persuaded to give an interview that spread over three weeks of the Sunday rag. Ten thousand pounds was the fee for this poor little girl, who, feeling remorse, threw herself out of a window of the London Hilton.

Gyp and I got a call one afternoon. It was John Lennon. He said, "I just got a call from a friend. I'm going to be busted. "I thought to myself, that's ripe; John gets called first. I said, "What are you gonna do?"

"You tell me. You're the experts."

"Gyp and I will be right over." I hung up and turned to my young comrade. "John had a call. The squad are gonna bust him, and he wants our help." Gyp laughed as we grabbed our coats and jumped in a car. We pulled up at John's house in Esher, a large bungalow on an estate out of London, a home that Brian Epstein had found to isolate his charges from the fans. John opened the door, and we followed him into the large living room, softened with Persian carpets and comfortable leather chairs. John was swaggering like a sailor, his long hair flying, angry and ready to fight. He had an actor friend with him, who sat in a large chair, a bemused smile spreading over his Latin features.

"What do we do next?" John growled at me.

"Leave it to Gyp; he knows what to do." I smiled.

On the long glass coffee table lay three pyramids of the best Californian sinsemilla. We had never seen such splendor. A rich American groupie, it seems, would bring it in every three months or so, hidden in the wings of a custom painted Mercedes SL.

John left it to Gyp and went into his den, where the largest jukebox in the world took up one long wall. The records were LPs, of every blues, soul, and rock-and-roll classic in the world. John grinned at me and selected a Howlin' Wolf disk.

Then Gyp and I cleared the coffee table of all the lovely grass onto a tray and with a reluctant sigh flushed it down the toilet, along with some other substances that Gyp found in a curious inlaid box.

Gyp then walked to the French windows and stepped into the garden. I tried to follow, but Gyp turned and put his finger to his lips to indicate Stay! I watched him walk down the garden path, then went back into the room and sat with the actor, expectant, and, yes, a little stoned. Just then the doorbell rang.

John stormed to the front hall and opened the door. There stood Sergeant Pilcher and his men.

"What d'ya want?" John barked.

"Good evening, Mr. Lennon, we have a warrant to search your premises for drugs." The bold sergeant smirked.

John opened the door wider and shouted, "Come in, then, and fookin' search."

The squad entered and began. The coppers were everywhere, looking for the stuff. Curiously enough they were far more placid than they'd been during our own bust, not destroying any furniture or trying to rough us up.

John tore around behind them, effing and blinding. 'What right do you fookin' 'ave to come in 'ere and treat us like bloody criminals; you should be out finding soom real villains. You bastards are all the same!"

Gyp had returned and stood ready to ward off any cop who might dare to grab me again.

Then it was over. They had found nothing.

Sergeant Pilcher assembled his men in the hall and said, "Next time we'll get you, Lennon, mark my words." I thought John was going to nut him then and there, but Gyp held him back. As the cops filed out of the door he held it open for them, then crashed it shut with a 'Good bluddy riddance. Fook off, you bastards!'

And they were gone.

John walked back into the long, lovely room where Gyp, the actor, and I sat. "Where's the stuff?" he asked.

"Down the loo, John," said Gyp.

"You what?" exclaimed John. "All that lovely grass gone?"

"Where else could it go?" I smiled.

John slumped into a big chair.

Gyp waited a beat, then said, "Don't worry, man. Follow me." He stood and opened the French windows, beckoning us all to follow. John, the smiling actor, and I walked single file behind Gyp as he walked down the garden, the twilight slowly falling over the soft summer lawn. We arrived at the goldfish pond around which three gaily painted smiling gnomes stood sentinel. Gyp knelt down and motioned us to do the same. "Roll your sleeves up, boys, we're going fishing." He laughed the laugh he was famous for.

We all did as we were told. Then, when Gyp plunged his hand into the water, we all did the same. "Ah!" Gyp raised his eyebrows. "What 'ave we 'ere?" Slowly and with ceremony Gyp raised his hand, turned over his palm, and there lay two ounces of slick black hashish. Our eyes popped. "I couldn't see this disappear now, could I?"

We four young bohemians walked up the garden path again and into the house, where Gyp rolled a large English joint. And another adventurous day in the life of Gyp, Donno, and John softly came to a close.

Sky of Blue and Sea of Green

Back in London, the Drug Squad concentrated on their next victim.

Patti told me about George's bust. One afternoon, Sergeant Pilcher and his squad drove out to Esher with a search warrant again. Patti opened the door and asked what they wanted.

Sergeant Pilcher asked, "Is Mr. Harrison at home?"

"No," replied Patti. "He's in London and will be home soon."

The sergeant thought about it for a moment and asked, "Do you know exactly when your husband might be home?"

"No, but would you like to come in and wait for him?"

All very civilized. The policemen sat quietly in the drawing room, behaving themselves this time, and Patti even served them tea. This English rose knew how to set a drug squad at its ease.

Then the sounds of a car on the gravel outside announced an arrival. Sergeant Pilcher stood and so did the rest of the squad. They smoothed down their suits and straightened their ties. It was, indeed, George.

For some reason the squad all left the drawing room, opened the front door, and walked down the path to meet George, Patti close behind. As George got out of the car, he saw the group of men waiting for him.

Patti told me that George took one look at Sergeant Pilcher's boots and smiled, figuring out everything at once. He was not at all scared.

Sergeant Pilcher walked right up to him, and they stood looking at each other. Eventually the sergeant said, "I am Sergeant Pilcher of the London Drug Squad, Mr. Harrison, we are here to search your premises for illegal drugs." As he handed George the search warrant, a photographer leapt from the bushes where he had been hiding and flashed his camera, catching a photo of the famed Sergeant Pilcher and George, the quiet Beatle.

And that was the way it was. Sergeant Pilcher was collecting celebrity busts like a fan collects autographs.

I would visit Paul McCartney in his St. John's Wood, London home, where he lived with his love, Jane Asher. Paul and I were kindred spirits, but we found it hard to write songs together as we both were just too prolific.

Any ideas that I had he would immediately riff off into an idea of his own and vice versa. He was so full of songs, I swear that if he fell on the piano, by the time he picked himself up he would have written three new melodies.

Paul's Liverpool humor kept me laughing as he gibed me about my own attitudes. He took great delight in calling me Philip, my second name. I guess "Donovan" seemed exotic to him, and this was his way of teasing me about it.

I did not see it at the time, but I was becoming a close friend of Paul's, a rare confidant to him in his increasingly private world, as fame separated him more and more from so-called reality. The loss of privacy that fame had brought gave us a common ground.

One quiet Sunday I was alone, recording new songs on my little Uher tape machine, when the doorbell rang. It was Paul on his own. He played a couple of tunes to me on his Martin Acoustic six string. One sang of a strange chap called:

> Ola Na Tungee,
> Blowing his mind in the dark with a pipe full of clay—
> No one can say . . .

The tune was "Eleanor Rigby" but the words had not all come out yet. Songwriters sometimes sketch in the lyric with any old line, then come back to it.

Another song he sang to me was a little ditty with a chorus about a yellow submarine. He was missing a verse for the tune and asked me to get one in there. So I said, give me a minute, and left the room. What I came back with was not world-shattering, but he liked it.

Sky of blue and sea of green
In our yellow submarine . . .
—Donovan Leitch

We played a few more bits and pieces we were both working on there in my little Japanese room, the sunlight filtering through the lace curtains.

Then the doorbell rang again. I went to see and found a young policeman. He said a car had been left parked outside illegally, at an odd angle, the doors open, and the radio still on. Paul came to the door and the policeman said: "Oh, it's you, Mr. McCartney. Is it your car, sir? A sports car?'

"Sir." mind you. Paul gave him the keys, and the DB6 was parked by the starstruck policeman, no less! In those days the Beatles were treated like royalty. The copper came back with the keys and saluted. Saluted, would you believe! "Lord Paul" left soon after, and drove off down the long, winding road.

The *Sunshine Superman* album was still being held back from release, and Mickie Most said I should not play Paul any of the tracks for fear of some of our ideas leaking into Beatles sessions. This was a real fear in those days, but I had played tracks to Paul and I knew the classical/jazz arrangements impressed him.

Mickie Most later said that the music we made in late 1965 and 1966 influenced the Beatles to experiment more adventurously on *Sergeant Pepper's Lonely Hearts Club Band*. This may well be. I also stirred the Celtic cauldron and encouraged Led Zeppelin to express himself with images and sounds from our Celto-European roots.

Perhaps my contribution was that I helped to define British music, separating us and making us distinct from the strong American influence we had all grown up with. I gave our music the name "Celtic Rock."

Van Morrison and Georgie Fame did not miss the breakthrough of the strong jazz elements into my composition, vocal performances, and Cameron's arrangements. We were bringing back jazz to popular audiences.

The music rag *Melody Maker* once again questioned my credibility. The headline ran: DONOVAN, POET OR POSEUR?

Of course I *was* very full of myself. Young artists tend to take themselves too seriously. But they have to because no one else does. In retrospect I see that what was really happening here was that I was a channel through which flowed a spirit encouraging "self-realization" and that spirit was meeting extraordinary resistance.

Brian Epstein brought an act to Britain that summer that would change the face of popular music forever. Earlier in the spring, Brian had given an interview to the American DJ Murray "the K" in which he had told Murray about a new star on the horizon, a young black guitar player named Jimmy Hendrix. Hendrix had been playing around Greenwich Village in New York for some time, but nobody in America had taken a blind bit of notice until Chas Chandler, the bass player of The Animals, brought him to London. Epstein told Murray to be ready when Jimmy (his name would soon be shortened to "Jimi") came back to the States.

So Chas called Gyp and asked us if we would like to meet a new guitarist from New York who was really amazing. Jimi was just about to fly in. Gyp and I were staying in the Bayswater Hotel, a rather rundown establishment where bands used to stay. This new pad was not much to write home about, but the boss was tolerant of the shenanigans that we pop chappies all got up to. It lay just off the Bayswater Road over which one could easily cross to the park, as the dawn came up and the trip came on. Chas had booked Jimi into the same hotel.

Chas and Gyp went to the airport to pick up Jimi. I stayed at the hotel, talking to a beautiful blonde Swedish girl named Yvonne, who was also staying at the hotel. Her best friend Lotta was dating Chas. Gyp was very attracted to Yvonne. We sat in the funky little reception lounge with its tatty carpet, plywood bar, and mock Grecian urns.

"Do you like Gyp?" I ventured.

"I don't know. He's quite different, isn't he?" the Swedish beauty replied.

"Yes. Gyp is rather unusual—he's an artist, you know."

"So am I," Yvonne said.

The taxi arrived and Chas whisked Jimi up to his room as Gyp blustered into the lounge, filling the room with his wonderful presence. Soon he had sidled up to Yvonne on the fake leather seats.

Chas came back and asked if I would like to meet Jimi. I was intrigued after all that Chas had said about this new musician's style, which, I must admit, Chas had difficulty describing. When Chas and I found the room, Jimi opened the door and there we were in a tiny "single" with a tallish black boy, dressed in tight trousers and a colored shirt. On his feet he wore Annelo Daride ankle boots. A Fender Stratocaster guitar case was propped up against the wall.

If he stretched his arms Jimi might touch the floral wall with both hands, so small was the space. He would soon touch us all with his electric wand, his ecstatic stage presence, and his shamanism. When I got to know him a little bit, I saw that he did not feel particularly black inside, and later I found out that Jimi had thought me a bit of a fool before he met me. He said that he'd seen photos of me posing, looking all pretty with my velvets and silks and lacquered fingernails, and he'd thought "Damn me." Then he'd met me and, as he was to say later in an interview, he found I was the nicest person in show business he'd ever met!

Chas Chandler, Jimi's manager, had found two musos to play with him. A unique bass player from Folkestone named Noel Redding and a drummer who had played with Georgie Fame, name of Mitch Miller. A band was born—not just a band, an "Experience."

The first London show of The Experience was in the hip club The Bag O'Nails. At the sound check, Gyp was thrilled to see his new Swedish girl friend who had painted an abstract above the bar. That night everyone was there. Chas had *made sure* that those who needed to be there were there.

The band took to the stage, and the universe changed forever. Jimi Hendrix had arrived.

So many black guitarists had stood down stage (as it were) to the likes of Brian Jones and Eric Clapton, the white boys getting to "blow the blues" to the great white audience. But here came Jimi Hendrix. Watch out, you white boys, "Dig the Slowness!" He was going to reverse the process and take center stage as the African guitar wizard.

The Jimi Hendrix Experience band was then booked to play Brian Epstein's new venue the Saville Theatre. Gypsy and I went down to dig the scene. The theater was filled with on eager audience and a huge turnout of stars for the opening night of the week-long engagement. The Beatles and The Rolling Stones sat in opposite boxes over the stage. The Experience performed The Troggs' song "Wild Thing" and an amazing version of the title track from *Sergeant Pepper's Lonely Hearts Club Band*. Both blew us all away as Jimi took the tunes into the stratosphere on his Stratocaster guitar.

The three-part sound of the Cream band (with Eric Clapton, Jack Bruce, and Ginger Baker) had also just arrived and Pete Townshend, Keith Moon, John Entwistle, and Roger Daltrey of The Who were smashing guitars and destroying drum kits. But the bass-guitar sound that Noel Redding created for Jimi, relentlessly driven on by the jazz-rock drums of Mitch Miller, was the most exciting Anglo-American fusion to appear in 1967. A lot of stormy heartache followed, and Jimi would be swept away on the tide. The music lives on, and who knows where the wind blows? It may even cry . . . Mary.

The Road Again

❖

Sunshine Superman continued to run into legal problems as my new manager Alan Klein tore up the deal I had with Pye Records. As a result I was sued by Pye, and there was no possibility of release soon. It seemed that my innovative work was to be shelved indefinitely and, what with the bust, it looked like my career was over. I told George about my problems. "The illusion is very strong," he said mournfully.

Gyp and I decided we should just leave the whole game and go back to our travels. I had left home to find freedom, and now that I was losing my freedom I felt I would have to leave fame behind to find it again.

"Where shall we go, man?" asked Gyp.

"World's our oyster," I replied. "Greece sounds like it to me."

"Yeah, man," Gyp agreed.

Ever since I had taken Linda to see the film *Zorba the Greek* in St. Ives the previous year, I had fancied Greece. And so I asked Anita, who was a full-blooded Greek, to set me and Gypsy up for a visit.

Meanwhile I wrote a poem and sent it to Linda to try to persuade her to come with us. I'd heard she'd come back to England to see Julian. She was feeling disillusioned about LA. She loved the sun, but hey, how many tans can one girl get?

> I love the girl in white
> And the Sun flashed gold in a rose sky
>
> Come
> I will show you beauty
> Enough to swell your heart
>
> If I run follow me
> Time is on our side
> a mile wide
> there's the cloud to ride
> In Greece
>
> a little sweat in your palm
> dry your hand on my hair
> if I shut my eyes I can
> Wrap you in turquoise silk.
>
> —Donovan Leitch,
> *"I Love the Girl in White"*

I packed a huge trunkful of books, then down to Granny Takes a Trip for a white sharkskin suit and a panama hat. The bootmaker Lobbs of St. James had already become my cobbler, and I now sported a pair of two-tone canvas shoes. I think I got my movies mixed up a bit—inside I felt like Alan Bates, but on the outside I looked more like Bob Mitchum in *Macao*.

So Gypsy and I were on the road again, but this time first-class train down to Brindisi, Italy, there to catch the ferry over to Greece. Soon we were pulling through the dark, silent countryside past tiny stations with hurricane lamps burning on the platforms.

We went down to Piraeus harbor where Anita asked a shipping clerk for the most unspoiled island in the Cyclades. We boarded an old tramp steamer headed for the island of Pàros. Nineteen hours later we disembarked into a small boat with our trunks. We landed on the bare sand of this undeveloped island. Anita asked for a hotel. There was no hotel. "How about rooms then?"

Anita asked our guide. There were no rooms, but our guide had an old house and he would let us rent it. He led the way up a road packed with rocks, cleared from the fields of this arid island, the animals expertly picking their way slowly up to the empty house standing on its own, its nearest neighbor some way below. It was perfect, a large, flat-roofed dwelling. Wooden shutters opened on the valley below and a panoramic view of the island. There was a nice little veranda with a low wall. A clutch of scraggly chickens lived in the barn, and a small outhouse served as a toilet with a hole in the ground.

We returned for our stuff, stopping off at a hardware store in the white-washed town to buy supplies. We would need mattresses, a hurricane lamp, teapot, and kitchen utensils, not forgetting a large flagon of wine in a tall, woven basket as well as goat's cheese, tomatoes, and batteries for the portable briefcase cassette deck and record player, the first of its kind from Japan, three vinyl records, The Beatles, Leonord Cohen, and my own "White Label" pressing of *Sunshine Superman*.

Soon we had the place in some kind of order, had our first meal and a glass of wine. I had already fallen in love with Greece.

The next day Anita fixed us up with a donkey named Serafina that had one good eye and, on its back, a rough wooden saddle with a worn, padded seat.

Photographs show that at first we posed in our city-slicker clothes, squinting in the bright sunlight, with white skin and nice, clean shoes. Soon the pictures tell a different story as we bought Greek shirts and waistcoats, sun hats and sandals, relaxing into the slow pace of the islands.

I badly wanted my work released in the UK, but the machinations of the business world in London had worn me down. Time was passing, and the "Now Music" of Donovan would soon become the "Then Music."

I also missed Linda terribly. I was lonely and hung out with a couple of girls down on holiday.

One morning Gypsy and I woke up to see a basket of figs in vine leaves sitting on the low wall of the patio. We ate the delicious purple fruit and wondered who had left them. The next morning the figs were there again. We saw our neighbor below us. He waved and we knew the figs were his gift to us. He was a silver-haired gentleman who lived in the farmstead close by. He lived alone in a tidy little farm below and rode an immaculate mule. He himself was always very cleanly dressed in simple clothes with neat hair and an aristocratic bearing. Baba Costa was his name. He sat with us in the evening while I played my songs. Neither of us knew the other's language, but with smiles and miming Gyp and I communicated to him that we really loved the island. We would marvel at the sunset and he would nod, his eyes knowing. He had seen thousands of sunsets up here on the mountain.

> And here I sit, the retired writer in the sun.
>
> —Donovan Leitch
> *"Writer in the Sun"*

One day I was searching the landscape for birds through the small pair of pearl opera glasses I had brought from London, and the old man was evidently curious. I handed him the Edwardian glasses, and he looked into the lens. He started back, surprised to see his little house so close. Was it possible he had not used a lens before? Was he kidding? Many Greeks go to sea, and he would surely have seen binoculars before. But then, maybe not, from the way he carried on, so pleased did he seem with the discovery.

On one of our trips to town with Serafina, Gyp and I were jeered at by some less friendly villagers (our long hair, perhaps). Just then the old man came into view on his mule. He stopped to greet us, and the town saw that he had done so. From that day forth we were never again treated in an unfriendly fashion.

The summer glided on through glorious days and star-filled nights. Gyp and I would take turns riding Serafina down each day to the little taverna on the seafront.

One day as we sat in the taverna the owner told us that we were to receive a call on his telephone, the only one on the island. The call came through eventually; it was from my manager, Ashley. We spoke over the noisy wires and Ashley said, "Don, come back. It's all been sorted out. *Sunshine Superman* has been released—and it's number one all over the world!" He continued: "There're two first-class airline tickets waiting for you in Athens. Get there as soon as possible—the whole fucking music business wants you!"

The line broke up, and I replaced the receiver. Gyp and I were blown away as the taverna's owner came up to the table and wiped it, asking, "What was that all about, boys?"

"My record is number one everywhere, and we have to get to Athens on the next steamer."

The taverna's owner laughed, not quite believing. We emptied our pockets of coins onto his table. Number one all over the world, and not enough money between us to get back to Athens on the weekly steamer due in a few days.

"You boys are broke?" the Greek islander asked.

"We are" Gyp said.

"Listen, guys, I have an idea," the taverna's owner said. "That briefcase record player you got—I'll give you the steamer fare for it. That will get you to Athens, at least."

Gyp and I toasted our luck with a few retsinas that day, rolled a few joints, and thought about a change.

The deal was done. Gyp and I wandered up the mountain to our little house in the sky to pack.

We embraced the old gentleman. I gave him the Edwardian opera glasses, which made his face light up. The ferry pulled away from the harbor, and we saw him slowly waving, "Adio, adio, adio," he called.

It was a great change in life when I stepped onto the Steamer to Piraeus that summer. Never again would I be as free.

But the world lay at my feet. My music was playing on every radio on the green rolling earth.

There was no going back. I strode into a glowing future and embraced fame and fortune, but not without one last melancholy look back at the old man of Pàros, who smiled and slowly waved good-bye. And I also waved as I bid a sad farewell to a way of life I could never live again. I took one more languorous look at the boy who was fading away.

Electrical Banana

And so I flew to London. I was back from Greece and back on the charts—the U.S. charts, that was. I dropped by the *Melody Maker* offices and chatted with Bob Dawbarn. He congratulated me on the gold disk, and he wondered when it might be gracing the racks of Britain's music shops?

I couldn't tell him, but I let it be known that I was back to work, refreshed from living in a stone house on Pàros with windows full of mountains. I wanted to record again, and the songs were ready to go. I knew I would have to pedal backward a bit to let the UK audience catch up with me, but I felt serious about communicating. In one of the new press articles I gushed:

> We've been through the "it's in to be way out" bit, the "it's in to take LSD" bit, now it would be "in to love," because that's the product of it all. Through all the best writers there is the "music-strain" of love—they have compassion.

"Love and Compassion"—I was still considered a trifle foolish for talking about such things. The constant gibes in the British press about my love of beauty has long left a false impression of my work.

The truth is I wished to present the possibility of self-change, and it was to this end that I directed my energy. My early reading of *The Diamond Sutra* when I was sixteen years old was still with me as I suggested that only through self-change could the whole world change. This was very clear to me.

My songs encouraged introspection, and soon millions of young people would join my search for the way within.

In 1965, two years before the Beatles' "Love, Love, Love," I had sung:

> The magician, he sparkles in satin and velvet,
> You gaze at his splendour with eyes you've not used yet.
> I tell you his name is . . . Love, Love, Love.
>
> —Donovan Leitch,
> "*Sunny Goodge Street*"

The magician being none other than your higher consciousness, which some call Merlin.

I also claimed that reincarnation is a reality. The tree never dies as the seeds live on. All through 1966 my message continued to be viewed as suspect, but what did I care? So much fine music would be created by so many fine new artists those last months of 1966—you only have to spin a few disks to dig the drift. You had to be seventeen million miles west of nowhere to miss the point.

It was clear that the Maida Vale apartment had had its day. George Harrison led Gypsy and me to our next quarters, the home of London sculptor David Wynne, who lived on Wimbledon Common and worked in an atmosphere far from the usual pop music world.

We moved into his comfortably bohemian lifestyle with pleasure. It is with great affection I recall the time I lived in the old rambling house that was the family home and studio of Gilly and David Wynne.

David had met the Beatles in their Paris hotel during the crazy early days of Beatlemania. He had sketched them for a bronze sculpture that he would cast. David would sculpt four heads, each head joined to the other, as they were in their life at the time. Other sculptures of his include *Boy with a Delphin* on the banks of the Thames, *The Tyne God* in Newcastle (for which Gyp had been the model), and *Girl with Doves* in Sloane Square, London.

There is another curious work by David Wynne that millions of people touch every day in Britain. It is the relief on the 1973 fifty-pence coin. There, on the reverse side, a circle of hands. Without prompting I guessed the owner of each hand correctly, it was a member of David's family. Gilly, his wife, Johnny, Eddie, Roly . . . and, of course, David himself.

David worked in his studio, Gypsy wrote stories, and I composed songs. One day David expressed his interest in sculpting a head of Joan Baez. I called her up, and she readily agreed.

Joaney would sit for David in the large studio as he made the clay model from which he would cast her head in bronze. David was a fan of the new music that we were all making, and he liked to play the harmonica with me when his day in the studio was over.

He had also completed the portraits of the violinist Yehudi Menuhin, the painter Oskar Kokoschka, and many fine studies of animals and birds. And yet it was his large-scale marbles that impressed me most, in particular *Awakening Earth* and *Embracing Lovers*.

A terribly handsome man, twenty years my senior, David Wynne was our mentor. Many an evening we spent around the generous table, his marvelous wife, Gilly, serving dinner with the children all around the pine board.

Later on in the evening out would come my guitar, and I would sing. I needed to be part of this family for I knew that pop success endangered my well-being in many ways. David was very clear on one point when I asked him what an artist should beware of in early fame. He replied in an instant—mediocrity. I would only realize later just how true his advice was and only after I had allowed myself to be seduced by my own fame.

Sometimes David would take down a volume from his shelves of books and read to me the great lyric poems of our islands and reassure me that I was from the tradition. He would then ask me to sing a ballad from the past, to which he would play his harmonica, pieces like "Mary Hamilton"—he knew I could render it in the true feeling.

David would make a bronze sculpture of me, too. Of course I was very pleased, and when my mom saw the bronze head she wanted one. Such portraits are usually finished in the dark green "aged" look. My mother asked for a copy in clean red bronze. How else could she polish it? she asked. "The green yin is awfully dirty-looking, son."

I bought Gypsy a full-sized billiard table for his birthday. David would climb in through the windows of the large ground-floor room to play the master of the sport. Later, when they found out about it, the rest of the family would stand and stare as Gyp smashed the balls home.

Gyp was seeing the young Swedish girl, Yvonne, who had captured his heart with her soft Scandinavian charm, and she moved in. Feeling lonely, I asked the young American girl Enid over to stay.

What did we need ladies to move in for? Surely they could not be thinking we wanted the evening to go on beyond the dawn? But Gyp had met a chick and I had met a chick; one thing led to another and soon both girls had moved in.

The first problem was the kitchen. The second and third problems followed after. The affable Gypsy Dave and the easygoing Donno became irritated with each other. For the first time between us there was heard a cross word, and the word was . . . chick.

Not that we didn't love the "little darlings." How could we not, as they floated in and out of bedrooms and bathroom in no more than a top and panties—bath time would never be the same. Not that we didn't like the variety of meals that were prepared for us, open-face shrimp sandwiches on black bread, or chicken soup and delicious goulash. Quite a change after beans on toast. It was just . . . it was just . . . they were always *there*.

So it was a changed scene, man. We young men would take sides. Factions formed. Looks were seen on faces when things were not quite right. What was right? What was wrong? Gypsy and I had never given it much thought before now. Everything was either cool or a drag—certainly never worth getting all fussed and bothered about.

But life had changed, and something had to be done about it. What that was we could not figure out as we guzzled the fine wine and smoked the good herb that late summer of 1966.

That same September that the *Superman* album reached number one, the Beatles released their new album *Revolver*. The last track of the record announced the teaching that John had been reading in *The Tibetan Book of the Dead*. John taught that we should turn off our minds and surrender. Then we could learn the meaning within ourselves: "It is not dying. . . . It is being."

George's song "Love You To" was accompanied by his Indian music. He and I had developed the use of the sitar and drone sounds that year.

With the *Superman* single and album riding high in the charts all over the world, the first record of the New Age, Mickie Most put me back in the studio. The title track of the new album was to be very much the opposite way, a cheeky little number called "Mellow Yellow." I had written this as a sing-along at private parties, nothing else, a throwaway, but Mickie picked this one as the follow-up single.

It is almost always best not to try to define what a song means. It is melody that moves us the most, but in the case of "Mellow Yellow" the lyrics have been much interpreted. So I will give some idea of where I was coming from, man, if you dig my drift.

Once again a song of mine was described as "drug-orientated." I was said to be singing of smoking dried bananas. I certainly was not! Years later the San Francisco singer Joe McDonald told me this story. He and his band, The Fish, devised a promotion for their local San Francisco club date. They would put the band on a truck and drive around Haight Ashbury playing music. Joe found a giant banana on an old Carnaral waste lot and hoisted it on the truck with the band. To add a little twist, Joe released a story to the radio that one could get high smoking dried banana skins. "The stunt would have lasted a weekend," said Joe. "But that weekend, Donovan, you released your record 'Mellow Yellow.'" And the two events were connected for life. This was a radical act from Joe, as he had formed his band to be a political entertainment. Joe was the founder of the radical *Rag Baby's* magazine. But what I really meant by the phrase "Mellow Yellow" was that I was a laid-back kind of dude, smoking the safe little green herb. The electric banana in my song was a reference to the "vibrators" that had become available through mail-order ads in the back pages of certain types of periodicals.

Then a Boston radio station banned the song, saying I was singing about abortion. How bizarre. The truth was that I had pasted word images together from newspapers, billboards, and magazines, collage-style, like pop artists have done since the painter Braque saw the peeling posters of Paris in the late nineteenth and early twentieth centuries. My friend John Lennon was doing the same. The rest of the lyrics come from saffron-robed monks, saffron cake from Cornwall, and a reference to my teenage girl fans at the time, mostly fourteen and just mad about me. To the day he died, my favourite uncle, John Hunter, was convinced that I did not sing "e-lec-tri-cal banana." He insisted I sang "I like a treacle banana." Same song, different reading.

The session to record the single "Mellow Yellow" was set, and this time the young John Paul Jones would arrange the track.

I had been to New Orleans and heard the old cats of jazz play in Preservation Hall and wanted a New Orleans Jazz feel, a march with a "mellow mood." Many of the best horn players in London were in the studio that day, and these jazz fans were in a mood of celebration. Once again I was bringing together cats who had had very little chance in the 1960s to make the music they wanted to make. I tuned down the acoustic guitar to a D-major drone, like the slide-blues cats. Electric bass and guitar would thump along with me and the horns would vamp.

I sang live in the studio. We recorded a few takes and went up to the control room to listen. I sat in the corner and listened. Something was wrong. Mickie came over and asked what was up. The arrangement? No, the parts were perfect. A strained atmosphere developed between me and John Paul. I couldn't put my finger on it. Then a horn player spoke up as I tried to explain the problem with the sound. "I know what Don means," he said. "He means we should put the hats on."

The "hats" are horn mutes shaped like bowler hats. The musos all went down into the studio, put the hats on, and played. A soft "mellow" sound wafted out through the speakers. This was it. John Paul smiled, and I laughed as the track was recorded. The sound before the hats had been like a stripper's song in a nightclub. It wasn't "mellow." Now it was. John Paul Jones and I would go on to make more good music.

And Mickie knew he had another hit. He always knew.

I used to invite Paul McCartney to many sessions, even though, as I say, Mickie was worried that the experimental sounds we were making all through 1966 would leak over into Beatles albums. But we were all absorbing each other's music so fast that it didn't really matter. Record releases were pretty well continuous then and often only months would pass before the Beatles, the Stones, or myself released another.

Paul came into the "Mellow Yellow" session and, contrary to what people say, he did not sing the "whisper vocal" that goes "Quite rightly." I sang this piece and Paul joined in on the "party" parts. (Paul and I did play together on other stuff, notably in Apple Studios with Mary Hopkin.)

The other tracks I recorded for the *Mellow Yellow* sessions were "The Observation," "Hampstead Incident," "House of Jansch," "Sunny South

Kensington," "Museum," "Sand and Foam," "Young Girl Blues" and a song recently composed in Greece, "Winter in the Sun."

"Sand and Foam" and "Young Girl Blues" were both a return to solo acoustic, but all the others had the new jazz-classical flavor with Latin, folk, rock, and poetry fusions.

The lyrics of these songs provide a diary of my changes then. Linda Lawrence had been present in most of my songs on the *Sunshine Superman* album. I thought she was less apparent on *Mellow Yellow,* but she *was* there, even though I had tried to forget her.

Melancholy pervades the Gothic splendor of "Hampstead Incident." "Young Girl Blues" is Linda in her disillusionment as a model in Los Angeles. A certain lovely sea sprite wandered through "Museum." And the blues singer Beverly Chamberlain, Bert Jansch, and I were three points of a triangle for a time in the "House of Jansch." Fleeting affairs—there were lots of party girls floating in those days. If I couldn't have love, at least I would have fun. The sensual artwork for the *Mellow Yellow* cover showed where I was headed. A painting shows a sexy party girl smoking something in a long holder, probably pure Humboldt Indica marijuana of the highest quality. I was both sensual and spiritual that year.

How else can we live in this age that the Hindus call Kali Yuga (the Age of Iron)?

John Cameron arranged some tracks, and he continued to excel in following the fusions I wanted. The lineup of musicians was the same as for the *Sunshine Superman* sessions.

We had nine tracks in the bag, and Mickie wanted a tenth. I played him a new song that I had written about Enid. This tune was not especially unique, a basic blues progression with an old-fashioned turnaround, but Mickie liked it and we recorded it with horns, expertly arranged by John Cameron. Big Jim Sullivan provided the raunchy blues-guitar riffs.

> I tidied up my last affair,
> I lost so much I don't care
> Felt like a fool in a foolery—
> But I'm well on the way to repair.
> —Donovan Leitch,
> *"Bleak City Woman"*

The "bleak city" of the title was Enid's hometown of New York, but the lines "I tidied up my last affair, I lost so much I don't care" spoke of Linda, the girl who I felt had wounded me, and oh, how I refused to heal. Neither was I "well on my way to repair," as the song boasts. Did Enid know that our love could only end with one of us crying?

The *Mellow Yellow* sessions were complete, and the album ready to follow the latest singles into the U.S. charts. Yet still the *Superman* album had not been released in Britain, nor was it when the *Mellow Yellow* album went straight into the charts in the States. That winter saw Donovan Leitch and Gypsy Dave still living on Wimbledon Common, a short eighteen months from roughing it on the road, but now with five hit singles, two hit EPs, three hit albums, and two new hit singles sitting high on the top of the American charts. Not bad for two kids from the white ghetto.

Jenifer Juniper

My return to the London stage in 1967 was a sell-out concert on 15 January in the Royal Albert Hall. I presented the new songs and the new sounds with John Cameron and the ensemble from last year's albums. I was very pleased to be back.

John would conduct and play all the keyboards, Tony Carr was on drums and percussion, "Candy" John Carr on percussion, with Shawn Phillips on twelve-string guitar and sitar. Harold McNair was on flute and sax, Danny Thompson on concert bass. Cameron had a string quartet of the finest players from the London orchestras under his baton.

This concert at the Royal Albert Hall was the first time I had realized my own complete production. Delighted to be talking to the media about this ambitious show, I said, "This is the first (live) idea completely conceived by myself."

I wanted to create a concert that was a multimedia event. This concept was new. I wanted the lights to mean much more than a "follow spot" to catch the singer. It should be remembered that pop shows up to this time were usually brightly lit affairs with no sense of color or stage craft. Now I wanted to present a new experience in sound, color, images, and vocal inflection.

I enlarged some of the illustrations to my songs as "backdrops" on the stage. There would also be a tattooed dancing girl. Her name was Vali, the young woman who had graced the walls of my beatnik bedroom in Hatfield. I was grateful that this character from the Paris bohemian scene was now a friend. When I asked her what she would like to be paid for dancing, she said, "One Nubian goat."

My father had invited John Lennon to the concert, but John declined saying "Beatle Mania" would take away the attention from me when he was spotted in the audience. A sensitive friend of mine was John.

I walked on stage to a roaring welcome back to my homeland. The first part of the concert I performed solo except for appearances by Shawn on sitar and twelve-string and "Candy John" on percussion. That night was the first time any audience had seen or heard the sitar on a pop stage. Shawn sat in the cross-legged position on a carpet and awed the audience.

For the second part of the concert, I brought on the small combo and the string quarter. Shawn returned with his sitar to play the riff for "Sunny South Kensington." The London audience appreciated the London images in my songs, and the Gothic ballad "Hampstead Incident" brought the house down. I had pulled off a folk-classical-blues-pop-jazz-poetical-ethnic jam of far-reaching influence in the years to come, totally "world music." All music is one music.

No one had made such a fusion yet. The concert was a great success, and the press wanted to know where all this was leading me. They wanted to know all about the "psychedelic mind" with which the U.S. media had tagged my music. The heightened states of perception that the psychedelic drugs produced were, of course, described in my lyrics. My music is gentle and soothing in its affect on the listener, encouraging a reflective mood.

I am indebted to many fine artists: the visual artists Sheena McCall and Mick Taylor, the musicians named above, and especially Mickie Most and John Cameron, who had so wonderfully realized my musical dreams on the two albums *Sunshine Superman* and *Mellow Yellow*. These two albums would encourage leading artists of the day to experiment in all the other musical forms that we had fused together so successfully.

I was still living with Enid in Wimbledon, and in February of 1967 Enid told me she was pregnant. I was pleased to know that I would be a father.

While the single "Mellow Yellow" was rising in the charts in Britain that February, we released another single in the States. Mickie had selected a new song I had written called "Epistle to Dippy"—my strangest single yet. This song was, as its title suggests, a letter to my old school chum Ron "Dippy" Gale. I had lost contact, so I released a single record that might get him to call me. It worked. He called from Malaysia where he had signed up for nine years in the army. I asked if he wanted out. He did, and for a few thousand pounds he was out free, as a soldier could do then if he didn't want to complete his term.

The arrangement was written around a ragalike riff I played on the guitar, which I had tuned down to a modal chord, my interest in Indian music showing again. John Cameron scored a string quartet, which blazed along with the chords in an exciting Gypsy form, complementing my melody perfectly. The lyric opens with:

> Look on yonder misty mountain.
> See the young monk meditating rhododendron forest.
> Over dusty years, I ask you:
> What it's been like being you?
>
> —Donovan Leitch,
> *"Epistle to Dippy"*

But the wheel was turning and insisted that we experience the dark side.

Our wonderful Wimbledon pad had become something of a "salon." Friends would drop by and play a chorus or two. Graham Bond was a favorite of mine. He had formed the early blues outfit The Graham Bond Organization with Ginger Baker (later with Cream) on drums. Graham and I would sit and discuss the "Color Organ," an eccentric invention that he was interested in. Each note of the keyboard would be a shade of color, the octaves the key colors and the shades the scales. I asked how the color chords could be formed. Who cares? said Graham. Who said anything about chords?

And, of course, he was right. Anything goes, if you want it.

Except that the strain that had appeared when Gypsy's lover and my own had moved in now worsened. Enid's pregnancy had begun to show, which added to the pressure. The atmosphere at Wimbledon was becoming unbearable. And rather than lose my friendship with Gyp, I decided to find another pad. Where would I go? I wondered.

My father found a tiny cottage for sale near where I grew up in Hertfordshire. Very secluded, just the job. Down a winding lane that spring I passed over a stream to view the sixteenth-century cottage, nestling in a hidden glade below a dark forest.

Bucks Alley Cottage was very rustic but the roof was new. A deal was struck for the paltry sum of £12,000. I moved in with my books, my guitar, a couple of bits of furniture, two Mucha prints, and Sugar, my Afghan hound. Enid loved the place and settled in to await the birth of our baby. My excitement grew as the baby grew inside Enid, and I threw myself into trying to make this relationship work.

The old cottage in the woods was a delight to me. I cut logs for the big inglenook fireplace. This was the first home I had ever owned—the first any of my family had owned, for that matter. There in the gentle glade, creatures visited the back door and chiffchaffs chirped their birdsong. Magpies tilted their tails at me as I sang my poems to the greenwood.

The spring was coming:

> Rain has showered far her drip
> Splash and trickle running
> Plant has flowered in the sand
> Shell and pebble sunning
>
> So begins another spring
> Green leaves and of berries
> Chiffchaff eggs are painted by
> Mother bird eating cherries
>
> In a misty tangled sky
> Fast a wind is blowing
> In a newborn rabbit's heart
> River life is flowing
>
> From the dark and whetted soil
> Petals are unfolding

From the stone-y village kirk
Easter bells of old ringing
—Donovan Leitch,
"Lullaby of Spring"
Donovan Music, London

My music was full of love of nature. I was writing songs of a different color. This did not mean that I had left the world of pop, only that I had sunk deep inside myself again, storing power. The songs I wrote in this cottage as the child formed, as the spring expanded once again, were full of feelings of rebirth.

Back in Wimbledon, Gyp and Yvonne decided to marry. We went out to The Desert Rose on the Cromwell Road to celebrate. The owner, Sabba, was a good friend of ours, and he was especially fond of Gyp.

This unusual Persian had a wife and family who never came to the restaurant. A flame-haired Scottish lass lived in upstairs.

There we were, clapping our hands and stomping our feet to the Arabic drums and zithers, drinking Egyptian wine. The room was filled with cool and rowdy friends alike, sitting on the typical low seats, gathered together to send Gyp off into nuptial bliss. The hookah pipe was constantly attended to as we enjoyed the revels of Gyp's wedding.

A break in the music came, and I stood to make a speech. Everyone hushed as I started with the best man's jokes.

"Well, well, well," I began. "We are gathered here together . . ." I was in my cups, of course. "I am Gyp's oldest friend, and in all the time I have known him I would never have thought . . ."

I was getting to some point that I could not quite articulate when I blurted out, "Gyp is not the kind of guy who should marry, really . . ." Laughter from the crowd.

Then it happened! Sabba thought that I was cursing Gyp and Yvonne's wedding. He flashed a curved dagger into the air, about to plunge it into my heart.

Quick as lightning, Gyp grabbed Sabba's arm and gripped it hard. "Sabba!" Gyp shouted. "Don did not mean it that way!"

The gathering gasped, then were silent, awaiting the outcome. Gyp stared into Sabba's wild eyes, and it was a few moments before smiles appeared on their faces again. Gyp took the dagger and placed it on the table. Sabba and Gyp embraced, and the music began again. I, too, laughed and embraced our Persian host.

Gyp had saved my life as I had saved his back in Mexico in 1966.

I missed living with Gyp. We were still very close and we would work together again; he reminded me with a glance across the crazy rooms of fame just where we had come from. He would still look out for me and check out the danger in all our partying. But a change had come into our young lives. Were we growing up at last?

> The road went ever onward
> Down many a devious way
> Through the valley of the shadow
> A traveller astray
> Till a light shone in the distance
> To lead me to the heights
> And by this star, I journeyed far
> Through the gay and crowded nights.
> —Donovan Leitch,
> *"To the West and the South"*

The world of music then was a small one. The media did not find out that I was about to be a father, but the "in crowd" did, and the news soon reached Los Angeles. Linda had listened closely to my music and heard the obvious references to herself, the insistence in the title track of the *Superman* album.

> It'll take time, I know it,
> But in a while
> You're gonna be mine, I know it,
> We'll do it in style . . .
> —Donovan Leitch,
> *"Sunshine Superman"*

Now she learned that I was living with Enid, and that Enid was pregnant. Linda waited to see my reaction. No marriage followed, and she told Cathy, "If he loved her, he would marry her."

This was true. I was in the best possible position to care for a kid, unlike many of my generation who just could not afford to support an unplanned child. The father of Linda's boy, Julian, had not looked after her or his kid, even though The Rolling Stones were fast becoming the number-one white R & B group in the world; but I wanted to see to it that my child was provided for. I think Enid knew I would not marry her, but this did not seem to matter to her at the time.

Soon I would convince my parents to move, too. They were still living on the council estate. Mother was pressured by the local housewives, "When is your famous son going to buy you a house, Mrs. Leitch?" My fame was changing my family's life as well. Reluctantly, my mother agreed to move, but my father was more keen. I bought them an architect-designed bungalow, high on the hill of a private estate. The Leitch family was now officially out of the working class. My mother would miss the shops and the gossip. My father never did.

Meanwhile, I decorated my little cottage in the woods and wrote the nature-inspired songs for the double album to come. As the full impact of my two hit albums *Sunshine Superman* and *Mellow Yellow* reached the huge U.S. audience, I was becoming the hottest concert ticket in North America.

Money would roll into the coffers in a major way in 1967, and I would rise to such heights of fame and fortune that even the skylark would wonder who was flying above him. And dig this, an illusion it might be, but I would go for it. My mission continued to present the cure for society's illness by introducing the Bohemian Manifesto into popular culture.

Demand for my work was coming in from all areas of the entertainment world. My penchant for penning romantic poetry had not gone unnoticed by the classical theater. That spring of 1967 I was approached by Sir Laurence Olivier to compose melodies for his new production of William Shakespeare's *As You Like It* at the National Theatre. I was delighted to be asked and composed tunes for "Under the Greenwood Tree" and "Shall I Compare Thee to a Summer's Day?"

This production was to be a modern version, starring Olivier. I gave "Greenwood Tree" a light, rocking musical form and kept the sonnet in the troubadour style.

Outside the cottage, up the winding lane, even the UK music business began to react to the enormous U.S. success, and the work poured into the offices of my new management. Ashley Kozak aligned me with Brian Epstein's
company, NEMS Enterprises, under the guiding hand of the managing director Vic Lewis.

Brian Epstein was, of course, the discoverer and manager of The Beatles. I remember I had almost met Brian Epstein in Spain, back in 1965
when I was on a long photo shoot for an article with *Fabulous* magazine.
There in the sunshine of the Costa del Sol I drank sangria, swam in the sea,
and visited flamenco clubs. I could not be dragged away from the Gypsy
music.

> Donovan loved it (flamenco music) and sat in front of the stage tapping
> his feet and clapping his hands for hours. And they loved him—the gypsy
> girls were making the most outrageous eyes at him.
>
> —Sheena MacKay,
> Fabulous *magazine*

In 1967 Brian Epstein had bought the Saville Theatre in London's West End
to create *the* new music venue in the capital. I was booked to do a week-long
engagement in this art-deco hall. Dozens of new music stars were there as I
played to capacity crowds through the week of 10 April. Incense floated
around the theater and I appeared in a red velvet cloak with silver satin
blouse, my jazz-classical orchestra in attendance.

A large sun image on stage seemed to upset the press. They still resented
the spiritual influence in my presentation. But if the soft and gentle approach
I took to my music annoyed some of the reporters, the fans were much simpler. They just enjoyed the sounds.

I was, in fact, presenting certain thoughts of musical, visual, and sensory
harmony, in a time-honored way, to center the mind and contact our higher
selves. We young successful singer/songwriters were the modern shamans in
action. Most journalists missed the connections. Of course, this was all just a
load of cheap theatricality to the uninitiated. . . .

I sang a selection of songs that included "Hey Gyp," "Sunny Goodge
Street," and a tune I had composed for a poem by the British poet Christopher
Logue, "September Song." Christopher had admired my poems, and we two

had taped a television documentary from his home in London's Portobello Road. We collaborated on this fine poem of his, retitling it "Be Not Too Hard," which Joan Baez recorded.

Other songs I sang that week at the Saville included the jazz version of "Young Girl Blues," "Sweet Beverly," "Season of the Witch," and "The Tinker and the Crab" (a favorite of Logue's), and a song from my new nature series, soon to become the album *Gift from a Flower to a Garden*.

In June 1967 my *Sunshine Superman* album was finally released in Britain, a whole nine months after it had topped the U.S. charts. My new sounds were now heard by my British fans. The only trouble was that the new release would be made up partly of the *Superman* tracks and partly of the *Mellow Yellow* tracks The track list that made up the British release included:

> "Sunshine Superman"
> "Legend of a Girl Child Linda"
> "The Observation"
> "Guinevere"
> "Celeste"
> "Writer in the Sun"
> "Season of the Witch"
> "Hampstead Incident"
> "Sand and Foam"
> "Young Girl Blues"
> "Three Kingfishers"

This was a compromise so that the British fans could catch up with the last two albums. This selection did not include the tracks "The Trip," "Bert's Blues," and "The Fat Angel" from the *Superman* album, though "The Trip" did get out on the B side of the "Sunshine Superman" single in Britain back in December of 1966.

The arrival of this album in Britain caused a stir as I had departed so radically from the folk scene in many reviewers' opinions. Of course to me it was a natural progression and wholly intended as I "fused" all world "art forms" into a brotherhood and sisterhood of music. True "social" sounds.

I toured the Continent that summer, taking in Scandinavia. There were also tours of Australia and the Far East. In Germany, especially, I was welcomed as one of their own. German fans would be my most ardent followers in the years to come, so well do they love Scottish and Irish fusions in music. It was Germany, of course, that had recognized the Beatles first when they played in Hamburg in the early 1960s.

The *New Musical Express* covered the Windsor Festival, which was one of the first outdoor events I played. The bands performing included Eric Burdon & the New Animals, The Move, the Small Faces, The Crazy World of Arthur Brown, Zoot Money with Dantalian's Chariot, the Cream, Al Stewart, Paul Jones, and P. P. Arnold.

Among the guests in the audience were Jeff Beck (with his Afghan hound), Stevie Windwood and Traffic, Chris Barber, Andrew Oldham (The Stones' manager), and Geno Washington.

There were many problems with this festival, and most of the bands received a mediocre welcome from the huge audience.

The writer Norrie Drummond (*New Musical Express*) said of my Sunday afternoon performance, "To be fair, this seemed to be Donovan's Festival." Drummond wrote that I had sung poetry for nearly an hour that afternoon while "the cellos, violins, bass guitar, pianos of the session men floated on and off the stage, painting musical backgrounds to his songs." And he said it was to my credit that the likes of Stevie Windwood, Andrew Oldham, Denny Cordell and Eric Clapton (with all his hair and a very striking young lady with a very orange coiffure and tall white legs) watched from cramped corners where the amplification was distorted, before leaving for the refreshment tent. "Don wound up with "Mellow Yellow" and "Catch the Wind" and then seven thousand spectators stood on their seats and cheered."

In fact, Eric Burdon had a great show and so did Paul Jones. The Small Faces, on the other hand, were really pissed off as their amps were unplugged on the stroke of midnight—they were being punished for turning up late. They had only done twelve minutes and three numbers.

I knew and dug all these performers. It's hard to do a show under terrible circumstances.

Norrie Drummond of *New Musical Express* commented on the results of this brave attempt at a festival: "Windsor was a nice try, but not an answer to

Monterey. Only a quiet reply." Norrie was referring to the American festival Monterey Pop, which had begun the festival craze and had seen the arrival of many a fine band, in particular The Jimi Hendrix Experience. I had also been invited to Monterey, but due to my recent "bust" I was not allowed to enter the States.

Derek Taylor, the Beatles's press officer, would write:

> Donovan became an established hero-figure of the counter-culture, seemingly serene and very successful. By 1967 he was strong enough to be a 'must' as a headliner for the Monterey Pop Festival of which somehow I was a founder and the press officer. But Monterey was not to be for Donovan, visited again by the Raiders of the Great Herb, that exotic plant without which there would have been no counter-culture and no Monterey and Woodstock, for that matter.
>
> His visa for travel was removed and the festival compensated itself and paid tribute to Donovan's ranking by making him one of the 12 "Governors" alongside Mick Jagger, Paul McCartney, Roger McGuinn, Brian Wilson and Smokey Robinson, among others.
>
> —Derek Taylor,
> *Troubadour Box Liner Notes*

That August, I released another single in the States—"There Is a Mountain." It came out of my interest in Eastern religion and the practice of meditation, the lyrics adapted from a Japanese Haiku that Derroll Adams had taught me.

Again I fused two seemingly impossible combinations, Zen and Caribbean music.

> The lock upon my garden gate's a snail, that's what it is.
> The lock upon my garden gate's a snail, that's what it is.
> First there is a mountain, then there is no mountain, then there is.
> The caterpillar sheds his skin to find a butterfly within.
> Caterpillar sheds his skin to find a butterfly within.
> First there is a mountain, then there is no mountain, then there is.
>
> —Donovan Leitch,
> *"There Is a Mountain"*

Melody Maker carried a review by Stevie Wonder. Apparently he had commented upon first hearing it: "Yeah! Cut it off, I know it. No, leave it on—I'd dig to hear it again. I like that very much. I've heard most of his things. Out of sight; he's just out of sight."

"There Is a Mountain" only reached the No. 11 spot in the States, but praise from Little Stevie is praise indeed.

Initiation

August saw the arrival in Britain of a teacher of Yoga who had come from India to conduct a series of lectures. This Yogi was named the Maharishi Mahesh Yogi.

Patti, George's wife, had been introduced to transcendental meditation on her first trip to India with George, when he was studying Sitar with Ravi Shankar. Upon her return she had become enrolled in the Spiritual Regeneration movement and began to attend meetings once a week. She had opened the door to another universe, inviting in four young musos from Liverpool.

The world thinks it was Maharishi who turned us all onto yoga and the path to meditation. Wrong. We were reading the key books beforehand but needed a yogi to show the way to meditate.

My personal belief is that as reincarnated Celtic bards, George, John, Paul, and I knew of the spiritual plane before we met Maharishi. How else, apart from initiations in previous incarnations, could we be such powerful makers of magic? Patti now recalled George to the path, and I believe Linda was calling to me from the other side of the Atlantic to return to the quest.

Maharishi was giving a lecture in Bangor, Wales. Patti had been invited by the SRM organization and encouraged the four Beatles to join her.

Ringo did not plan to go and meet with the Yogi, as he was at Queen Charlotte's Hospital with his lovely beatnik wife, Maureen, to welcome their second son, Jason, to the material plane. But both Gyp and Ringo would come to India later, two Cancer star signs, sceptical and amused at the whole affair.

Quite rightly!

So John, Paul, and George met the Maharishi in London and were overwhelmed. Soon they were making plans to visit his ten-day course at the seaside resort of Bangor, Wales. The press had a field day, and a puzzled world read about the most popular music group in history setting off to renounce their fame on The Mystical Express.

The Maharishi was very pleased to have these latest converts and held a press conference where the Beatles announced that they had given up drugs to give meditation a go.

Brian Epstein did not attend the Yogi's course down in Bangor and had not given up drugs or the odd bottle of fine wine. That Sunday of the bank holiday weekend Brian was found dead, locked into his bedroom after a night of heavy drinking and too many sleeping pills. Jane Asher, down in Wales, answered a phone in the dormitory where the Beatles were sleeping. Paul McCartney was called to the phone and Peter Brown (Epstein's assistant) broke the news. Brown says that all of the band were "shocked and saddened but strangely sedate."

Had the band already learned to meditate very deeply that week in Bangor? Had the Maharishi explained to them the transitoriness of all living forms, the doctrine of reincarnation, so that death seemed less sad? I don't know, but it seems that Yogi actually sent the Beatles "giggling" to face the press, if Peter Brown's account is correct.

Back in London, Brian's barrister, David Jacobs (the barrister for my drug bust the previous year), handled the press who swarmed around "Eppy's" house waiting for the story to unfold.

On the airwaves my new single beamed out its quirky lyric:

> The caterpillar sheds his skin to find a butterfly within.
> Caterpillar sheds his skin to find a butterfly within. . . .
> —Donovan Leitch,
> *"There Is a Mountain"*

Soon the four young men would find that life without Brian was a ship adrift. A chapter in their amazing tale had closed, and a new one was opening.

When the news of Brian Epstein's death arrived in New York City, my business manager, Alan Klein, may have felt his dreams about to come true. This ambitious U.S. manager had wanted for some time to manage The Beatles. After a suitable period had elapsed, Klein would board The Beatles's flagship and command the fleet.

On August 16th, a boy was born. Enid named him Donovan Jerome. I delighted in the wee babe and recorded his tiny cries for the track "Song of the Naturalist's Wife."

Even though I was up there at the top of the charts, filling the world's concert halls and creating new hit songs almost each day, I felt dissatisfied and wanted to take a new creative direction. Full of love for my baby boy, I told Mickie Most I would make an acoustic album of nature songs for children.

And so we had a falling out, and that September I went back into the studio without Mickie and recorded song after song for the selection that would later be titled "For Little Ones."

I evoked the spirit of nature and sang of the sea and the mystery of Mother Earth. My inspiration had, of course, come from living in the country; but I also called up a simpler and happier time when I had lived on the beaches of Cornwall with my only possession an old beat-up guitar.

> The Magpie is a most illustrious bird
> Dwells in a diamond tree
> One brings sorrow and one brings joy
> Sorrow and joy for me
> —Donovan Leitch,
> *"The Magpie"*

My cottage was visited by the birds many times as they flew into the garden and sat in the trees after the rain. The old carpenter who mended my cottage door had given me the traditional rhyme:

One brings sorrow, two brings joy
Three brings a girl and four brings a boy

The fourth magpie certainly had brought me a boy.

I envisaged a double album. One would be for the children and the other for the parents. I wanted to release both albums in a set, singing for my generation, our hopes and wishes, and also for our children.

A band was formed, and I recorded a set of songs that would become the second LP in the box set *Wear Your Love Like Heaven*. The title track recalled my love of painting, and the chorus called to my generation to wear their love like heaven, to spread compassion around the world.

I completed the double album and sent a copy to Clive Davis of Epic Records, explaining the concept and showing him line drawings that my artists Sheena McCall and Mick Taylor had made for the children's part of the package. My project would include poetry and illustration. I needed a box. Clive was not pleased at first. Boxed sets of records were for classical music. I would also need to work out my differences with Mickie Most, as he was signed up as my producer. I was not yet trusted as producer of my own songs.

Meanwhile I prepared to do the first giant tour of North America. With The Beatles retired from live concerts, I was the hottest concert ticket of that "Summer of Love" in 1967.

During a pause in the West Coast end of the tour, I was invited to one of Maharishi's lectures by a young fan. This fan was smart, in a suit, short hair, and one of the Maharishi's disciples. It seemed that the Yogi's people were for the most part very straight indeed.

I was in Los Angeles at the time and arrived at the college hall where the guru was conducting one of his introductory shows for the students and anyone else who wanted to come. It was free, after all.

I arrived and took a place in the back of the auditorium, not wanting to be recognized. On stage was a podium behind which hung a large black-and-white photograph of a powerful Yogi, the Maharishi's own teacher, Guru Dev. The Maharishi sat cross-legged on the platform, a microphone before him and a few flowers in his hand, with which he caressed his face now and again. He spoke eloquently about the science of being, presenting the possibilities of his transcendental meditation in a most entertaining way. His infectious laughter punctuated the discourse, and this helped endear him to the assembled multitude. For my part I could not but like this guy.

Just before the Maharishi finished his "show" (and it was very much a performance), the fan in the suit came to fetch me and asked if I would like to go backstage and meet him.

Now I very rarely visit artists backstage. They are bothered enough by fans. But I was curious.

Standing in the wings, I watched as the Maharishi wound up, inviting the audience to join him in his movement and discover the hidden potential within us all. I saw him rise from his podium and leave the stage to a round of applause.

Moving sedately, he walked slowly to the wings, dressed in a flowing cotton robe, his long dark hair and beard flecked with silver strands. As he clicked on his wooden sandals nearer to where I stood, I heard him ask his aide, "And who is this?" in his singsong way. I heard the aide reply, "Like The Beatles."

Well, I was flattered to be compared to my friends.

The Yogi came to meet me. Moments of embarrassment followed as I stood in the presence of a guru. Sensing my plight, the Maharishi invited me to visit him where he was staying in Beverly Hills. "Come and see me soon."

I had an impression of his soft, brown hands holding mine, his lucid eyes looking at me with a detached gaze. My next impression was of his aides, hovering around him in a most fawning manner that irritated me. But I said I would visit him, and he floated away with his entourage of admirers and a periphery of press people seeking an interview, eager to get the story of The Beatles's conversion.

As I slid into my limousine, I thought, Why not? I'll go see the guru. I lit up a joint and gazed through the dark glass as the limo moved through the long, lazy streets of Hollywood to the mansion in the hills.

Some days later I arrived at the address the disciple had given my chauffeur. It was a large home in the lower flats of Beverly Hills, below Sunset Boulevard but still a chic location. The sprinklers hissed on the perfectly manicured lawns as I disembarked and entered the house, escorted by another aide dressed in a suit of indeterminate color.

We took off our shoes upon entering. Inside were other guests sitting on the floor, awaiting an audience with the Maharishi Mahesh Yogi. I took my place along the wall. The furniture, I now saw, had been removed. The atmosphere was one of reserved piety, and older American women in saris floated around the quarters, probably earlier converts to TM (transcendental meditation) from when the Maharishi had first come to the States.

It seems that he had contacted establishment figures on his first visit. He had never made any bones about his mission in the United States: he wanted to infiltrate the power structure of the business community and alter their views.

Along the wall of the sparsely furnished room, I noticed a group of long-haired musos in outlandish gear and strange attitudes. Other, more conventional types sat waiting to be called into a small breakfast room that the Maharishi had secured as the Initiation Cave.

Knowing nothing about initiation, I waited my turn. I did not recognize any of the musos and was surprised when I was called in to see the Yogi out of turn. It seems that I had been upgraded when the Maharishi knew I was there. I was ushered into the dimly lit room. The Maharishi sat cross-legged on a deerskin on the carpeted floor. His aide departed and the Yogi motioned for me to sit likewise. He adjusted his cashmere shawl and settled himself, his limpid eyes bidding me to relax. I did so and entered his vibe.

A calming influence came over me as the Maharishi gazed down at the floor and spoke of the attitude I should adopt to receive my initiation. He breathed long and slow, and I became aware of the stillness in the room. The windows were shaded, and the world outside seemed to slip away. He said, softly, "Close your eyes and breathe as I do." I followed his instruction and drew air into my lungs through my nose, expelling my breath slowly. With no effort at all I entered his world, and then he said, "Say this word to yourself." I repeated the word after him. "No," he said. "Say the word inside." I felt myself fall deep down within and kept falling, down and down, into a place I had never gone before. I gave myself up to his instruction, remembering that total obedience to a guru is essential.

After a time, which I had no way of measuring, the Maharishi spoke again and said, "Slowly open your eyes." I opened my eyes and returned to the world. But it wasn't the same world. I felt displaced as I came to and realized that I had been initiated.

Somehow an aide knew it was over, entered the room, and said, "The Grateful Dead are next." Maharishi laughed and said, "They should not call themselves The Grateful Dead, they should call themselves The Grateful Living."

I left as "The Dead" entered.

Back in the hills, I mused over the initiation experience. I had been led into the spiritual world of the superconsciousness without the use of a sacred plant. So there *was* a way within without getting high from herbs and acid! This was momentous. And how could a mere man lead me into divine states of being that I had only read about?

Shamans were said to be able to lead their tribe into the other world, and I knew that the magic of music can lead us within. But this was different. Was this Yogi one of the few who had journeyed beyond ordinary reality, pierced the Veil of Maya, and lived to tell the tale? And, more to the point, was this Maharishi Mahesh Yogi my long-awaited guru? I would practice his method of mediation and discover the truth for myself.

Each morning and each evening I sat alone, practiced the breathing, and recited the mantra.

Meanwhile, somewhere else in LA, the girl from Windsor sat watching the parade of British bands touring the country. She watched my progress across the States closely as I sang to thousands of fans songs that I had written for her. But Linda knew I was still angry with her and that any approach by her would meet with immediate rejection. She did not visit backstage or try to contact me.

And it was time. I was adamant. She had gone out of my life and I would make the best of it, looking for another girl who would love me on my terms. Not exactly the sensitive way to look for love, but I was young and confused and an arrogant young sod, a rascal.

Linda had thought long on what had happened to us both and now knew for certain that she really loved me and wanted us to get back together. But by this time I had steeled myself against her. I see myself backstage on that 1967 tour with very young girls, me almost as young-looking as them. Here I was on the road, and I didn't feel that Enid was part of all this, anymore than she was part of my spiritual quest. Enid's father would not understand why I could not marry his daughter, but I believe her mother knew.

After many days of meditation I took to it quite naturally and became aware of another state of consciousness, different from anything I had experienced before in a waking state. The slow-breathing technique and the mantra placed me in a very relaxed frame of mind as I sat alone each morning and evening for the twenty minutes suggested by the Maharishi.

I had, of course, felt introspective states after smoking the herb or ingesting mescaline, both of which did slow down ordinary thinking, pause logical reasoning, and, at times, quiet the constantly active mind. This meditation was different.

But my first observation was that I very easily lost the will to recite the mantra. Other "thoughts" constantly occupied my attention. It was frustrating to know I could not repeat a simple word at least three times in a row without forgetting the fourth. I returned to see the Maharishi to be "checked," appraised. The Maharishi explained that thoughts are constantly rising and falling and can be allowed to pass gently. Then you recall the mantra and reintroduce it as you sit with closed eyes in the semi-darkness of your room.

I continued and found it was indeed difficult not to become attached to the various thoughts of the day previous, the next day; the week, month or year to come. I recalled a Buddhist text from my schooldays:

> The mind is fickle, it flies after fancies
> wherever it likes. It is indeed difficult to restrain.
> —The Dhammapada

This, I realised, was the explanation of a much-used word in the teachings: "Detachment"—not only "Non-Attachment" to objects and people as belongings, but "Non-Attachment" to outcomes, fears, concepts, conditioning and, of course, all 'thought' which might bind us to any of the foregoing.

I knew how the breathing rate increased with attachment to certain thoughts. Here it was in reverse: "Non-Attachment" to thought, producing deep relaxation.

The Maharishi's Transcendental Mediation teaches that great results can be achieved in any walk of life when you contact this deep level of relaxation, this Creative Intelligence which is the actual source of all thought. He calls this the "Unified Field."

In describing my first introduction to meditation, I am trying to conjure up first impressions and experiences which were so much a part of my life that year, many, many years ago. All the world was young and the possibility of World Peace was in every gentle heart.

Prince of
Flower Power

❖

My time in California came to an end and the tour moved off around the country. The show was on the road, and I appeared in all the best venues from coast to coast, including the New York Philharmonic, where I set new attendance records. I was described in the media as "The High Priest of the Peace Movement." Fashion-conscious articles described me as a Victorian or Edwardian figure, dressed in velvet and lace, somewhat like Oscar Wilde or a Pre-Raphaelite child of the Romantic Period.

At most of the halls I was expected to create the same havoc as usually happened at all pop shows, and therefore rent-a-cops were always standing by, though cops were often the biggest cause of trouble, shining lights in faces and generally being difficult with the audience. I would handle any problems with a finger to my lips and a soft word through the PA system. It is very effective to whisper; the audience try to listen.

The curtain rose each evening. The audience gasped. Lights glowed, and incense curled up into the darkness. I had invited my father into my life on the road and after the curtain rose, he came on stage to introduce me each night. He wore a suit until I bought him a silk-embroidered robe of a golden color. He can be heard on the *Donovan in Concert* album of 1968 where he announces: "Ladies and gentlemen, your evening star!" I moved through the songs with my ethnic-jazz ensemble, string quartet and sitar accompaniment.

I prepared to do two huge sell-out Los Angeles concerts at the Hollywood Bowl open-air amphitheater. While my staff and crew were busy preparing the production, I walked alone up into the hills above the Hollywood Bowl, with a shepherd's crook which I had found in an antique store in England. It was natural-wood, but I considered it a magic wand as I sat on the hillside looking down into the amphitheater. I could hear distant music from the sound check drifting up to me.

Rain had been forecast—rare for California. I made a circle of semi-precious stones and laid my wand in such a way as to point it skyward. I would ask the spirits and fairy beings of the Native Americans to bless my concert and keep the rain from falling.

After the ceremony I returned to the bowl to finish the sound-check and oversee the stage set. I had envisioned a flower mandala, and had ordered white and blue irises from every flower shop in the Los Angeles area. The mandala would cover the entire stage—a huge space. Some seven thousand flowers were needed. Very soon my aides told me that the flower shops were now saying that I had bought every available iris. And still we needed more.

Just then the US tour manager said that he had also ordered some from Hawaii, and the flowers would be there on time.

That night I sang in the center of the largest flower mandala ever seen in the Western world. The gentle audience sang along. The clouds came over, and it did indeed begin to rain softly. I asked the eighteen thousand souls to clap their hands once on the count of three. They did as I bid. The rain stopped.

Some fans were so excited that they broke through barriers manned by the local cops. One cop chased a fan, and they both fell into the small lake that curved from side to side halfway up the amphitheatre bowl. The crowd cheered. When the two got out, the cop was smiling. He took out his pistol and shook it to show that it was wet. He gave a good-natured shrug of his shoulders, and the crowd roared their approval. The cop was surprised when another fan took a flower and placed it in the muzzle of his gun. He danced a little jig as I started the next song.

The LA concert cops were not like other police officers. They were into the swing of that 1960s "thing."

Next day a reporter from *Time* magazine coined the phrase 'Flower Power' in his review of my concert.

As the tour moved though October, the American press gave major coverage to the story of two actresses who had become impressed with the Maharishi Mahesh Yogi. Shirley MacLaine, on holiday in India, announced she would like to "return to India for a stay with the Maharishi at Rishi-kesh in the Himalayas." Asked why she was disillusioned when she had so much, Shirley replied that it was due to the West's "moral affluent decay, the perpetual slick discomfort." She said that Madison Avenue's subliminal propaganda "had taken over even the churches, and the movie sex symbol Marilyn Monroe had committed suicide due to such an ersatz atmosphere." The reporter Prakash C. Jain went on to say: "Shirley has turned to India, 'for the people here introspect and search'." She was asked, "Search for what?" She said she did not know, but what was important was the search.

Mia Farrow was the other actress reported by Associated Press to be leaving "husband Frank Sinatra behind and flying to India for a month of meditation with Indian mystic Maharishi Mahesh Yogi, her studio said today." It seems Mia had been introduced to the Yogi by her sister, Prudence, around the same time that I met the Maharishi in LA.

My massive tour rolled on across the plains of the Midwest to the teeming cities of the East Coast. When I played in the capital city, Washington, a story in the *Washington Post* highlighted my appearance in the city. "Washington-area teenagers, attending a concert last evening by Donovan, England's foremost folksinger, rummaged for apparel to express their own personalities."

Performing in Constitution Hall, I was described as "a portrait of sensitive calm, contemplating a small bouquet of pink-and-white flowers, while two thousand teenagers waited for the doors of Constitution Hall to open."

I had been led by Joan Baez to expect this venue to be the epitome of fascist bullshit in the American establishment. My "sensitive calm" as I arrived was, in part, due to the breathing I had practiced in the dressing room prior to my performance. I strolled onto the stage and realized that the negative vibes were being dispelled by the joy of the young audience smiling up at me.

That night at my concert I sang:

> I will bring you gold apples, and grapes made of rubies
> That have shone in the eyes of a prince of the breeze
> Bright cascading crystals, they danced in the sand dunes
> On the beach of no footprints to harpsichord tunes.
>
> —Donovan Leitch,
> *"Legend of a Girlchild Linda"*

My record producer, Mickie Most, and I had become reconciled, and he selected two tracks from the double-album sessions I had completed. The song "Wear Your Love Like Heaven" was the single, in his opinion. He was right again. Adding Harold McNair on flute and reproducing the sound, Mickie presented the work to Clive Davis. It would be released as the tour came to a close and follow the previous single "There Is a Mountain" into the charts.

The U.S. press noted that I had changed. As they said of me:

> At 21 he has been through the Kerouac pilgrim phase, tramping around the English industrial countryside in denim. He's played the ardent young rebel, singing BBC-banned anti-war songs at Newport. He's dabbled in magic, been busted for drugs, and once appeared in the British Press, with his friend Gypsy Dave, going like saints to the lions, to meet the magistrate.

And they repeated the story about how, when I was arrested, I had jumped, nude, on the arresting officer's back, shouting obscenities. "Donovan was on his way to being the Brendan Behan of the pot generation," they said.

One of the verses of "Oh Gosh," the B side of the single, says:

> With the future safely dreamed of
> And His kisses on your brow
> You may rest assured peace is coming
> To think upon all that is

Fair to look upon and to touch
Oh Gosh, life is really too much,
You'll see
Soon, soon, soon.

—Donovan Leitch,
"Oh Gosh"

I was preaching Peace while 1967 screamed to a close with:

Nine thousand, four hundred and nineteen Americans dead in Vietnam.

Over three hundred thousand antiwar demonstrators in New York and San Francisco.

Antiwar protesters storming the Pentagon.

Ten thousand people mobbing the Oakland, California, draft induction center in the "Stop the Draft Week."

Secretary of Defense McNamara calling Vietnam bombing a failure and being promptly replaced.

Muhammad Ali stripped of his title for refusing to be drafted.

The CIA compiling a list of three hundred thousand names of members of antiwar groups, suggesting ties with "foreign interests."

Nearly half a million foreign troops in Vietnam by year's end.

Riots in thirty U.S. cities, the worst in Detroit—forty-three dead, two thousand injured.

Five thousand homes burned.

National Security Adviser Walt W. Rostow saying of U.S. involvement in Vietnam: "It looks good. The other side is near collapse."

And all this during a year that also saw the Apollo 1 spacecraft fire (killing its three-man crew) and the Republic of China detonating their own H-bomb, increasing fears of World War Three. Is it any wonder a generation sang of Peace and Love? But of course the papers continued to portray the youthful rebellion as hedonistic and without substance.

Critics of my gentle approach to music were still missing the point. In contrast to the wild exuberance of rock and roll, I was soothing with my songs. Peaceful music was needed then. Even more so now.

Soldiers returning from Vietnam met with me later and spoke of the effect the music had on them. Many returned damaged and became lost in the great peacetime that wanted to forget.

On tour I spread TM brochures around the foyers of the halls for my fans. Over in England the Pye label released a collection titled "*Universal Soldier,*" and a younger generation turned on to the songs of protest. As the tour moved toward its triumphant conclusion, I was amazed at the reception that my music got. Themes in my songs were being welcomed by the tens of thousands who felt a similar ache for a new way of seeing. In 1967 it truly looked like anything was possible.

On the surface everything looked good, but underneath I was slipping into a crisis situation. I knew the message was being commercialized. Moreover, although I welcomed the success, I had left my beginnings and was adrift on a greater ocean with no home port to return to. Almost a year had passed since Enid had moved into my cottage, and the incompatibility between us was now impossible to ignore.

There were worrying signs within the movement, too. A sinister vibration began to make itself felt. As early as the Summer of Love, in San Francisco, the center of the American peace movement, needle drugs and synthetic pills of powerful potency appeared. No longer would the soft drugs of marijuana and LSD lead the seeker in the search for the true behind the false.

George Harrison journeyed to San Francisco to see for himself the "expansion of consciousness" and was disillusioned when he saw the movement degenerate into bad drugs. Shirley MacLaine's comment on the "West's moral affluent decay, the perpetual slick discomfort" rang true.

Did Transcendental Meditation offer an antidote to the malaise beginning to appear in the consciousness of a generation? Could the drift toward negativity be countered by TM? I came out and declared that I had given up drugs.

An article in the *New York Times* of Sunday, 17 December 1967, ran:

No longer the Brendan Behan of Pot.

Along with such notables as the Beatles, the Rolling Stones and Grateful Dead, Donovan has discovered the Maharishi Mahesh Yogi, swami to the stars, advocate of Bliss-Consciousness, and perhaps the most influential Indian export since hemp.

The article went on:

Under the Maharishi's tutelage, Donovan has given up drugs in favor of meditation and, in a pamphlet slipped into the dust jacket of a recent 45-rpm release, has asked his fans to do the same.

Little did this writer know that I had come to this decision completely on my own—I was not asked by my guru to drop drugs—and neither was my decision as simple as he suggested. I still believed that the soft drugs, cannabis and magic mushrooms, were far safer than alcohol and tobacco.

Before I left New York City to return to the cottage, I stepped into the offices of the Epic label to see Clive Davis, together with my manager, Ashley Kozak. A secretary gaped as she saw me floating through the corridors in Arabic robe and bare feet. Soon I was sitting with Clive, trying to convince him that the double box set of *Gift from a Flower to a Garden* was commercial.

Clive still had serious doubts. The package was expensive, he said: the seven color separations needed to print the artwork, the actual "box" to house the two LPs—the costs, the costs, the costs. Then a dear gentleman by the name of Sydney Maurer came to the rescue and championed my cause. Sydney was the cover-art designer for all Epic products, and we took to each other immediately. He saw the package idea and loved it. Soon he convinced Clive that the uniqueness of the project and the respect that the label would receive for such a release from such an artist made it worth doing.

Clive went for it, but with conditions. I would pay the extra costs of the package, and the two albums would come out as separate releases before the box. Fair enough. I agreed. Sydney went to work, and fine and lasting work he produced from original artwork by my illustrators Sheena McCall and Mick Taylor.

For the inside sleeve the color photography would be on the new film stock, infrared, which reveals colors that the human eye cannot consciously detect. The photographer, Karl Ferris, shot the sessions at Bodiam Castle in Sussex. The photograph on the cover itself was taken in Cornwall.

I enjoyed my own boy Donovan, only five months old, but I was rarely at home. His mother and I were seeing less and less of each other. I cared for them both and felt guilty for involving Enid in my crazy bohemian life. She was a lovely young woman with dreams of her own, and I loved her, but I did not love her as she wanted to be loved. I felt guilty, too, that my son would not know me as well as a son should know his father.

As the year ended, the first album of the double box-set was released on 30 December in the States. It only went to No. 60 on the charts.

The second part of the package, *For Little Ones,* came out next. This mainly acoustic set of songs appeared in the stores the first week in January, only reaching No. 185 on the *Billboard* charts, bearing out my original expectations.

On 13 January, the double box-set, *Gift from a Flower to a Garden,* was released in the States. The full-page advertisement in the trade magazines *Cash Box* and *Billboard* read:

Produced by Mickie Most
Donovan
The smash new Donovan single—now an exciting new album "Wear Your Love Like Heaven."

Donovan

From Donovan to the little ones of all ages. An album of irresistible appeal for all children, from preschool to old school. "For Little Ones."

Donovan

His music, his art, his poetry . . . all in a magnificently designed volume that includes the two LPs, a beautiful art portfolio, complete lyrics, and full-colour photographs.
"Gift from a Flower to a Garden."
A totally unique concept that only an artist as excitingly different as Donovan could accomplish . . . and he does . . . on Epic.

—*Epic Records Ad*

The complete double-album set would enter the Top Twenty and reach No. 19, very good for such a new way of seeing and hearing pop music. My original idea was now realized, and the belief in the project by Clive Davis,

Sydney Maurer, and the staff of Epic Records was totally vindicated. I felt a sense of achievement in "fusing" musical and visual arts in this materialistic business of entertainment. The album set soon went Gold and has become a collectors' item.

Some years would pass before another 1960s artist would emulate this package. George Harrison would present his own box-set, *All Things Must Pass* and *Concert for Bangladesh*. Apparently, when his record company was initially reluctant to allow him a box-set, he said, in that doleful Eeyore-ish voice of his. "Well, Donovan's got one." George and I continued to follow a similar path towards self-realization in the years to come.

I still believe that Clive Davis and Epic Records made a major faux pas in not releasing this package for the Christmas market in 1967. I also want to draw attention to the fact that, apart from the two tracks "Wear Your Love Like Heaven" and "Oh Gosh," I alone had produced this double album, Mickie Most being credited as producer.

On the back of my box-set was the picture of the Maharishi and I, taken during those weeks in LA when he initiated me. Soon I would be heading for his ashram in India to continue my studies.

Yogi

❖

Nineteen sixty-eight saw hurricane-force winds lash my homeland of Scotland, killing twenty. The weather was atrocious in the North Atlantic, and the world was stunned to read that a bomber, carrying four nuclear bombs, had crashed into the ice off Greenland while trying to make an emergency landing. It was not clear what had happened to the bombs, and the U.S. Defense Department said that the bombs were not armed and were "probably" under the ice. Far away in Vietnam, heavy casualties were suffered by both warring factions as the conflict continued unabated.

I continued to meditate. Enid still did not seem to me to show any interest in my changes, and we continued to drift apart that winter.

In fact my time with Enid was over. I felt bad for Enid, but I was determined not to abandon her and the child financially, as Brian had abandoned Linda. We had been together so little over the fifteen months since we met, and now it was with great pain that I asked her to leave.

Later George, Patti, and I sat with our eyes half-closed and meditated, feeling strangely excited to be entering our own inner paradise. We let our thoughts disperse; our thoughts turned to the East and the ashram that awaited us by the ancient Ganges River.

When I told my father I was going to India and that my music engagements would be stopped for the trip, he smiled and shrewdly said, "You're not going to study meditation in India, son; you're following that wee lassie Jenny."

Yes, I was going to follow both paths: Yoga and the strange attraction I felt for Jenny Boyd.

"Will you be going to India?" I remember asking Jenny.

"Oh, gosh! I hope so," giggled Jenny in a delightful way. "Will you, Don?"

"I want to. I feel it's very important to me." I smiled at her.

"Me too," Jenny said.

A fairy arrow seemed to fly toward me, glancing off my heart.

A few days later, I heard through mutual friends that Linda was having a hard time back in Los Angeles, passing on the many offers of marriage that came her way. She wanted true love and could not sleep around and snare a star like many Hollywood chicks. For my part I could not swallow my male pride, my pain, and ask her to come back to me. As for Brian Jones, he had collapsed on stage, and the Rolling Stones were recording without him. He hated the musical direction the Stones were taking, and bad drugs were eating him up. He had a nervous breakdown and checked into the Priory, the first of several visits.

I met Jenny Boyd at George and Patti's home in Esher. Younger than her sister Patti, Jenny was a fair-haired English rose. So young-looking was she that I felt like I was about to rob the cradle. I was also attracted to Patti, but she was with George. Jenny had her sister's manner—a middle-class maid with long, silky hair and bright, curious eyes—and she was obviously attracted to me. We would sit and look at the spiritual books that George and I were studying that year.

My interest in Jenny showed me that I was leaving Enid. I recall I had taken Enid to stay at George's house once but went on subsequent visits alone, leaving her in Wimbledon. I could not continue to grow with my American love in all the ways I explored with my spirit-brother George and his wife and with George's sister-in-law, Jenny. It was at George's home in 1966 that the photograph of me in the white sharkskin suit had been taken for the *Mellow Yellow* album cover. I wanted what George had, to share a home and a spiritual path with my kindred spirit, yet I could not bring myself to call Linda.

Jenny was seeing a young man at the time, Magic Alex. Alex was John Lennon's friend and a kind of Rasputin at the Court of Apple, the Beatles' ill-fated business venture. When George heard Jenny's song "Jenifer Juniper" he was bemused and asked, "What's this all about?" He knew Jenny and I had not slept together.

George, Patti, and Jenny were making plans to go to India to study with the Maharishi, and was invited by the yogi too.

"Are you going to India, Don?" asked George. We sat on the Persian carpet. He had a book in his hand. "This is a gift. Have you read it yet?"

It was *Autobiography of a Yogi* by Yogananda, new to me.

"It's amazing," said George. "It's the first time a Yogi has written his autobiography."

"Thanks, George." I would value his gift. "Yes, of course I am going. I want to dive deeper into meditation."

Flipping through the front pages of the book, I read the account of the Yogi dropping his body, and the corpse remaining unspoiled for some weeks after. The morgue report was printed in the book. "Yogananda was displaying his control of the physical plane," explained George. I looked into George's sparkling eyes, so bright and excited about the path we both shared. I, too, had extraordinary books to share with my friend.

"Have you read *The Diamond Sutra?*" I asked.

"Buddhism is from India. I prefer going straight to the source, the Vedic teachings—more pure," answered George in his Liverpool drawl.

"I feel that Buddha took it forward for the future," I said.

Cross-legged on the carpet, his favorite incense curling up into the still air, we both laughed at this gentle jousting on the difference between the Hindu and the Buddhist paths. We both knew there was no difference, only different ways to the same goal.

My record producer Mickie Most and I resumed our amazing collaboration with master arranger John Cameron and recorded the song I had written for Jenny Boyd, "Jenifer Juniper." Once again, we fused classical and folk elements with delightful results. The introduction of the classical instrument called the Cor Anglais created a perfect complement to my vocal range. Very English indeed.

It was fun to sit in the studio with John, conducting the "straight" classical performers on one side of the sound baffles and the "cool" jazz cats on the other. Two groups of musos who would not normally be invited to play in such a fusion—only in my sessions.

The single "Jenifer Juniper" was released that February in Britain and flew into the charts. With this lyric, the remaining tenuous ties to Enid were finally broken, it seemed, and I began to court Jenifer Juniper in earnest.

Meanwhile, Linda Lawrence was working for Jonathan Debenham in Hollywood. Jonathan had invented a crazy little game on TV called *The Dating Game*. She would look after his house, and this created the first stable environment for little Julian to live with her.

Jonathan received a visitor from India one day, his friend Richpal Singh, grandson of a Sikh spiritual leader in northern India. Richpal had read with amusement of my and the Beatles' intention to give up "Western" temptations and study Yoga. He was headed in the opposite direction, to dive straight into all the temptation and have a good time in Hollywood!

Soon Linda could be found wearing a lovely sari as she cooked Indian meals for Jonathan, recipes that Richpal had taught her. She watched with frustration as I took my leave of the West to enter the ashram. But she noted, too, that Enid was not going to India with me. Linda wanted to learn to meditate.

An Austin Princess limo picked me up at the cottage and cruised to Heathrow Airport and the flight to Delhi that sixteenth day of February 1968. It was with a light heart and a wistful air that I said hello to the VIP air hostess when she opened the door to my car on the pavement of the largest airport in the world. Her uniform was immaculate as she ushered me into the terminal, asking whether I'd had a pleasant journey down from Hertfordshire. She escorted me into the firstclass lounge to await departure. Those were slower days, and the crew met us on the curbside. It was a happy bunch of campers that sat in the jet that day: John and Cynthia, George and Patti, Paul, Jane Asher, Ringo and Maureen, Jenny Boyd, Mal Evans, Gyp, Yvonne, and myself. Our expectations were high, and we were all looking forward to the weeks ahead in India.

When we arrived at Delhi, wild monkeys leapt around the airport and onto the terminal roof. They cavorted and pranced about like they owned the place. We musos had each brought an acoustic guitar—except Ringo, of course. George would order up a tabla for him when we settled in. This was to be an amazingly good opportunity to write a whole new bunch of songs.

Soon our party was traveling by taxi to the distant village of Rishikesh on the banks of the Ganges. Then it was Jeeps and eventually the backs of donkeys. When the path became too treacherous for the animals, we walked the last half mile, crossing a narrow rope bridge over a muddy chasm, and reached the gates of the ashram. Our luggage came after us on carts drawn by oxen.

This was the first time in years that the Beatles had been totally cut off from the rest of the world. The news agencies had carried the story of our quest, and they waited for us to return to the West with our discoveries.

We checked into rustic stone bungalows that turned out to be quite comfortable, with all the modern conveniences. There in the large compound we were welcomed by the staff of the Yogi in a most cordial manner. After a wash and a brushup, we were called to the Maharishi's own modern bungalow to be received officially.

Slowly we filed into the room, and an awkward silence followed. John, always the humorist, decided to break the silence. He walked up to the Maharishi as he sat on his deerskin, patted him on the head, and said, "There's a good guru." We all laughed, relaxing into what would be a strange and momentous period in all our lives.

Our days were spent in serious meditation, and the practice became longer and longer each time we sat alone in our rooms. Our meals were taken outside at large tables under trellises, where we would eat vegetarian dishes prepared for us by the chef. We exchanged our experiences of meditation as the monkeys tried to steal our grub and the shrieks of wild peacocks came from high up in the tropical forest.

We had been joined by Beach Boy Mike Love, the fine jazz musician Paul Horn, Mia Farrow, and her sister, Prudence, plus some European students and various Americans. A few older Swedish women were already there in the ashram, converts from previous years. Shirley MacLaine had not been able to attend due to her busy film schedule. She was continuing her quest in her own way.

As the soft evenings descended on the ashram, we would slowly gather around the lecture hall and await the arrival of the Maharishi to speak to us and extol the virtues of meditation. One such evening, Paul was finishing a cigarette as I stood by the doors of the lecture hall. The Yogi was approaching. Paul said, "Fags out, boys. Here comes the teacher." Paul had not been totally convinced about the benefits of TM. John was into it, and George, of course, was ready for anything Indian. Ringo still reserved his opinion, but, like Gypsy Dave, would give it a go.

I struck up a friendship with Paul Horn and we would play together during the hours of dusk after the lecture. We both shared a love of jazz fusion and I marveled at his wonderful alto flute. He and I discovered that the vocal range of my songs could be complemented most harmoniously by his playing, and we became fast friends.

One night I was awakened in the wee hours by a weird rustling of leaves outside my window. I sat up, the moonlight streaming in through the open casement. After so many long and silent sessions of meditation, I followed the Maharishi's instruction and fell into a waking reverie. An exquisite stillness pervaded the gleaming room, and I began to compose. Lighting a candle, I focused my half-closed eyes on the space between the worlds.

> Seek ye the mystery
> Through all this energy
> To set your soul bird free
> For Deathless Delight
>
> There are so many ways
> Forms upon which to gaze
> Live in a Divine Daze
> Of Deathless Delight
>
> I have had some tingles in my time
> Never dreaming them to be a sign
> Be a sign
> Out on the lonely road
> Living a warrior's code
> Ev'ry where thine abode
> Of Deathless Delight
>
> —Donovan Leitch,
> *"Deathless Delight"*

Clear and cool the moonlight shines, soft and still she shines upon the myriad creatures. All is calm and soon the day will dawn and we will all awake to be ourselves again, whoever we are. Meditation is difficult to describe, for one must experience it to know it properly. To give you an idea of how difficult it is, I would ask you to describe the taste of water.

Next morning, the Maharishi announced that we would now embark upon an extended period of meditation, during which we would not be allowed out of our cabins. Meals would be passed under our doors as we continued to "fathom the infinite." I was moved to a small cottage on the periphery of the compound.

I would be disturbed softly by a member of the Yogi's team when he or she (I knew not who) would slide the food into the room. I was not locked in, but it was clear that I would not be allowed to exit. Arising from my reverie, I would take the food in my hands and place it into my body. The distance between waking and sleeping became less and less. Sometimes I felt that I was not here or there at all.

One day or night, I knew not when, the soft shuffling by the door of my chamber became the Maharishi, and he entered. Bidding me continue my stillness, he asked how I was doing. I replied that the stiffness in my bones sometimes necessitated that I lie down and sleep. He said that was quite all right, for such sleep was needed by my deeper self.

After a time, which I had no way of measuring, I was called out and joined my fellows in the ashram; they, too, had been sequestered away in a prolonged session. Not wanting to compare such strange experiences, we became flippant once again, joking our way through the warm and lovely day.

During my absence, the media of the world had arrived at the ashram gates and had camped out on the doorstep. All of the main papers and TV stations were there, and we famous few wondered whether they would gain access. Maharishi quelled our fears, and we sat in our gardens, going about our business of being.

One day I was sitting playing my guitar on John's little patio, while he was sitting next to me washing his hair. Suddenly he leapt to his feet, effing and blinding as he chased a photographer intent on getting a photo. This incident upset John, who gave the photographer such a chase and a tongue-lashing I guess he'll never forget it. John then stormed off to the Maharishi's bungalow and gave him a piece of his mind also. The Maharishi laughed, and the day went on its own inimitable way.

In the bungalow next door to John's, George was receiving visitors, a group of Indians delivering various instruments: a sitar, one tamboura, and a set of tabla drums for Ringo. George picked up the sitar, and proceeded to tune the instrument. So well did he succeed, that soon we were chording a new song or two.

George then went through the scales that Ravi Shankar had taught him the previous year. He explained that the position that must be assumed to cradle the sitar is a very difficult one to perform, as if the music itself was really secondary to a half-lotus position. This sounded so much like the basic problems of meditation.

George gave me the tamboura as a gift. I picked it up and realized that this four-string gourd was about as much as I could master. I began to make a tune of my own that related very closely to the "airs" of my Celtic past, and what I played would later evolve into my song "The Hurdy Gurdy Man."

The next day I walked down to the gates of the ashram. There in the gatehouse sat an Indian gentleman wearing a pair of dark, creased trousers and a white cotton shirt without a tie. I engaged this very articulate intellectual in musical conversation. Having my guitar with me, I proceeded to give him a rendering of the tunes I had written. The first song I gave him was the jazz rock "Sunshine Superman." He listened most attentively, then, after a pause, he said, "Ah yes, I know the raga, eighteenth-century raga in the Muslim mode."

Shocked, I said, "No, I wrote that one."

"No, I beg to differ; this tune is very old raga."

Not wanting to be pedantic, I sang the next song, "Mellow Yellow." He listened to the various chords that I played, then he said, "Ah yes, I know the raga, seventeenth-century, which was improvised in an evening raga of a great sitar player, court musician to His Highness the Maharaja of Jaiphur."

Now I was getting pissed off. There he sat in the small gatehouse, belittling my contribution to popular culture. I could not let this white shirt do this to me, so I hit him with a very left-field composition that even an Indian intellectual could not underestimate: I gave him "Isle of Islay." Without any apparent remorse, he stated that my heartfelt tune was another raga from the Aryan music of his own history. I humbly replied that I realized that music is truly universal.

Mia

I found I didn't miss the alcohol, didn't miss the street, didn't miss the hashish. I missed a lover's bleat; I missed a lover's bleat. Yes, in all this meditation I still felt sexual desire. Surely this was a sin in an ashram? But then again, lovely young women were walking about the place in the most scanty apparel.

One day Patti asked the Maharishi if she and the other women could go down to the town. He giggled and replied that it was impossible. Patti insisted that she and the girls were adamant.

He said, "No."

When pressured for the reason why the girls could not visit the vicinity of the Ganges that day, Maharishi gave in and explained. "If you walk today by the caves of the swamis in your miniskirts you will become a great temptation. Today," he explained, "the swamis who have been meditating for many years in their caves will be coming out, and I cannot be responsible for their actions."

Giggles followed his explanations. So much for self-control, I thought.

Although it was part of the rules that we were not allowed out of the ashram, I very much wanted to get out, and soon the Maharishi would actually take me out himself. One day he asked me to attend him on a journey to another town. Not knowing what to expect, I arrived in sandals and cotton clothing to do his bidding. Three weeks into our course we had discarded the wardrobe we had arrived in and adopted pantaloons and pyjama tops.

A very rickety taxi awaited the Yogi on a side street up behind the ashram, and I wondered why we had not arrived in our own taxis at this entrance. No doubt this was the Yogi's secret exit. Maharishi barked and the driver opened the door to the old jalopy. I adjusted the deerskin in the passenger seat for the Maharishi, then took the backseat as we moved off in a hurry up the jungle road. The taxi driver was very uptight as he maneuvered the hairpin bends on the higher land. It seems he was concerned that the Maharishi would not be pleased with him. Perhaps he thought that this was a Yogi of very great yog, and that his family would suffer should he not serve the enlightened soul in the time-honored way.

As we swerved to avoid large pats of elephant dung, the Maharishi urged the driver to go faster and faster as we approached the bends. At one particularly dangerous curve, the driver quite rightly slowed down. The Maharishi seemed to be in a hurry and said, "Don't worry; nothing is coming."

I looked at the driver, and he turned to the Yogi with a smile and pushed his foot into the floor. I believed him, too. And you know what, nothing was coming.

We arrived at a gathering of at least a hundred people. Someone had died. I don't remember what happened next, but the Maharishi was said to have been at two funerals that day, one in the province he and I had visited and another many miles to the west, all in the same day. This feat is said to be an accomplishment of realized Yogis. Who was I to question it?

As the sun went down each lovely day, we musicians would gather to play and sing. Songwriting came easy. Paul Mac never had a guitar out of his hand. He let us all get a few songs in though, and you can hear the results on the records that followed, the Beatles' *The White Album,* and my own "The Hurdy Gurdy Man."

"How do you do that?" asked John one day as we were sitting playing guitars in the shade of a jacaranda tree; he meant my fingerpicking.

"It's a pattern. Wanna learn?"

"Yeah, I do. When do we start?"

"Right now, if you like. Here, lemme show you. It'll take a few days though."

"I've got days," John said, in his nasal tone.

So I gave John the wisdom taught me by Dirty Phil. "OK, choose a chord of six strings—E's good, as it's two open strings."

John did so.

"Now, thumb and third finger lie on fifth and second strings."

My new pupil went to it with a will, and he learned the arcane knowledge in two days, faster than I had done from Dirty Phil. In this way John began to write in a whole new way, composing "Dear Prudence" and "Julia" in no time flat. John asked me for some help with the lyrics of "Julia," a song for his lost mother and the childhood he'd never had.

George showed an interest, but he preferred to stick to the "flat pick" and "finger style" that he had learned from Chet Atkins's records. Paul picked up little bits from looking. He did not have the application to get it, but he still wrote some lovely ballads under the influence of my finger style. Many songs, written during that time in India, were influenced by that guitar style, my own descending bass patterns turning up in quite a few Beatles' songs. George has also said that the songwriting on *The White Album* was influenced by our daily playing together, and George and I wrote together in India. In particular, he wrote a verse for a song I was working on: "The Hurdy Gurdy Man."

One day we were called to the flat roof of the Maharishi's bungalow. He wanted to know how we were doing with the "sitting." John told him that he sometimes found it hard not to write songs when he was in deep meditation and asked what he should do. The Yogi laughed and said John should slowly come out of the meditation, write the song down, and return to the mantra. This pleased John. We all laughed, and the world would now hear Lennon songs that came from his deeper self. He was feeling for his lost mother in a most loving way when he wrote "Julia."

George was forming music and songs that would surface in the years to come as the finest spiritual sound, while Paul was entertaining us all with his funny little ditties like "Rocky Raccoon" and "Back in the USSR," and, of course, melodious ballads just poured out of him.

I don't recall Mike Love of the Beach Boys ever getting on the guitar, but he was very witty, ever smiling. Mike and I would keep up our friendship for a time in California until the walls went up between us all. But that was to be far in the future. "Big Mal" Evans, the Beatles's famous road manager, was my mate also in that holiday camp of an ashram, working together on my song "The Sun Is a Very Magic Fellow." He had previously added lines to many a Beatles' song.

Ringo and I got on well and he would tap on the tabla drums, making those metal bowls sing.

On my own in the stone cottage one night, I was staring at a small plaster cast of a swan. There was a girl entwined around the long neck of the swan, and they were kissing. The myth of Leda and the Swan. I picked up the guitar and wrote:

> She in her boat long hours
> He in his royal plumage
> She threw him some flowers
> In the reedy river
>
> Sadly they mourn and sigh
> Whilst in evening twilight
> Two swans glide
> and fly . . .
> O'er the Reedy River
> O'er the Reedy River
>
> —Donovan Leitch,
> *"The Reedy River"*

I was longing for my Linda, wherever she was.

I placed a chord while composing the song that I had seen Paul Mac use (G-minor 7th + D-flat bass). Then, when I played "The Reedy River" at our daily get-together, Paul became somewhat possessive over the chord. Perhaps it was the "lost chord"? Perhaps it was just the tendency in Paul to wish to lead us all? Perhaps it's just downright bossiness?

Rather like me, in fact. I am just as bossy and cocksure. Ask anyone close. We who were on the firing line had to be sure of ourselves; no one else was. Kate Bush would record "The Reedy River" in the future. I am honored.

McCartney and I remained friends though, and we had many a great little jam together and a few laughs about the craziness of it all.

One day Paul Horn and I went down to the local town of Rishikesh, having convinced the Maharishi to let us out. Once in the busy little street, lined with shacks and open-air barbers, stalls of Indian fast food, metalworkers banging pans, and droves of bicycles that nearly ran us down, we headed for a shop to buy some writing materials. I always buy notebooks in every country I visit. The Indian school jotters were rather good affairs on cheap yellowed paper with an Indian scene on the front. In the stationery store, which was also the grocer and the haberdashery, we gazed at the full-color posters of deities, Krishna and very sexy goddesses. One lady in particular looked absolutely awesome with a necklace of skulls, Kali the Destroyer. I know girls like that, I thought.

We bought copies of the posters on shiny paper and were also amazed to see on the stalls that ads for products that actually incorporated the spiritual figures. I particularly liked the elephant god Ganesh. The Jimi Hendrix Experience would offend some of the Hindu community when they used Ganesh heads in a painting for an album sleeve, yet in India the religious pictures are used on ads and calendars.

Back on the street, the sad-looking beasts drew carts up and down, an occasional car honking to disperse the constant flow of animals, bicycles, and people on foot. The smells were incredible. Foul stenches from open sewers contrasted with the incense. Two smiling lads with no hands begged from us, their family so poor that they were forced to deform themselves. I shuddered. I noticed that after we had passed by, the lads lit an Indian cigarette, using their stumps.

Then I caught a glimpse in the back of a street stall of a tiny girl-child with jet black hair and dressed in gaily colored rags. She stared at me with eyes lined with thick kohl, which gave her a theatrical air. Seems the eye makeup is not just to keep away the flies but to prevent blindness, so harsh is the Indian sun.

A perfectly healthy boy latched on to us. He was, say, twelve, although it is hard to tell the precise age of young Indians. He spoke perfect English and wanted to be our guide. We took to him and told him we were up in the ashram; he knew the place and explained that there were thousands of gurus with their ashrams all over the country. He seemed to respect the Maharishi though, even fear him. This lad wanted to go with us to America or England, anywhere away from that Indian town. He would be our servant, assistant, anything. Of course we could not take him. He spoke of the wonders of our Western world and asked us to send him, of all things, a few drip-dry shirts.

Paul and I bid farewell to our clever little friend and planned to take another trip in a few days up into the foothills of the Himalayas to visit the hill town of Dehra Dun.

Paul Horn went on to record an album in both the Taj Mahal and the Great Pyramid of Giza. Between the two of us, we probably invented what is loosely called "New Age Music," music that induces a meditative state.

Paul and I would tour together, sitting cross-legged on stage. I found in him the flute friend I lost when Harold McNair dropped his body. Paul also became a TM teacher.

The Yogi moved me to one of the new bungalows he had recently completed, overlooking the Ganges. The bungalow smelled of fresh wood and paint. I moved in, delighted. Next door, I discovered, was Mia Farrow. She also had just moved into one of the new bungalows. That night, beautiful Mia and I got to know each other; I found her to be an innocent and charming girl. Frank Sinatra was a lucky man. My obsession with Jenny ended.

Back in the ashram, Mia Farrow was concerned about her sister Prudence, who had been deep in meditation for a long time. The Maharishi had apparently seen her disturbed frame of mind and separated her from us all. This long therapy prompted John to write "Dear Prudence," asking her to "come out to play." When she eventually came out, Prudence got well and said that the meditation had been the cure.

Mia and Prudence's brother John arrived one day, more on holiday than to study, I think. He took me aside and showed me a great lump of hashish someone had brought into the ashram. My eyes widened as I thought of the press getting wind of it—after all, we were officially off the herb and the juice. I took it from him and flung it far into the swirling waters of the Ganges. He just stared at me. After a few days I confessed to him that I might have been a trifle hasty.

The day arrived for our trip up-country, and John Farrow would join Paul Horn and me to film a bit of the trip on his Super-8 camera. I would record the music on my tape recorder. We would travel by car to the town of Dehra Dun, there to visit a school for the deaf that was run by an energetic American lady. As we traveled up-country, the air became cooler and our heads lighter as the altitude increased. Far in the distance we could see mountains. Reaching a washed-out dusty town, we set out on foot to find the school. There, standing in a run-down colonial garden, our hostess introduced us to the smiling students, all Indian boys, all deaf.

Then she took us on a tour of the classrooms and showed us the out-of-date headphones that were used, and the simpler balloons the students would make ba-ba sounds with, pressing their lips to the stretched rubber. The children were also put through their Hatha Yoga postures. The woman shouted to them what to do. It seemed that they could hear *something,* or perhaps it was just the wave of good cheer emanating from their mistress that vibed them. They loved her so.

It was time for us to play, said the teacher. "Play?" I asked. "But the boys are deaf." She insisted, so Paul and I began. The long, sonorous notes of his alto flute filled the air, and I joined him on guitar, singing one of my little tunes for the kids. Immediately they ran to me and pressed their fingers against the sound box, moving in time to the beat. They could hear (or feel) the music quite well. Marvelous.

We took our leave of the kids and their eccentric American teacher and headed for the road higher up to visit a family of artists who lived near the Colonial School, built for the Europeans who had lived and worked in Mussooree during the Empire days.

Now we really were high up. We sat taking tea with a gentle family, looking at their drawings, and I sang to their children as the majestic sun set in the west. Next day we returned to the ashram, for George was having a birthday, and party plans were afoot, something of a surprise.

The evening before George's birthday, the Maharishi announced that the whole ashram would take a trip on a barge down the river. We were all excited as we followed the Yogi through a tiny village to the riverbank. There were long stalls laid out with those incredibly sweet and sticky Indian candies and deserts made from rice, thick with sugar syrup. Yuck! But we all ate them happily enough. In the village square a small silver screen had been erected, and a projector flashed a romantic Indian movie in the twilight. The high, squeaky vocal soundtrack delighted the two or three kids sitting Indian fashion in the dusk.

The Maharishi moved slowly as if on a "walkabout," with all his students in tow through the fading light of the day. The stars began to appear in the sky as we boarded the barge and took our seats along its sides. The Yogi was positioned aft, and two large, bald-headed "chanters" in brown robes sat in the bow. The Maharishi said they were able to alter the weather with their chanting. They began to give us an example, the one starting a drone very low, the other joining him with a slightly off-key dissonant drone. This vibration was said to break up cloud formations and release rain in the dry season. They looked like Tweedledum and Tweedledee, and I could well believe their claims.

We jolly campers were joking and having a great time—even though we were not taking drugs or drinking. We all were healthier than we had been for years. Someone noticed a star moving across the heavens and thought this was a very auspicious sign—the Golden Age was coming to the world—until one of the more down-to-earth students murmured that it was just a satellite. The Maharishi laughed with us, and life was good as we slid on the black surface of the water under the great starry firmament. I had brought my guitar and sang the lines I had begun and which would become an anthem for meditation, "Happiness Runs." This song vocalized our thoughts of being like little boats upon the sea of being. The Yogi liked it and I became his minstrel that spring as we all delved deeper inside, looking for ourselves.

> Happiness runs in a circular motion
> Thought is like a little boat upon the seas
> All our souls are deeper than you can see
> You can have everything if you let yourself be.
> —Donovan Leitch,
> *"Pebble and the Man"*

This song would later appear on the *Barabajagal* album and has been adapted as a prayer by Yogi Baghwan and other spiritual schools across the world. I have letters from children's schools where they sing it. This is the type of fame I prefer.

That night all of us slept soundly in our beds. But changes were coming that would taint our innocence and alter our lives for ever.

Far away in America, Linda was bringing up her boy Julian and wondering if his father, Brian Jones, would ever see him again. Brian's health was worsening. John and Cynthia Lennon also had a boy named Julian, who was back home in England while his parents studied with the Yogi.

Seek ye the mystery
through all this energy,
to set your soul bird free
for deathless delight.

My studies in the ashram might have gone on forever, but of course I had to go back sometime. I told the Maharishi I had a life in music. He was saddened and asked me to stay. I was sorely tempted as I know, deep down inside me, that Yoga is one of the keys to understanding. But, like him, I had a mission. Empowered by his teaching, and the teaching of his own Guru Dev, I would continue to make music that lifts the sensitive heart and soothes the troubled soul.

I would not go on to build a University of Transcendental Meditation in Edinburgh, as the Maharishi asked me to. But I went on to found an invisible school of self-awareness in the hearts and minds of those gentle souls who love my songs.

As a seeker on the path, I knew my "Liberation from the Wheel of Becoming" was going to take a lot longer than three short months in an ashram in India. Still, as *The Tibetan Book of the Dead* proclaims, any meditation is better than none when death comes around again.

The essential nature of Yoga is described in the Yoga-Sutras of Patanjali as "Yogas' citta-vrtti-nirodhah" (Yoga is the inhibition of the modifications of the mind)—*The Science of Yoga: A Commentary on the Yoga-Sutras of Patanjali* by I. K. Taimni; the Theosophical Publishing House Adyar, Madras, India.

This second aphorism of Patanjali might seem such a simple task, but try it yourself, dear seeker. Try to stop your thoughts consciously.

Imagine a "scene," a moment of great beauty—a dove-gray sky with smoky pink clouds—a dusky purple mountain. Let this scene put you in an exulted state.

Will this exulted state to continue.

Understand that this is why we get high—to increase the exultation.

And yet, this is our natural state, which is why we want it—bliss.

The Beats speak of saving the world by turning everybody on. This might appear to be a cop-out. Wanting to help the world and tripping out on drugs do seem very different on the surface. Experiences of exulted states achieved through meditation, fasting, or "holy plants" are described as "hallucinations," as "visions," or as "paranormal," as if they are unnatural. As if the petty and mean-spirited people who disapprove of such things live a *natural* way of human life!

But these two apparently very different desires—the wish for the exulted state to continue and the wish to save the planet—are not so contradictory as one might think. The exulted state is a state of no conflict, of pure beauty, of "one-ness" with the spirit of all things. If everyone felt exulted, there would be no need to have a peace movement. There would be no war if everyone knew that they were killing themselves by killing the so-called "other." As John put it: I am he as you are he as you are me and we are all together.

John's sublime lyric expresses Oriental wisdom with his characteristic northern bluntness.

And as well as through meditation, fasting, and holy plants, the state of exultation can be reached through music and poetry. But to experience the "one-ness" in all its reality requires bravery of an extraordinary kind. Great inner strength is needed to "detach" subjective thinking from experience and "be" what you experience, so that you may realize that all that you see, you are. It requires a painful "leaving" of conditioned thinking, modes of behavior you have been taught to regard as "normal." It is a lonely, narrow path where even your closest loved ones cannot be with you.

Of course, ultimately, you will realize there is no difference between your loved ones and you, and so you will be reunited.

You cannot "take" love; it must be given. Similarly, you cannot be taught "one-ness." You must "experience" it.

Are you experienced?

As we were leaving the ashram, John gave me the gift of a drawing to thank me for teaching him. It is a beautiful study of a girl with long dark hair, her hand to her mouth in a secretive gesture. Only later would I recognize this girl as Yoko Ono.

The Hurdy Gurdy Man

❖

Upon my return from India I sat in my cottage and sang the songs I had composed out there. There was one powerful tune: "The Hurdy Gurdy Man." This was once again a departure from anything I had written before. I could hear the acoustic chording down the song, but I could also hear absolutely wild electric guitars—lots of them. I thought of Jimi Hendrix, of course. I had met Jimi, and dug him. I wanted to give him the song to record.

When my producer, Mickie Most, heard the tune he flipped and said not to give it to Jimi, as it was my next single. I suggested that we should at least get Jimi to play the power riffs on his guitar. We called his manager, Chas Chandler, and found that Jimi was off somewhere gigging that week. I was disappointed, but Mickie said we would find another guitar wizard, or two.

The guitar wizards were my old friends, Jimmy Page and Allen Hollsworth, a session guitarist who had played with Blue Mink, among others.

John Paul Jones and I had worked together before, and he arranged and played on the "Hurdy Gurdy Man" session. We were joined by drummers Clem Catini and John Bonham.

A warm acoustic opening led into a blazing rock fuzz–guitar sound with manic drums, my vibrato vocal vibing with the tempo. Most people would think we used an effect on the voice, but it was natural. Layers of guitar were added by Page and Hollsworth, and a new kind of metal folk was created. The term *metal* had not been coined for music yet, but perhaps Jimmy Page, John Paul Jones, and John Bonham were inspired by this session to form Led Zeppelin.

The ethnic instrument called the "tamboura," which George Harrison had given to me in India, provided the drone. I strummed this four-stringed gourd as I sat cross-legged on the studio floor. I had created "Celtic Rock."

As I mentioned earlier, while I'd been jamming with George in the ashram, he had written a verse to "The Hurdy Gurdy Man."

> When the truth gets buried deep
> Beneath a thousand years asleep
> Time demands a turnaround
> And once again, the truth is found

But singles in those days were rarely longer than three minutes. The exciting power-chord riff solos by Page and Hollsworth were too good to be cut short, so George's verse was left out. The missing verse did finally get recorded, however, when I released a live album *(The Classics Live)* in 1990.

The new single was ready to go, but before it was released, the box-set *Gift from a Flower to a Garden* arrived that spring in Britain, following its earlier debut in America. Some of the British press were taken aback by its wide-ranging concept and unique packaging. What makes me proudest of it are the hundreds of letters I have received from parents and schoolteachers from around the world who played the songs to their children, helping to introduce them to subtle nature and a peaceful vibe. My Taoist feelings spread through the children, as I had dreamed they would.

To present the new selection of songs, I gave another concert at the Royal Albert Hall in late March. I would be joined on stage by the superlative Harold McNair on flute and tenor sax; Danny Thompson on double bass; Tony Carr on drums; and arranger, conductor, and keyboard wizard John Cameron. John had arranged many fine string parts for the classical section, who came dressed in immaculate evening suits and bow ties, a wild contrast to the romantic frills of the rest of us.

The majestic concert hall was filled with five thousand people eager to hear of the new experiences and musical discoveries that I had brought back from my sojourn in the East with the Beatles.

I was supported that night by two up-and-coming new groups, one sweet folk outfit called the Flame and a duo led by Marc Bolan called Tyrannosaurus Rex. My friend Graham Nash was also there that night, and he gave me a book of the incredible graphic drawings of M. C. Escher.

In the exciting backstage area of the Royal Albert Hall that night the two jazzers, Danny Moss (tenor sax) and Les Condon (flugelhorn), gazed around at the flowers and miniskirts and wondered whether they were too old for all this. They were not, of course, and later dressed themselves in the most colorful gear they could find.

My good friend on double bass, Danny Thompson, stood there in a flowered shirt, warming up the jazzers—Harold McNair, Danny Moss, and Les Condon—with bebop licks as the chaos mounted. In another crowded room backstage, the strings and woodwind ran through snatches of Bach and Mozart to get in the mood.

I am proud to have been an influence on acts like Van Morrison and Led Zeppelin, who went on to dominate the 1970s. As I say, the support act that night was Marc Bolan's fledgling group Tyrannosaurus Rex. Marc had one acoustic guitar and a percussionist named Mickey Finn.

People say that Marc borrowed much from me—Celtic fairy lyrics, my look, even melodies.

Well, the thing is, I told him to!

Small of stature, Marc looked like the Artful Dodger. He was mischievous—his long, coiling hair could have hidden elfin ears for all I knew.

Later we recorded a heavy version of my song "Lalena" with Marc on electric guitar. This recording was lost. If anyone finds it, please tell me.

I saw all this as I arrived dressed in a white cotton jacket and trousers, as relaxed as I always was. In the dressing room, wearing an Indian shawl, sat a very young-looking Mia Farrow. We hugged and kissed hello.

Calling Harold McNair into a smaller dressing room, we tuned the guitar to his flute for the solo songs we knew so well. I was pleased to see him and taught him a new song in three minutes flat, so close were we musically in those distant, heady years. He is sadly missed.

John Peel was emceeing. It was time for me to go on, and I felt the audience welcome me back to London. The stage was decorated with flowers. I was very pleased to be back. Sure of myself as ever, I strolled through the tender ballads and steamed into the jazz numbers with my great band of musos, the classical section giving loving performances under the baton of John Cameron. When Georgie Fame hit the stage with jazz singer Jon Hendricks, the crowd went nuts.

I gave my thanks to the wonderful audience and all the fine players who had made it possible that night, especially John Cameron. The show came to a close, and I gave an interview in one hot and crowded dressing room, so hot that we had to retire to one of the old Victorian bathrooms to finish the piece.

Soon the jazzers were heading for the bar.

Disillusion

After this exciting beginning, I was off around Britain, doing more concerts. Nineteen sixty-eight would see me working harder than ever, with festivals in Europe and tours all over the world. This year would also see five singles and four albums released, with the accompanying promotion of TV and radio on two continents.

In all this work I found time to see my little boy, Donovan, but the relationship between his mother and me was full of pain. Enid was taking it quite badly, I felt rotten, but I just didn't love her. I wrote a second song for her. The first had been our "meeting" song, the second a "leaving" one:

> And the child feels the pain in the dream that swims by
> And he may or may not know but he will when he hurts his own
> Lady of the Lemon Tree
>
> Sails on the sea, wheels on the land,
> Cannot carry me further than I stray from your hand,
> And the gift I must leave you is the burden you carry

My Lady of the Lemon Tree
My Lady of the Lemon Tree
—Donovan P. Leitch,
"The Child"

On 4 April, Martin Luther King was shot dead in Memphis, Tennessee. His last words to Jesse Jackson had been, "Be sure to sing 'Precious Lord' tonight, and sing it well." Within hours of his death, there were riots in dozens of towns and cities all over America. In Detroit two policemen were shot, and a white youth was burned to death in Florida. There was burning and looting within three hundred yards of the White House.

May also saw a violent mass uprising of students and workers in Paris. The riots began with the arrest of six students demonstrating against America, and the workers soon joined them because of their own grievances. Back in March the American Embassy in London had been surrounded by eighty thousand demonstrators.

I still felt that my own protest should soothe instead of agitate:

Histories of ages past
Unenlightened shadows cast
Down through all eternity
The crying of humanity

'Tis then when the Hurdy Gurdy Man
Comes singing songs of Love
Then when the Hurdy Gurdy Man
Comes singing songs of Love
—Donovan Leitch,
"The Hurdy Gurdy Man"

Again, the press did not link the song with world events, saying I had come up with another dreamy song of wonderland, and they continued to have fun with my use of the word "beautiful."

I honestly didn't realize that I colored my conversation with this adjective so often. After all, I had not been brought up in a protected shell, hidden from ugliness. Yes my parents had given me a loving upbringing, yet being a young boy with polio had been hard; and although the small tenement had been warm and cozy, the streets of Glasgow were full of poverty and oppression. All around the city in the late 1940s the ruins of the war, empty, wallpapered rooms open to the wind and rain, were monuments to man's violence and suffering.

Rather than take the easy way out, get a job and settle for an apprenticeship and a wife, I had taken to the road at the age of sixteen and slept rough under the stars. I was not doing this with money or a decent pair of boots. I was out there alone, fending for myself, without the relative security of the Welfare State.

I want my children to see my fame and success in contrast to my beginnings. I want them to know where I—and therefore they—came from and to remember that when a man or woman of good heart rises above their background there will be those who will want to cut them down. In my case, what hurt was when people did not believe I was genuine and honest in my work. Yes, I took myself too seriously at times. As I say, this was when no one else would. Pop music is supposed to be frivolous and fun for the most part, and yet I felt and still feel that popular music is a medium through which important new ideas and values can be introduced.

The liberal attitude of the 1960s opened many doors of perception, not mainly through the use of mind-expanding drugs (though they played a good part), but through the deliberate spreading of ideas and the new ways of seeing that flooded popular culture in those days.

Do not be led into believing the propaganda of the British establishment, which says that the youth culture of the 1960s is responsible for the dire straits the Western world finds itself in now.

May 1968 saw me in the studio again, recording a set of songs that would become *The Hurdy Gurdy Man* album. This LP was not released in Britain for some reason.

Once again I was accompanied in the studio by Harold McNair, Danny Thompson, Tony Carr, and John Cameron. Mickie Most produced the album in his masterful way. Gypsy Dave wrote "A Sunny Day" and "Tangier" for this album, and my old friend and mentor Bert Jansch visited the studio to play the superlative acoustic picking on "Tangier." It was on this track that

I played the harmonium, a small keyboard box with bellows that I had bought. This is what Indian families play when they sing their hymns together. "Candy" John played bongos.

I also played the harmonium on "Peregrine," a song I had written for George. The lyrics spoke of our quest to discover ourselves, using the Maharishi's description of our thoughts being like boats upon the sea of being. I sang of how George's thoughts in his own songs were very beautiful to view. Permeated with sadness and longing, this song also sang of the bright future time when the world would be a kinder place.

The opening lines were Celtic images of mountains and falcons:

> Peregrine falcon, hooded and flying
> Whither you go blindly over the mountain
> Oh your boats upon the sea are very beautiful to view
> By me, by me, by me, I hope by you.
> Once I tried to be your friend, But I was undergoing change
> The same as you, the same as me, The same as you,
> The same as me, The same as you.
> Oh, oh, and there will come a time
> When to each other we'll be kinder
> Than we were, than we were
> And there will come and there will come and there will come
> A peace of mind, a peace of mind, a peace of mind.
>
> —Donovan Leitch,
> *"Peregrine"*

Freely I keened the ancient melody while the master of the ethnic bass, Danny Thompson, was intoning and bowing in his antique way. Danny and Bert Jansch would create their own fusion group called Pentangle with John Renbourn, Terry Cox, and Jacqui McShee.

Later, George Harrison took this song to India to record it as an instrumental with Ali Akba. Kahn and other musicians gathered about Ravi Shankar in those days. I was delighted.

Harold McNair played most wonderfully on "Sunny Day." "The Entertaining of a Shy Girl," and "Sun Magic." He and I continued to be a delightful duo on acoustic guitar and flute. "Sun Magic" was the song that Mal Evans and I had worked on in India in the ashram. Harold showed his roots on "West Indian Lady" when he played the riffs that carried the track, the music of his Jamaican origins. He also surpassed himself when he softly played the saxophone on "Get Thy Bearings."

> Get together work it out
> Simplicity is what it's about
> All the world knows what I'm saying,
> All the world knows what I'm saying,
> The world knows fine well.
>
> —Donovan Leitch,
> *"Get Thy Bearings"*

Here again I was taking the Taoist position that all the world really knows what is going on even though we might think we are powerless to alter it. My drummer, Tony Carr, flipped when he heard the tune. He loved the chord structure and the freedom for the band to play jazz fusion. He gave one of his most memorable performances on this day.

Business hassles have always dogged my career, especially in my homeland, but "The Hurdy Gurdy Man" single did get released in Britain, and I was glad to be in the Top Ten again. It also reached No. 5 in the United States in June of 1968. I was glad that Mickie Most had convinced me to record it myself and not give it to Jimi. This first experiment with heavy sounds convinced me to try similar fusions in the future.

I began to do the summer festivals in Europe. In May 1968 I was booked to headline the "First International European Pop Festival" at the Palazzo Dello Sport, in Rome, Italy. This extravaganza was planned to run from 4 May to 10 May, and fifty-five artists were invited. As with many Italian gigs, the promoters had bitten off more than they could chew. The Italian way is always full of bravado and "Invitations to perform at this largest Pop Festival in history have been (or are being) extended to the following"—so ran the advertisement:

> Donovan with . . .
> Herb Alpert and the Tijuana Brass
> Barbara and Dick

Bee Gees

Big Brother and the Holding Company

Blossom Toes

Blues Project

Bo Diddley

James Brown

Buffalo Springfield

Paul Butterfield Blues Band

Captain Beefheart and his Magic Band

Judy Collins

Country Joe and The Fish

Crazy World of Arthur Brown

Crome Syrcus with "Astarte" Ballet

Dalida

Dantalion's Chariot

Doors

American Flag and American Music Band

Equipe 84

Fairport Convention

Family

Freddy

The Grateful Dead

John Handy

Françoise Hardy

Incredible String Band

Jhaveri Manipuri Dance Group

Roland Kirk

Living Theatre

Charles Lloyd

Lovin' Spoonful

Mireille Mathieu

John Mayall

Steve Miller Blues Band

Move

Moscow Radio and TV Big Band

Muddy Waters with Little Walter

The Nice
Wilson Picket
Pink Floyd
Procol Harem
Robati (Five Up)
Il Rokes
Buffy Sainte-Marie
Sam and Dave
The Seekers
Ravi Shankar
Soft Machine
Mercedes Sosa
The Tages
Traffic
Vanilla Fudge
Dionne Warwick
and The Who

This show promised to include fifty-six one-hour performances, fourteen shows, and light shows from Britain, America, and the Continent. Also to be featured were avant-garde and experimental events, electric-blues-jazz-folk-soul and contemporary music.

At the event, Julie Driscoll and Brian Auger performed a rendition of my song "Season of the Witch" in grand style, Brian blasting it out on the Hammond organ. I also recall Captain Beefheart and the boys blowing us away. My friend Tony Foutz swears that The Stones also played.

In spite of all this success, feelings of disillusionment were never far from the surface, and I asked my father to go to Scotland to look for some property in the Western Isles.

I was dropping out again.

The Lord of the Isles

My thoughts were drifting to the wild and windy land of my birth. I had some crazy notion of starting a commune with my artist friends, to pick up the threads of an early dream, to be a poet and a painter. I felt that musical fame had led me astray.

My father Donald traveled north and viewed property for sale in the islands. One day he called me from an isolated telephone booth high above Waternish Bay on the Isle of Skye. I could hear the wind whistling around him as he shouted a description of the panorama from where he stood. The sun was going down over three islets, he said, all of them with property for sale: Isay (Isle of Harris), Mingay Isle, and Clett. He told me to come up right away to see for myself, and I joined him in Scotland. We traveled up the coast, staying in small hotels, sampling the local fish, and spending rare time together, just the two of us.

He showed me many hidden beauties of our homeland. At the most far northwestern point of Cape Wrath, we walked a windswept strand to a small graveyard on the dunes. There, near where the Vikings had first navigated the Western Isles, we found a tomb. The great stone sarcophagus lay half-submerged in the sand. Runes had been carved, perhaps for a Nordic chief buried there a thousand years ago.

We journeyed down the coast again and landed on the Isle of Skye. Soon we were gazing down on a beautiful little bay, the sun setting and the evening still. Shimmering silver shone on the placid sea, the three isles just visible in the distance. The peace and tranquillity of the scene moved me.

From far down the sea valley, the sound of pipes came drifting up to us. The local piper played a slow and noble air as he walked the strand, piping down the sun. I heard a call to my deepest feelings.

We would stay in the village that night, talking with the old lady who ran the Stein Inn. The next morning we would meet the owner of the islands, the Laird MacDonald.

The little old lady was from Glasgow, in fact, and she and my father chatted about the old days. Then a young crofter was coaxed into singing a haunting tune in Gaelic. My father was visibly moved. I, too, could barely restrain the tears.

Next morning, the sun was shining, and after a hearty breakfast of kippers and eggs and strong black tea, we heard the sound of an ancient Land Rover pull up outside the inn. The hereditary heir, MacDonald of the Isles, had arrived to meet us.

There are two branches of this clan in the Western Isles, the old man we met being the chief of the poorer of the two. With clear, sparkling eyes, he was very much a farmer in his tweeds and wore nothing to indicate his noble origins. But he evidently commanded great respect and carried himself with an air of importance, introducing us to a local man who, he explained, would take us to the islands. Alec the Fisherman was his name.

The Lord of the Isles departed, and soon my father and I were moving over the morning sea in a tiny boat, the outboard motor churning the waves. Alec sat at the helm, steering us toward the three islands. Above us the clear blue vault of the sky arched, while to the west no clouds were to be seen. I trailed my fingers in the black waters and felt the wind pull my long hair back over my forehead. I felt peaceful and centered. Seals surfaced around us as we passed a dark rock, halfway to our destination. My father sat gazing with a far-off look in his eyes. We were happy just to be there. We were in our element.

The sound of the outboard geared down as Alec reached the landing. No pier on this isle, just a low tidal approach to the dry land. Carefully, Alec eased the boat into the shallows on the pebble strand. We had landed on the Isle of Harris.

Long ago there had been tenant farmers living here and ruins of many cottages could still be seen, the long sea grass growing in and out of the stone. Alec led us up over the small beach to view a field of blue iris, waving in the northern breeze. The largest ruin had once been the summer home of the MacDonalds, and—although it was small compared to many castles—we could see that it had been quite a substantial building in its day.

Only the gulls inhabited this island now, and they circled and dived upon us, screeching and cawing. They did not welcome our arrival. This was *their* isle. Their eggs and hatchlings were in danger.

Somewhere back in the real world my fame continued to sell records. Agents called my number, but I was not there. Reporters called my manager, but I was away, ostensibly on holiday, though it was much more than a holiday. The illusion of Maya had loosened its hold on my consciousness since I had learned how to meditate, how to detach myself from the perception of the show called life. In between the absolute and the relative, I was floating away. I was *literally* disillusioned.

My father and I sat on thick tussocks of sea grass in the ruins of the old castle as Alec the Fisherman plunged his arm into the clear, clean waters that caressed the Isle of Harris, gathering the carrageen seaweed, which is so valued in the Western Isles for sweet making and medicine.

I walked the length of the long island to the cliffs. Then we took a turn around the two smaller islets, Mingay and Clett. Clett was a rock sanctuary for hundreds of seabirds that nested there. It was completely covered with eggs and young fledglings.

Once again on the main island of Skye, my father arranged to buy the three islands, and we journeyed back down the coast again to Fort William, Glasgow, and London.

Although there is a five-year difference in our ages, my brother, Gerald, and I found some common ground in the music business at this time. Gerald worked on the Beatles's Apple Studio and also completed Rampart Studios, The Who's recording complex. He went on to help create The Who's successful Laser Company. He still does some laser shows, notably the recent London

Millennium Celebrations of 2000. My brother finally married his love, Vanessa, and they have two dear little girls, my nieces Katie and Rebecca.

I was booked to play at the Woburn Music Festival on 6–7 July, courtesy of His Grace, the Duke of Bedford. Other artists on the bill were Pentangle, The Jimi Hendrix Experience, Fleetwood Mac, and John Mayall. I played on the Sunday afternoon. Later, Bert Jansch and Danny Thompson of Pentangle and I hung out, jamming into the night.

My continuing interest in jazz took me to Majorca to join such greats as The Bill Evans Trio, Georgie Fame, Johnny Dankworth, and Cleo Laine. This festival was called "Musica '68" and also included The Byrds, The Jimi Hendrix Experience, and The Animals. Solo artists Sandie Shaw and Scott Walker were also there. My festival calendar then took me to Peterborough, Paris, Geneva, and Montreux.

That same July saw Gypsy and I attend the wedding of my friend Alexis Mardas to his Greek sweetheart, Eufrosyne Doxiades. I was joint best man with John Lennon as we placed a double tiara of forest flowers on Eufrosyne during the ceremony in the Greek Orthodox Church in Bayswater. The forty guests included Yoko Ono, George Harrison, and his wife, Patti. It was the first time any of us had met Yoko Ono.

According to the press clippings in the archive my father kept, it seems I was sociable that summer and joined The Beatles, The Rolling Stones, Marianne Faithfull, Cilla Black, and Georgie Fame to see the great American singer/songwriter Tim Hardin at the Royal Albert Hall. I knew Tim from earlier days and had recorded his "Green Rocky Road" the first day I was in a studio in 1964.

The premiere of the film *Yellow Submarine* at the London Pavilion Theatre brought me out again to join The Beatles, Yoko, Grapefruit, Keith Richards, Julie Driscoll, The Animals, and The Move. My little contribution to the lyrics of the title song of this first animated rock film gave me much pleasure.

More changes had come to the Beatles's camp as Jane Asher, Paul McCartney's girlfriend of five years, announced that they were splitting up. The rigors of the fame-game had put too much strain on another relationship.

John Lennon told the press that he really did love Yoko Ono, and the criticism of pop's most celebrated couple began in earnest.

The live tapes of my U.S. tour in 1967 were now released that July of 1968 in America. The album, *Donovan in Concert,* reached No. 18 in the *Billboard* chart.

A second big tour of North America was set for September, and the prospect of playing live again helped cheer me out of a growing depression. I would present my new song bag. I would throw myself into performing live, the work I do best. Here again was the grueling round of one-night stands and endless press and media interviews set for me by the record company and my managers. I love it.

The success of my live TV performances had not escaped the notice of Stanley Dorfman, a BBC television producer. Stanley had called me, and we made a show: *An Evening with Donovan.* So began the series of TV shows that cemented my relationship with a wider audience.

I had always felt at ease in the TV studio. Floor crews saw I was willing to join the team, and they always gave me the best sound and lights possible. This beginning with Dorfman on British television also caught the attention of the two popular American TV shows, *The Andy Williams Show* and *The Smothers Brothers Show.* I had no qualms about performing on so-called "variety" TV shows. In those days there were no twenty-four-hour music shows like MTV and VH1, and I wanted the musical and spiritual ideas I was presenting to be heard and seen by the largest audience possible.

It was *The Smothers Brothers Show* in the States that was the most radical, booking folksingers and political comics. Tom and Dick had the best sound recordings of any TV show, a four-track tape recorder and FX to rival a recording studio.

Over in London, Stan Dorfman also made a series of shows with the talented American singer/songwriter Bobbie Gentry, and I was a guest on her show. I also joined Dusty Springfield on her TV show, which was a high spot for me as I had been a fan since the beginning of her career. I also guested on the *"This Is Tom Jones"* TV series. These appearances led to a meeting with Sir Lew Grade, the king of UK TV at that time. Lew offered me my own TV series, but the thought of repeating myself every week in the same location did not excite me.

✥

I heard that Brian Jones was sliding alarmingly fast into depression and paranoia, and that Linda had flown into London to see him. News of this fueled
my own paranoia. Did Brian need Linda to be with him now? The irony was
that, although circumstances had made Brian my enemy, I sympathized with
him. I knew what he was going through. Brian had recoiled as the pressure of
his dream slammed against the reality it had generated. I was recoiling too,
yet refused the potion of forgetfulness that is always available to the hero of
his own myth.

The other irony was that, unknown to me and against all my expectations, Linda's friends were now advising Linda to marry me. The trouble was,
I was losing my own grip on reality: I couldn't see that the flow of events that
had kept Linda and me apart was now pushing us together. She was coming
toward me. It was as if I was being tested—and it was a test I was about
to fail.

Atlantis

September came around, and I flew to the States to begin a second big tour of North America. *The Hurdy Gurdy Man* album was still in the charts when I arrived in Los Angeles and checked into the Beverly Hills Hotel. During the tour it would reach No. 5—another smash hit.

A giant billboard had been booked to advertise that I was coming to play again at the Hollywood Bowl. Along Sunset Strip, endless lines of cars paraded beneath the scores of billboards that announced the new movies, albums, and, of course, the hottest musical shows in Las Vegas and Reno. These huge display advertisements towered over the street, the images on them painted by experts who could copy a photograph perfectly—superrealism. One billboard displayed a photo of me from the back of the sleeve of the new album.

My album-cover designer Sydney Maurer suggested I paint my own billboard for a change. This was a casual joke, but I thought why not? I would paint something on the side panels. I decided that I'd paint Mardi Gras figures with animal and bird heads. Sydney and I got into harness and stood on the work plank high above Sunset Strip, ready to go to work. Gypsy stood guard at the ladder in case any fan should put me in danger. The PR company let the press know, and soon a few hundred fans were blocking traffic. Police were hired to direct the flow, and the event went off without incident.

Almost.

One young fan climbed up the back of the billboard. Balancing with arms outstretched like a tightrope walker he slowly moved along the top toward me. Someone said he was stoned on LSD. I asked him if he was OK. He smiled, smoothly crossed the frame of the billboard, and came safely down with Gyp's help.

The billboard was above a tattoo parlor and across from the Hyatt House Hotel, called "The Riot House" by the many bands who trashed it. From the balcony of one of the rooms, the press had watched the billboard stunt. Unbeknownst to me, standing beside my manager, Ashley Kozak, was Linda. Ashley had invited her. I discovered this after we'd been lowered to the ground, and I went to the Hyatt. I felt betrayed and at first refused to talk to her. But then we said an awkward hello, and Linda invited me for a meal. She said she was staying in a large house in the hills, still housekeeping for Jonathan Debenham. Julian was living with her now. I accepted her invitation with some reservations. I didn't know what I felt.

That evening, I was dropped off in the limo at a large Spanish rococo mansion in the hills. It was to be a private dinner that she would cook. When Linda opened the door she was dressed in a beautiful self-made costume of Indian silk. Her Indian friend, Richpal, had shown her the secrets of the herbs and spices, the rice and vegetables, and she had prepared an elaborate curry. She floated ahead of me into the long drawing room and poured a cool drink.

Outside the picture window, the lights of Los Angeles twinkled after a rare shower of rain. Linda's hazel eyes looked searchingly into my own. Her long auburn hair shone in the candlelight. She looked as she had when first we'd met three years ago in 1965—young, fresh, flawless skin, and delicate long fingers, curved like those of a Burmese dancer. And I saw that she still wore the bloodstone ring I had given her. We sat at a small wooden table laid with an Indian print cloth, neatly folded napkins, and polished brass cutlery. I tasted the delicious vegetarian curry, small cups of raita to cool the heat. As she looked at me across the table, my heart began to pound with the old hurt. I recognized that look. She was hoping I would "feel" her thoughts.

I probably jabbered on about the tour, my music, and the craziness of it all. I was scared to be so close again, scared above all of being rejected again, just as she herself had once been scared of being rejected. Wasn't she there with me, for me? Wasn't she serving me Indian vegetarian food, showing me that she was searching for, like me, a solution? Linda was on the path that I walked.

After the fresh fruit salad and herb tea, I could see in her eyes that she wanted me to kiss her. But I was so fucked up, it all seemed like it might be some cruel trick. She means nothing to me, I thought.

At midnight the limo came to pick me up. I was leaving early the next morning to start the tour. As I paused on Linda's doorstep, she looked into my eyes as she had been doing silently all evening. I gave her an awkward kiss, brushing her cheek, and—young fool that I was—walked away.

The tour opened in San Francisco, this time in the Civic Auditorium. This was a good venue with an open stage, the sound fair, and the getaway safe.

The fans were so keen on getting to us, Don Murphet, my security adviser, and Gyp had to plan an escape route that would not harm the fans or myself. Before I sang the last song, the DJ or the promoter would sometimes tell the fans this, against Don Murphet's orders—very uncool. All of Murphet's carefully laid plans would then be blown out. I would go back on stage while he and Gyp quickly devised another escape route.

The excitement was so high that the promoters were often not able to figure out what was going on. Only Don Murphet knew how to organize the police and the backstage crew so that we could make it to the getaway car in time. Girls in fast cars would follow us to the hotel, trying to gain access. If Gyp let them, they would succeed. . . . Many did.

Murphet went on to create a company called Artists Services. This young man trained many of the "minders" who now protect the top stars from the dangers of too much fame. He went on to work for The Beatles, The Monkeys, and many others. I call him The Escapologist, and he was better than Houdini.

One incident where he displayed his split-second timing was at the Anaheim Convention Center. Murphet's instructions to the police were simple. Ten officers were to guard the doors to the foyer, as this was the only way he could lead me off the stage to the car. The police took up their positions.

The foyer doors were closed. After the last song, I ran down the steps behind the stage, Murphet grabbed me, and we started to cross the large lobby to where the limo was waiting. The fans rushed to the doors and surged through. Each cop was instantly trapped as they had taken up their positions against the walls between each of the ten doors. Halfway across the foyer, Murphet turned to see the first hundred fans trap the cops and flow like a tidal wave toward us.

He told me to run for the car, then he tackled a large young man and tossed him into the first wave of fans. This gave him and Gyp time enough to slow down the onrush, and we made our escape. We did not wish to treat the fans this way, and the slight toughness that Murphet had had to deal out that night was not his usual way of doing things.

The second night of the tour, I played the Hollywood Bowl in Los Angeles. I sat well back from the audience. They were in the distance across a small lake, twenty thousand strong. They were noisy. It was LA, and they felt entitled to be spoiled.

Police were situated around the small lake to prevent fans from swimming across to the stage. One eager girl stood to walk around the water, and a cop grappled with her. They both fell into the water, to the great enjoyment of the huge crowd. The young cop fished himself out to cheers. He took out his pistol and shook it good-naturedly, shrugged his shoulders, and threw it back into the water. The audience applauded him. As I mentioned earlier, LA cops on concert and movie duty in LA are usually easygoing. They're part of the entertainment.

The next night was Sacramento, a "pukka" stage with a curtain and very helpful sound boys. The hall got very smoky when I turned the airconditioning off. Pot, probably. This gig was very good, and the getaway was easy.

We then flew into Arizona and played at the Sports Arena in Phoenix. The large speakers were inadequate, but the promoters were on the ball.

In Salt Lake City, the lights were hopeless in the Terrace Ballroom, the sound no better. This Mormon town had enormous amounts of young girl fans. The musical lineup for the tour was the same as for the previous year, 1967. I would play a good part of the concert solo, then bring on the band for such songs as "Hampstead Incident," "Young Girl Blues," "Rules and Regulations," "The Fat Angel," "Mad John's Escape," and the hits.

We took the tour north to Portland, then Seattle and into Canada to play

Vancouver. We dived down into the States again to do Spokane, then swung east for Chicago and Minneapolis, after which we headed south for the show in Baton Rouge. The schedule was manic.

It was a pleasure to enter the United States again. We played Carnegie Hall in New York City. The concert hall is my best kind of venue, and here the audience was comfortable and the acoustics were perfect for my sound. Three good halls followed in Hartford, Philadelphia, and Princeton, before we returned to Los Angeles.

The tour finally ended in San Diego on 4 November. I sat in the hotel overlooking Shelter Island. It was over and no broken bones. I had released another single during the tour, "Lalena" from *The Hurdy Gurdy Man* sessions. This track was an acoustic ballad featuring a string quartet arranged by John Cameron, produced by Mickie Most. Harold McNair played fine flute; Danny Thompson, once again, played concert bass. The lady in the song was inspired by the German actress Lotte Lenya and the character she played in the musical *The Threepenny Opera,* written by Bertolt Brecht and with music by Lotte's husband, Kurt Weill.

As I toured I endeavored to improve sound and lights production as well as protect the fans from their own excitement, pointing the way to today's standards.

I had some time off in California after the tour and went into the studio to record some new tracks for another album. This was the second time I'd decided to go it alone without my producer, Mickie Most. I booked myself into the American Recording Company in the San Fernando Valley. Mickie stood by to see what I would come up with. It was not that I did not get on with Mickie, I had just moved into another scene. Mickie knew that he and I would work together again.

An LA-based producer named Gabriel Meckler had become a friend, and we started up the session together. I was bursting with new ideas and was in a real party mood, keen to experiment with poetry and rock sounds. Gabriel and I brought together a few LA musos to play my latest songs.

I was reading a book about Atlantis, *A Dweller on Two Planets,* written by a Victorian gentleman called Frederick S. Oliver, who claimed to have transcribed it under the direction of a spiritual being called Phylos the Thibetan. The book related that the Atlanteans were a civilization that predated Egypt and India, a people who had lived ten thousand years ago on a group

of islands once situated between the New and Old Worlds. In a great cata-
clysm their lands had sunk beneath the sea, perhaps due to a comet striking
the earth and a great Tsunami.

I found myself writing a song, a poem spoken to a set of chords. I had
also read in the ancient Irish legends of the Tuatha de Danann, the mystical
race who'd arrived in Ireland floating on a mist from the Western Ocean, the
People of the Sea.

The Ancient Indian Vedas also spoke of a bygone advanced civilization
and its power over nature.

I was moved by all these accounts to try and write of these people who'd
lived before the Great Flood.

> The continent of Atlantis
> was an island which lay,
> before the great flood,
> in the area we now call the Atlantic Ocean.
> So great an area of land
> that from her western shores
> those beautiful sailors
> journeyed to the South
> and North Americas
> in their ships with painted sail:
> To the East Africa was her neighbour,
> across a short strait of sea miles.
> The great Egyptian age
> is but a remnant of the Atlantean culture.
> The Antediluvian Kings colonised the world.
> All the gods who play
> in the mythological dramas,
> in all legends from all lands,
> were from fair Atlantis,
> Knowing her fate,
> Atlantis sent out ships
> to all corners of the earth,
> on board were the twelve.
> The poet, the physician,

the farmer, the scientist,
the magician,
and the other so-called gods of our legends.
Tho' gods they were.
And, as the elders of our time
choose to remain blind, let us rejoice and let us sing
and ring in the New Age.
Hail Atlantis!
Way down below the ocean
where I want to be
She may be.

—Donovan Leitch,
"*Atlantis*"

I read this piece over chords I had learned from Derroll Adams. Gabriel Meckler and I laid down a long track of music, with him playing piano. The small band would then kick in with the heavy chorus for the coda of the song.

We recorded the track for the agreed amount of bars, and the chorus exploded. The next part was tricky. We did not want to splice on the band, so I had to read the piece and arrive at the words "Hail Atlantis" just before the drum introduction. I took two passes at it and—Bingo!—I got it.

The slow and noble "air" under the reading needed "effects." These were early days, before synthesizers arrived. I wanted a steel sound like the antique Irish harps, so I strummed the grand piano strings with a quill, while Gabriel made the chord shapes on the piano with the pedal open. It sounded fabulous.

The heavy rock chorus had a "break," and I wanted a powerful guitar solo to build into the last choruses. We had no guitarist booked that day. I explained the kind of riff to Rick, our engineer. "A kind of Brian Jones–Stones thing," I said. He went into a back room and brought out his Fender Stratocaster, plugged it straight into the board, swung his legs up on the desk, and punched "record." He cut into the riff I gave him, and, man, did he blow it good. The years have fogged my memory of his last name, but thanks, Rick, for that day.

All that remained to be done was to lay on some more choruses and mix it. This unusual record was a dream of mine to combine a poetry reading with a rock track. It would reach No. 7 in the U.S. charts when it was released in the spring of 1969. (I had produced "Atlantis" with Gabriel Meckler, although Mickie Most's name is credited. I just could not get it released without Mickie's name, as had happened when I produced *Gift from a Flower to a Garden.*)

I was having fun and laid down a few more tracks that week in November 1968 in LA. The party mood continued as I recorded a song called simply "The Love Song." This would be an easy rock number with a party atmosphere in the bridge and coda. Friends would sing and clink glasses, that sort of thing.

During the tour, I had—as I have mentioned—been on *The Smothers Brothers Show,* a duo who had come from the folk scene and become hot property. I became close to Tom, and we hung out, as they say. One of Tom's comedy writers was Murray Roman, and he and I were inseparable for a few weeks. Murray kept me in stitches with his funny stories. He came down to the sessions in the valley, and I got him to do a funny DJ rap during the party section of "The Love Song"; I gagged him with my hand at the point the vocals returned. I had to—he couldn't stop the rap.

I began work on a third song, titled "To Susan on the West Coast Waiting." This was about soldiers in Vietnam. I thought of the "boys" (they were, too) out there in the jungle, facing death. The tender guitar picking I played was complemented by the soft drums and the warm bass. Gabriel played a gentle mouth organ part. The whole effect was one of combined melancholy and hope.

Outside the studio on the street, three young girls had been waiting for a few days, wanting to meet me. I invited them in and taught them the chorus for the song. They were delightful backup singers, and you can hear that it turned out well. "To Susan on the West Coast Waiting" would be released as a single in February 1969 in the United States and became a minor hit.

Each day in the studio turned into a party. "I Love My Shirt" was for all who cherish a worn-in, faded shirt or pair of jeans. It worked perfectly for the Smothers Brothers and me when we performed it on their show, Tom and I on guitars with Dick on stand-up bass. Tom's deadpan delivery brought out the humor in the lyric perfectly. Thanks, guys.

The last track I recorded with Gabriel and the boys was "Pamela Jo." As you can imagine, a young singer meets many women, some warm and tender, others tough and crazy. Pamela Jo and I met once, on a long day off during that hectic tour. A southern girl, she seemed like a friend from the past—perhaps previous lives. Lying in the shaded hotel suite in the afterglow, she talked softly about her life, and I forgot the massive pressure I was under. In the song I sing: "She looks just a little like a circus child . . ." Pamela Jo did indeed share some resemblance to Fellini's wife, Giulietta Masina, who played the circus character "Gelsomina" in the first Fellini film, *La Strada*. Pamela Jo, a lovely companion, that long ago afternoon.

I had made five tracks for an album that would not be completed and released until 1969. The album would be titled *Barabajagal*. The liner notes show that I thanked Gabriel Meckler but I failed to list the session players. Thanks to Jim Gordon on drums, Bobbie Ray on bass (I think), Murray Roman on "rap," many friends on "rave-up vibes," the three girl fans who sang backup, Rick "the Phantom Engineer," Gabriel Meckler, and, of course, Phylos the Thibetan, that shadowy figure who inspired "Atlantis."

I returned to England after the tour, but a week of engagements in Germany and Austria was waiting. The live concert album had prepared the audiences, and the single "Atlantis" was particularly successful in Germany, Austria, and Switzerland.

When I returned to the cottage in England, Enid called me from America, crying down the phone again, wanting to come back to me. I still felt bad about the whole thing, but felt I had to say no. Anyway, I was off on tour again straightaway. When my son was older, I hoped he would understand.

> There's surely been a mistake here
> Misinterpretation I fear
> There must have been a mistake here
>
> I thought I was where I was not
> I was cold and I thought I was hot
> Thought I'd nothing when I had a lot
>
> You can call headquarters
> On the telephone
> They will substantiate
> That I wasn't home

There must have been a mistake here
No coordination I fear
There must have been a mistake here

It's really quite disturbing me
When the dream is really dreaming me
It's a case of mistaken eternity

—Donovan Leitch,
"Mistaken Eternity"

My father, Donald, and I flew into Hamburg in the north of Germany. Radio Bremen was playing the single "Atlantis" as we pulled up in the Mercedes to the Hotel Atlantic. We had come in a day early to do media and advertise the small tour. The schedule was perfectly organized, in the German way. My day started at nine. Into the shower, coffee, and cold cheese; then off in the wagon by 10:15. I returned to the hotel at 9:15 that evening, after doing Radio Bremen, *The Beat Club* TV show, and two other studio visits, then called ZDF and NDR, not forgetting a *Stern* magazine photo shoot.

So began my long relationship with Germany, a relationship that continues to this day. The following morning's start was not so early, and we boarded the train for Düsseldorf to do the first concert. European trains are my favorite way to travel. I read a book after lunch on the train and took in the immaculate scenery. My constant reading at this time was a translation of *The Odyssey*. The myth of the hero seeking to return home after the sack of Troy was becoming more and more the tale of my own life. I was adrift on a strange ocean that was bejeweled with magical islands and haunted by beautiful sirens. But there was no Penelope waiting for me.

A show took place in the Kongress-Saal in Munich. This black-and-gold rectangular hall had a sinister atmosphere. The second-floor balcony ran the full length and breadth of the venue, with a frieze of mythological figures. Adolf Hitler had performed many a show here. I meditated before the concert, expecting a bad vibe, but the kids surged in, filling the somber hall with light and positive energy. The sins of the fathers did not visit us that night.

Down to Vienna, Austria. The Konzerthaus was a beautiful hall with perfect sound and terrible lights. Here in the old city of Vienna, I was not the first to experience fan-mania. Beethoven had stood on this stage. Vienna had long been known as the best city to try out new works. The audience were open to anything as I introduced myself with a display of finger-style guitar.

The next day we flew into the old German capital of Berlin. I recall going to a Russian restaurant after the gig. We entered through an old door set down below the street. A tiny hostess met us and led us through bead curtains. Once seated, we were "ordered" to order blinis to begin with. Caviar followed, along with frozen flagons of vodka immersed in blocks of ice. The clear vodka had herbs floating in it. Balalaika music played as costumed girls served. My moratorium on alcohol was broken when I heard the emotional cry of the Russian music.

A hostess with pale skin and jet black eyes flopped down beside me. "My name is not Natasha," she said with a German accent.

"Don't tell me—it's Verushka."

"How did you guess?" She spread ten tiny silver-ringed fingers on the table. "I do not like gold." Scent of patchouli. "Where are you staying?" she asked.

"With you, perhaps."

"I have a boyfriend." Astrid—or whatever her name was—lifted her shot of frozen vodka and clinked it against my own. "Here's to life."

Out of the corner of my eye I noticed Dad in a recess, deep in conversation with the Lufthansa stewardess of yesterday. It was tomorrow already as we staggered up into the gray Berlin dawn.

There are three cities that I found difficult to leave: New York, Rome, and Berlin.

The Death of Brian Jones

Following the tour, that winter of 1968 I began the Scottish commune I had been planning. This uncertain venture was in part an attempt to return to my roots, partly an escape from the crazy world of constant touring. I loved my work, and yet I was disgusted by many aspects of the music business. I was looking for something else. I bought a few old Gypsy caravans for myself and the four other couples who had joined me. Painter Dave and his girl-friend, Ro; Julian and Victoria; and my schoolfriends Sam and Lynn. Gypsy and Yvonne would come up later. In a symbolic gesture I gave my Daimler to my schoolfriend, Mick Sharman, and bought a Land Rover.

To walk away at the height of my fame seems a little rash now, as well as mixed-up. I made entries in a large leather-bound diary. They chronicle 1969, which began optimistically, but soon fell into more despondency. Eventually my agent and manager came to find me, and I returned to the fray. I had wanted to reunite my early bohemian friends—but artificially, it seemed.

Some of the lads and lassies worked very hard in the wild weather. Dave had led the way in creating a huge garden. Painting and composing and raising children in the far Western Isles of Scotland, my friends and I had probably experienced the last wilderness of Europe before the coming tide of development. All my friends were richer for this experience.

I had also invited Enid to Skye. One night, as the Pleiades arched over the Northern Hemisphere, Enid and I made love for the last time in my old gypsy wagon. Heaven blessed our love, and our second child, Ione, entered the earthly plane.

Of course, I did not know this at the time. I knew I was paying the bills. My father watched aghast, so in the end I gave Sam and Lynn the post office and sold the Isles to a Dutchman. Julian and Victoria had given birth to little Jasmine. The others went their own way. Many changes came in that beautiful wild island, not all of them happy.

John Lennon watched me buy the islands and bought his own. He bought a Victorian fantasy island celebrated in a classical piece of music, "Fingal's Cave," composed by Felix Mendelssohn. This rock was not habitable. John had bought it purely as a romantic dream.

Truth be told, I had bought my islands for the same reason.

> Dreams on the tumble of feathers made
> Rise up high and fall like lead
>
> Ladies to curtsy, Gentlemen bow
> Take your partners for the changes now
> —Donovan Leitch,
> *"Skye"*

At twenty years of age, I had had enough recognition and fame for any young man. So why was I so dissatisfied, so restless? It certainly wasn't money; there was plenty of that flying around. And I loved writing songs every day. I only had to pick up the guitar, and there they were. Perhaps that was part of the problem? I wrote too many to be able to record them all, and still do.

And I asked myself: Who am *I* in all this creativity?

Despite my No. 1 records all over the world, the millions of records sold, and the innovations I had made that were proving decisive in the English counterculture revolution of the 1960s—the introduction of poetic lyrics, Celtic images, and psychedelic images, and the introduction of jazz fusion and folk-metal fusion, I had no measure of my own worth. Most of my contemporaries concentrated on one style. My successes suggested I, too, should continue in one style, but I found it impossible to copy myself. My producer, Mickie Most, looked on as I went through my changes. He was amused by my angst.

But the deal I was being offered was simple: you love my music and I lose my freedom. There was a loss in all this gain. When Brian Jones and I had sailed out from our youth and hopeful dreams, we never could have imagined that the audience would want to love us to death.

"To Susan on the West Coast Waiting" was climbing the U.S. charts in spring 1969 as I returned to London. Mickie and I went into the studio to record more songs and complete the new album that I had begun in Los Angeles at the end of 1968. Mickie had thought of an exciting lineup for my new song "Barabajagal." At the time he was recording the Jeff Beck Group, and suggested to Jeff and me that we could work together. I thought this was a great idea, and the session was booked.

When I arrived in the studio, I heard Mickie Waller (Jeff's drummer) setting up his kit and doing a few paradiddles. He was steaming away at what I thought was my song "Barabajagal." I said "Hi" and told him that the part he was playing was just perfect for the track, thinking he had heard the song. In fact, he said he hadn't heard a bloody thing. Synchronicity at work.

Mickie Most had not let the musos know what they were doing until we all got together. So Beck, Ron Wood (bass), and Nicky Hopkins (piano) all came in with no idea at all of what was to happen. Mickie had arranged hors d'oeuvres and nice wine. I ran through the song, and Nicky sat at the piano reading a comic book—*Silver Surfer*, I recall. Jeff looked a bit vacant after a trip up north. The chords were easy to learn, all two of them.

Mickie asked Jeff to break out his guitar. Jeff was gazing around the studio, then he walked into the hall, then the control room. No guitar. He had left it up north, or the roadie had locked it away. He asked us to get him any good Fender—and we did. He was not put out at all and tore into the riff that would open the track. There was no bother in cutting this most different record of my career to date. Jeff Beck played amazing funky guitar, and I count this session as a major one in my career.

The jazz-rock sound worked well with the Jeff Beck Group and the background vocals by Madeleine Bell and Lesley Duncan moved the tune along fabulously.

This was to be a single. We ran through another song for the B-side. I had written another lyric for the melody, "Lay of the Last Tinker" from the *Gift from a Flower to a Garden* double album. This time I called it "Trudi" and added a different chorus. The jaunty "Bo Diddley" feel worked well with Jeff's band.

I was pleased with the results of this latest fusion. The musical world would be surprised, and at first some wouldn't believe it was actually me. Mickie and I had three tracks already recorded from sessions in May 1968 the previous year, and they would make up the balance of the new album. One was the song I had written in India called "Happiness Runs."

My friends Graham Nash (The Hollies), Mike McCartney (The Scaffold), and Lesley Duncan came down to help me out. The lyric spoke of the experience of meditation, prefaced by an introduction that described an encounter between a naturalist and a pebble on a beach. "Happiness Runs" would become a favorite with audiences as I asked them to take the various singing parts that Graham, Mike, and Lesley sang on this record. The dulcet tones of Graham, the childlike sound of Lesley, and the funny *bass-vox humana* of Mike made this song one of my favorite recordings. The track was just we four and my acoustic guitar.

Another track that Mickie and I soon had in the can was a powerful version of "Super Lungs." We had originally recorded this for the *Sunshine Superman* album of spring 1966 but dropped it due, no doubt, to its too-obvious marijuana reference. Now Mickie reminded me of it, and we rerecorded it. Owing to the lack of track listings, the names of the musicians who played are missing. It sounds like John Paul Jones on bass and Hammond organ, Jimmy Page and/or Big Jim Sullivan on electric guitar, and possibly John Bonham on drums. The third track we had from 1968 was a love song called "Where Is She?" Harold McNair played flute, Tony Carr was on drums, and Danny Thompson on double bass. A new member of the team was Alan Hawkshaw on piano. Alan played haunting piano chords to my heartfelt caresses on acoustic guitar.

> Springtime—for me has gone
> Where is she?
> Waking—in the blue dawn
> Where is she?

Someday—I'll say to her
I am he
Smiling—her words will be
I am she

I know she'll wait for me
I know she'll wait for *me,*
to come to her

—Donovan Leitch,
"Where Is She?"

With the tracks that Gabriel Meckler and I had produced in Los Angeles and the others recorded with Mickie Most, the *Barabajagal* album was complete. I designed the album cover for *Barabajagal* with Sydney Maurer. We used Victorian prints from my growing collection of books. The images were of children. Another photograph of me shot in infrared film was on the back. The album was not available in Britain, and I can only think the reason was the *Greatest Hits* collection that perhaps took precedence that year. It came out in February and contained all the "hits" from the first four years since 1965. I rerecorded "Catch the Wind" and "Colours" for the crazy reason that Pye Records would or could not allow the Epic label to have the original tracks. Although I enjoyed rerecording these songs with John Paul Jones and Big Jim Sullivan, I preferred the originals.

So as far as my British fans are concerned, three whole albums were still missing from my career at this time. Quite a slice of music and hard work featuring fine players and showing other sides to my songwriting. *Greatest Hits* would reach the No. 4 position in the U.S. charts that year.

That June, as my "Barabajagal" single arrived in the States, Brian Jones announced that he was leaving The Rolling Stones, the group he had founded. His replacement would be Mick Taylor, a guitar player from John Mayall's Bluesbreakers. Brian began to form his own band. He wanted to go back to his roots for inspiration, and invited drummers Tony Newman (Jeff Beck and my own records), Mitch Mitchell (Jimi Hendrix Experience). John Mayall, and even John Lennon and Eric Clapton were rumored to be interested in Brian's new band.

Three weeks later and two days before The Stones's first gig with the new member in Hyde Park, London, Brian was found drowned in his swimming pool. It was said at the time that he had died from an overdose of drugs and alcohol, and he was also known to be asthmatic. Much has been said about the circumstances of Brian Jones's death, and I advise my readers to consult the biography by Mandy Aftel, *Death of a Rolling Stone,* which sheds much light on the life and death of this complicated and misunderstood young man.

But in 1969 I was still secretly reeling from my rivalry with Brian Jones. I still felt he had done me down, and I felt rejected by Linda. Callously, my main feeling at the time was that the two of them had ruined my life. What a self-centered and insensitive fellow I was!

When Michael Aldrid, who had introduced me to Linda in 1965, rang her in Los Angeles to tell her the news about Brian, she took to her bed for three days. At first she said that she would not go to the funeral, but really she knew she had to. She had been the love of his life. She had no money, but friends bought her a ticket for the flight. She dressed in black and, with her golden-haired boy by her side, arrived in England. Friends had also bought her a necklace on which hung the Egyptian symbol of eternal life, the Ankh.

At the graveside were hundreds of girl fans mourning their loss. Linda laid a small offering of forget-me-nots on Brian's grave, with a poem her mother, Violet, had found—a Japanese haiku.

> Now my loneliness
> following the fireworks
> Look! a falling star . . .

As Linda stood there crying, with her little son, the Rolling Stones's girl-friends glared at her as if she had no right to be there. If anyone had the right, Linda did.

Of the people standing around the graveside, some would be tested by the death of Brian in a way that was yet to resolve itself. One week after he died, Marianne Faithfull lay in a drug-induced coma in an Australian hospital. With the death of Brian Jones, a dark shadow was cast over the decade of Flower Power.

Linda returned to America after Brian's funeral.

Karon

My third tour of North America was set again to begin in September to coincide with the release of the *Barabajagal* album. My success was reaching ever greater proportions. Some who met me commented that I was so natural, not fazed by it all; but deep inside, I was more than fazed. An emotional time bomb was ticking away inside me that year. Gypsy could plainly see it and was seriously worried for me. I flew into California to a large house in Beverly Hills that had been rented for me, so that I could be isolated from the fans. A Cadillac convertible and a Ford Mustang were parked outside this typical Tinseltown ranch, which boasted a swimming pool, a huge bar, and cavernous bathrooms. The place was stuffed with fake antique furniture, and there were even three film Oscars in the broom closet.

The tour would cover all the major cities I had played before and more. The media blitz began with a big PR bash at a nightspot called The Factory in Hollywood. My hostess and host were "Mama" Cass Elliott and Kirk Douglas. The guest list included Mr. and Mrs. Herb Alpert, Burt Bacharach, Jack Benny and Milton Berle and their wives, Sonny and Cher, Pat Boone and his wife, The Byrds, Dianne Carroll, and Leonard Cohen. Other movie and TV guests were Bill Cosby and Robert Culp, Jimmy Durante and Eddie Fisher,

Gene Kelly, Jack Lemmon, Jerry Lewis, Steve McQueen, and Melina Mercouri (who sat chatting with me about Greece). Musicians and singers invited included The Doors, José Feliciano, Noel Harrison and Jack Jones, Taj Mahal, John and Michele Phillips, Paul Revere and the Raiders, André Previn, Nancy Sinatra, Steppenwolf, Nancy Wilson, and Andy Williams. My friends, Tom and Dick Smothers, were also invited.

I was also pleased to see Jimi Hendrix, dressed in a white Nehru jacket. We sat and chatted about our earlier meeting and the song I had wanted to give him, "The Hurdy Gurdy Man." He vowed we'd try a tune together one day.

In a rare quiet moment at the party, Kirk Douglas asked me how I was handling it all. I lied, then Kirk asked me to sing. He said that my music was gentle and that I was a "gentle man."

There was one name I did not want on the guest list, the name of a young beauty who still caused me tight feelings in my chest whenever I got near to her. But she was there that night, with her friend Cathy, standing outside the club as the press party raved on. She could not get inside. She stood with scores of others denied entry to the hottest media bash in Hollywood that week. She had washed her hair and dressed in one of the Victorian costumes I had bought for her in London and was still wearing the bloodstone ring I had given her a lifetime ago. But I would not see her. My manager, Ashley, tried to persuade me, but I stubbornly refused.

I had told Enid she could come and see me with my three-year-old son. The next day I sat on a twenty-foot sofa overlooking the pool through a wall of glass. Don Murphet, Gypsy Dave, and my driver, Nikky Simpson, frolicked in the blue water, their temperature-zone skins still white. Far across the city, from eye to horizon, a vast blanket of smog lay, and below the garden a sporty car cleared its throat in the curves of Sunset Boulevard. It was early afternoon and I wrote a song, cradling my guitar, caressing the strings.

Sydney Maurer sat opposite, talking of artwork for the new album. "They'll do anything we want," replied Sydney to a question about creative control.

"And what choice typeface?"

" 'S all OK, man, forget to worry, you know the procedure. As long as you pay for it."

The doorbell buzzed. In tumbled my son, Dono, followed by Enid and another woman. "Hi, this is Karon," said Enid. "She drove me over in her bug. Say hello to Daddy, Dono—it's Daddy," said Enid excitedly. I had asked Enid to bring over Dono as I missed him so.

The boy became very still and stared at me. I felt the distance between us.

Karon curled up in a chair, slim ankles. She was a pale-skinned, dark-haired beauty.

"Would you like some tea?" I offered. "It's lemon with honey; I hope you don't mind."

The child had turned away now and was rolling a snooker ball along the floor, evidently fascinated by its momentum. I gathered him up and sat him on my knee. He was a feisty little character and every bit a Leo as he struggled free from this strange man.

Little Dono did not know yet that I had not married his mother, and I felt powerless to do anything about really being a dad to him.

Then Karon's lover called on the phone. I was a bit annoyed that Enid had been uncool with the number. The pale-skinned chick spoke in strained, hushed tones. "I'm with him now, Theo," she whispered. Pause, and a look at me. "Yes, he is; yes, I will." She handed me the phone. She said "yes" instead of "yeah."

Gyp winked at me. We both knew this might be a setup.

I took the phone in my hand and asked, "Is that you, Theo?"

"Yes, it is."

"Am I speaking to Karon's lover?"

"No, just her friend."

"You are performing at the Bowl?" He obviously already knew this.

"Yeah, I will invite Karon. Do you wanna come?"

"No, I don't go out much."

I would learn later that he was an up-and-coming artist, beginning to taste real success. Still on the phone, I asked Theo if he wanted Karon back.

"No, you can keep her," he casually remarked.

I hung up.

From out of the bedroom area strode a tall, long-haired woman named Rebecca. She had been sleeping off last night's revelries and yawned a hello to us as we sipped our lemon tea. Rebecca habitually talked with a sneer, cursed scandalously in Hebrew and English, and knew every star in the spangled society. She wrote for magazines and entertained us with her quick wit. She sat down to watch the action.

Wanting to see Karon again, I invited her to share a box with Enid at my Hollywood Bowl concert. Perhaps knowing that Enid would be there, she declined, but I guessed I would see this dark-haired young actress later on down the road.

The tour began in earnest. It was an event on the scale of the previous two years and even more successful. The last performance was in the Anaheim Convention Center, next door to Disneyland.

Before I returned home, Tom Smothers threw a party for me at Robert Redford's house. The guest list was as long as the press party with more faces. Tom took great delight in playing the "Barabajagal" single at full volume on the huge sound system, asking his guests who they thought the singer was. Everyone got it wrong. At the height of the excitement the crowds parted for a wild-looking chick with blazing eyes. She stuck her face close to mine. It was Janis Joplin.

"Just wanted to see what you looked like, Donovan!" And she was gone. Janis had gone back to the bedroom where all the musos were hiding from the "Hollyweird" crowd.

At the poolside there was a raffle, and the protest singer, Phil Ochs, won it. Everyone cheered as he went up to the microphone, but he was not pleased. He gave us all a tongue-lashing about Vietnam and the senselessness of Hollywood, this party, me included. Raising the huge basket of fruit he had won, he tossed it into the pool and left in disgust. Of course he was right, but the party went on regardless.

I climbed the rock waterfall high above the party (feeling a little like I also had been thrown away) and plunged into the pool to join the fruit.

It's Over

❖

The tour over, I returned to the cottage that November, exhausted. Each morning the woods would echo with the sound of the axe as I cut logs. Sitting in front of the inglenook fire, I wrote songs far into the cold night. After a while I felt discontent and gradually became enthusiastic about recording again. My work was becoming my only reality.

Although my relationship with Enid was over, I wanted to have our son educated in England. Enid flew over. She would stay with me in the cottage until I could set her up with a flat in London. Living with Enid for that brief last time may have made her feel that there was still hope of a reconciliation. She still wanted to live with me as my lover, but my feelings were dead. I took Enid to the Scottish retreat and we made love for the last time. When we returned to England, I knew we were prolonging the inevitable. It was finally and definitely over, and oh, how she hated me for it. I asked her to move out. She was a beautiful, wonderful woman. I had loved her and hated causing her all this pain. Tears and shouting accompanied the final showdown. I felt devastated for her. After she had moved out, she wailed her pain down the phone.

Some months later Enid told me she was pregnant with our second child.

I would care for Enid and both our children. I set her up in a large garden flat in Hampstead. It was a lovely location.

My last concert performance of 1969 was in the Royal Albert Hall with John Cameron and his orchestra. This venue had become my favorite in London. I introduced many new songs sprinkled among hits. My acoustic guitar remained the best vehicle for the poems that fairly poured out of me as the old decade waned. My love of curious wordplay had not deserted me as the new decade dawned.

It was time to make another album. Once again I wanted to strike out on my own and record without my producer Mickie Most, regardless of the contractual commitments to the Epic label in the States. And so I went down that January and February of 1970 to the newly fitted Morgan Studios in Willesden, London, booking an open-ended session. My engineers were Robin Black and Mike Bobac, young talent who would both excel in the art of recording in the years to come. We rolled the tape and I sang solo at first. It was as if I wanted to empty my complete songbook, so long were our sessions.

I invited "Candy" John Carr to play percussion. "Candy" now played a full kit of drums, and the lessons he had learned from the hand drums would benefit this new album. He introduced me to a guitar player named Mike Thompson, who also played bass. A three-piece Donovan sound emerged from the first rehearsals on tape. I played electric guitar for the first time, and in the freedom of the three-piece sound I found I could express myself instrumentally in a way I never could before. It was a revelation to me. Somehow the tracks recorded themselves. At the right time we invited the keyboard player Mike O'Neill, once a member of Nero and The Gladiators, a favorite instrumental group of mine, to join us.

The lyrics of the ten songs that I recorded in those first two months of the seventies reveal my state of mind at the time.

"Song for John" was a musical "letter" to my friend and fellow songster John Sebastian, speaking of my need to play with him again, of the easy sound of his soft acoustics and his great harmonica.

> Country ladies take us by the hand
> Soft-eyed and cotton-clothed

> Through "Parrish" meadowland
> And John and I can be the band.
> —Donovan Leitch
> *"Song for John"*

The song "Curry Land" describes a discontented young man, very successful and moody. A purchase of a sailing schooner, a need to leave his homeland to travel the world.

> Truly drowned in grief he did repair
> To haunted trinkets and gross despair
>
> All in white 'neath shade in bamboo chair
> Military discipline has replaced despair
> Anchored in the Bay of Innocence
> Is left a lonely man, lonely through and through.
> —Donovan Leitch
> *"Curry Land"*

Gyp and I had a 114-foot motor sailing yacht berthed in Athens, named *The Vagrant.* Our idea was to sail the world and make a film of the journey. The real reason was that I wanted out. The previous five years had taken me to the heights of fame, rivaling The Beatles, The Stones, and Dylan; and yet I wanted to return to the "Road." I had dropped out in Greece and on the Isle of Islay. This time it would be permanent.

The tune "Joe Bean's Theme" was a homage to the bossa-nova music of the influential Brazilian guitarist and composer Carlos Jobim. My song title was a wordplay on his name. The lyrics sing of that

> Long and lazy schooner
> In lapis lazuli.
> Aquamarina, in a southern sea.
>
> Soft and sensual sunset
> Somerset Maugham fun-set

The warm breeze of evening
Caresses silk dresses.
—Donovan Leitch,
"Joe Bean's Theme"

Here was a dream of sailing to the tropics, of an escape from winter in the north.

"Celtic Rock" was the song that gave the emerging Celtic folk-rock genre a name, separating it from the American folk-rock scene. I freely used Gaelic-style melody mixed with chants and rock rhythms. The lyric compared the miners of the British Industrial Revolution with the trolls of legend.

I was continuing to fuse traditional forms with the pop style of modern recording at the time. I had opened the door wide when I arrived in 1965, but I was still being ridiculed by the folk purists.

But folk music is for and of the people. It is the basis and the root of all popular music in any country at any time. We must return to the roots to nourish the "new." The spiral of creativity rises up into the future by drawing from the past, a truly Celtic pattern intertwining and weaving the sounds of life.

The "Season of Farewell" simply refers to the final leaving of Enid, and the leaving I was planning soon, far away from home, over the sea.

I also wanted to break the spell that hung over me, the binding spell of fame and false love.

Downstairs in Morgan Studios, Paul McCartney was recording his first solo album, following Lennon's lead. The Beatles were now apart for good.

Typically, Paul was playing all the instruments. His sound was curiously like the one I was making downstairs, simple and to the point. He was enjoying a freedom to experiment. Critics would say that his solo work did not carry the weight of his classic Beatles music. As the last song on my album said: "Change is life's characteristics / Bend and flow and play the game."

I borrowed Paul's Fender Strat for "New Year's Resovolution," We two did not collaborate on each other's albums that January and February of 1970, but it seemed that we were embarking on similar paths, winding away from that wild and crazy rock-and-roll Dreaming Decade called "the sixties."

Do what you've never done before
See what you've never seen
Feel what you've never felt before
Go where you've never been
Sing what you've never sung before
Say what you've never said
Bear what you've never borne before
Hear what you've never heard

All is not as it would seem
Nothing ever remains the same
Change is life's characteristic
Bend and flow and play the game
Lose your chain
And do what you like
Get on your bike and do what you like

So many times I was the one who stopped myself from doing things
So many times I was the one who grounded myself and clipped my wings
So I say

Do what you've never done before
For fear of losing face
You have nothing to defend now
In your state of grace
So get on your bike and do what you like

Love is the gift of man
Yet he will not receive
Within is the church of man
Yet he cannot perceive
Without is the realm of man
He yet cannot conceive

Man is the plague of man
Yet he will not believe

There go you go I
There go you go I
There go you go I

    —Donovan Leitch,
    "New Years Resovolution"

Of course this song was advice to myself. I felt elated when I sang it. The future beckoned bright. Everything was going to work out. In titling this album, I described my urge to travel in just two words: *"Open Road."*

The album reached No. 16 in the U.S. charts.

This success of the album was no doubt due in part to the fact that I was still handled in America by the formidable manager Alan Klein. His aggressive approach to the business has gone down in pop music history. The Beatles's record sales increased dramatically after he got involved. Alan Klein also played a major part in my career. Without this guy I might not have been a major player in the record industry. Sympathy for the Devil?

The new band had proved so successful in the studio that I invited "Candy" and Mike to join me on a Grand Tour of the world in my yacht *Vagrant.* My plan to tour the world for an extended period enthused my advisers. I was counseled to treat exile from Britian as a "drop-out" year (in other words, become for that year a tax exile), during which time I would earn all my income completely untaxed anywhere. Millions were involved. To benefit from this plan I would have to not set foot on British soil for one whole year from 5 April 1970 to 5 April 1971. I agreed to this, although my real reasons were personal, not financial. The British revenue were taxing all of us stars 98 percent. That's Ninety-eight pence to them, two to us. George Harrison wrote his song "Taxman" for the best of reasons. How much can one man possibly need? I was becoming bored with the whole fame game. All I needed was the exit sign. To anywhere, really. The weight of success and the loneliness it brought were becoming unbearable.

And with the end of the 1960s, a way of life was passing. Gyp and I had lived a life that could not be lived again. A sense of discovery was being lost in the commercial exploitation of a youth culture. When I look back at that decade, I now see that . . .

> It was in the time of innocence
> Before the media sold the world . . .
> —Donovan Leitch,
> *"Caprice"*

Voyage

The spring arrived and I left the little cottage in the wood to fly down to Athens, Greece, where the yacht was waiting. I would stay there for a few days, taking on provisions for the cruise to Crete. A villa had been rented on that distant island where I would rehearse with the band for the upcoming dates in Japan, first stop on the Grand Tour of the world.

I flew down to the yacht ahead of the band to settle in for the first part of the year-long tour. In the evening I sat alone on the deck overlooking the deserted marina. The distant music of a taverna came drifting over the water, and I picked up my guitar. The minor strain of a sad Greek tune started in me. As I watched the lovers courting in the shadows, I felt that same old longing.

> I see the lovers walking hand in hand,
> Late at night along the breakwater concrete strand.
> Side by side and arm in arm they stroll,
> I see them pause to lean against the wall.
>
> I watch reflections of the bright lamplight,
> Electric Moons upon the water.
> —Donovan Leitch, *"Electric Moon"*

My new song was composed in the Greek fashion, the bouzouki parts rounding off each verse with that distinctive flourish of notes. I turned in early. The band was arriving the next day.

In the morning the captain bid farewell to his wife, and we slowly moved out of the harbor and headed for the open sea. Nine hours out of Athens we arrived at Agios Nikolaos, a tiny fishing hamlet on the northern coast of Crete.

The villa stood on a high cliff some miles from the village. All of the gear was landed by tender on the tiny pier situated below the sheer rock face. Trunks, suitcases, amps, guitars, drums, microphones, speakers, brown rice, and two stray dogs were transported from the yacht to the villa. The band disembarked in the main harbor and came later in taxis. I sent the crew back to the yacht and looked the villa over alone.

The old dwelling commanded a magnificent position high above the shimmering Mirabello. It had lain empty for some time. A silence pervaded the courtyard and the olive groves. The sky was big and blue. It was hot and peaceful. A bee droned by in the still air. Impressions of my first visit to Greece returned. The main building stood highest, with a Gothic studded door. Inside the dusty Great Hall, a massive table, twenty feet long, dominated the room. It had curious, carved thrones at each end. A huge fireplace was fronted by a low, heavy table, served by wooden trestles. A thick carpet of great proportion lay rolled up on a stone shelf.

On the wall hung a large framed photograph from the past, an old Cretan in traditional costume smoking a *nagilla,* a waterpipe. A skull grinned from a recess. A vase of wild thorny plants sat on a windowsill. A small door led out onto a patio with a panoramic sea view. A litter of stray kittens mewed from an old oven. The precipice fell to the rocks far below.

I did not choose a room in the main quarters but took one of the guest rooms lower down, built into the cliff. It had a small cooking area, two single iron beds, a bathroom, and a neat little balcony with two arches and a sea view. Very austere but perfect for my mood. I moved in with my typewriter, paper, and a few books. Gyp and Yvonne stayed on the yacht.

The days were spent rehearsing up in the Great Hall, the electric sound reverberating around the stone walls. It would rise in the still blue air and sail along the coast and into the town.

But I knew in my heart it wouldn't work out with the band. I had been weaned on acoustic instruments. I found it hard to tune an electric vibration. True, I could record electric guitar in the studio, but that was at a much lower volume. Perhaps it was the hall, perhaps it was the levels we played at—or perhaps I had begun to lose interest in my music?

Candy and Mike would have continued jamming past six o'clock if I hadn't said something. I yearned for a fine quality of silence to soothe the weary soul.

I went down to my little room and lay on the bed, looking out past the shutters at the evening descending. Swifts came out, flashed and darted past the window, their squeaks echoing to each other. From behind me a golden glow shone on the land, touching everything. Far up in the hills a mule brayed. I boiled some rice for my supper, then shut the windows as the mosquitoes began their campaign. I lit some incense and meditated. After a while I stepped out into the velvet night and climbed the steps that led to the flat roof. The whitewashed walls of the villa were bright as day in the mysterious luminosity of a full moon. The black sea shimmered with liquid silver far below. I felt Her presence.

To Her I addressed my song, pausing to hear the notes return into Her silence. I felt observed and the hair on the back of my neck stood up.

> Who is she who haunts me, this lady so pale?
> Her sadness, her secrets, I would know her tale
> Her vision is fleeting, her visit it seems.
> Soon fades in the fashion of mists and dreams
> —Donovan Leitch,
> "The White Lady"

The Journal

❖

All my thoughts were of transitoriness, transitory lovers. I felt the need for a lifetime companion.

In a box of old journals I recently found the one from 1970, a large sketchbook. On the cover I had pasted a postcard of tropical islands and Buddhas. The entries are scrawled by a desperate man. Now I read the opening sections and I know that I was going mad at the time.

7 June 1970, Crete.
On a whim I called the American actress Karon yesterday. The one I met last year in Hollywood, when she came to my rooms with Enid and Donno. Invited her to stay with me here in Greece. She said she'd like to visit and I arranged for a flight.

15 June
A week has passed. Karon arrived Athens. I drove over the olive-grove hills, through ancient villages of proud old men and black-shawled widows beside the sea, to the little aerodrome of Iraklion. After a dizzy flight in an old single-prop plane, I landed in Athens.

Took a taxi around to the International Terminal and sat waiting for Karon's flight to arrive. Drank hot lemon juice and honey in the small restaurant. When I saw her she looked different. I was shocked for a moment. Was this the same young woman?

She was dressed in a loose, synthetic, trouser affair (I hate synthetic material), a green cashmere shawl, and sandals held on with the plastic netting oranges are sold in. She carried a small khaki knapsack full of drawing pens, ink, and junk. Scent of patchouli when I kissed her lightly on the cheek. She has a Syrian smile. Soon we were holding hands in the taxi back to the domestic aerodrome, I awkward, she jet-weary.

The private plane buzzed us over the Sea of Candia and landed back on Crete. In the taxi Karon dozed. I sat watching her, dark wisps of hair falling over her bare shoulders. When she saw the villa she was obviously enchanted. I whisked her away from the curious band and down to my little room over the rocks. She lay on the bed and slipped into a deep sleep. Her pale olive skin was translucent, like cloudy onyx. She *was* lovely.

The rehearsal came to a close. Karon noticed my frustration with the band, but it was more than that. I broke the news to the band that I would not be taking them to Japan, and that I would tour solo. I was retreating into what I knew was a safe acoustic position. It came as a personal blow to the two musicians, but they cheered up and we prepared to return to Athens from where they would fly on to London. We had, after all, recorded a fine album and *Open Road* would become one of my favorites.

The yacht arrived on the Greek mainland, and the following morning good-byes were exchanged. Karon watched as I stood on the white yacht, dressed in a white sharkskin suit, my white Mercedes sports car waiting. I turned to find her watching me with a strange smile. Was she thinking of me as a flash bastard, as I had once thought of George Harrison.

I was bound now for Paris to pick up the flight to Tokyo and the tour of Japan. I asked Karon to stay on the exile tour a little longer with me. I could see in her eyes that she was struggling to decide. . . .

1 July, Athens

It is all planned. After Japan I will meet the yacht in the Caribbean and cruise until the autumn. Then the tour of America, ending up in Hawaii.

The yacht by that time will have reached the Philippines, Siam, Burma, India, Ceylon, the Seychelles, Africa, Morocco, then through the Mediterranean, and back to Greece.

A new kind of madness had entered my life. The future was an unknown land. My journal became somewhat manic. I know now I was having a mini nervous breakdown.

This was a most unlikely venture. My yacht could not even navigate the smallest Greek island without problems. I was young and naive, gradually losing my mind—and not in the Buddhist sense.

Freaky

5 July, Paris
We circled Napoleon's star-shaped city. A Peruvian-French agent met us
at Orly airport and transported us in a Cadillac limousine to the Hotel
Angélique in Montmarte. Heavy drapes, gilt plaster ceilings, a four-poster
bed, red and gold brocade, a silk-covered suite, Victoriana bath chamber,
tiles, and a china bidet. We will stay here for a few days.

My imported lover Karon resented all this extravagance, yet enjoyed every
minute. That first night in the old hotel I dreamt a song:

> Hello happy Anna
> pigeon-English toed
> Jangling telephone ring
> go on with the show
>
> One-eyed gray-hairs waiter
> brings me Chivas Regal
>
> Drown my sorrows deep
> Dysney cheese and coffee

Part the dusty curtains
quiet-eyed to the street
Overcoated people
walk by wintry trees

Surfacing from deep sleep
unknown wilderness
Clinging in the dream state
to a thread of consciousness

Surrealistic still life
French mock-antique decor
Frozen in my doom bed
as the visions pace the floor

Sleep at last o'ercomes me
safety in defeat
Once again 'tis morning
car horns in the street.

—Donovan,
"European Dream"

The telephone woke us early. I picked up the heavy Bakelite instrument and ordered hot water, lemon, and honey. We were going to shop on the Champs Elysées. We stepped out into the teeming streets of Paris and got dropped at the Arc de Triomphe. Karon still wore those stupid little plastic sandals. I would buy her a pair of fine leather.

We returned to the hotel with a Leonard Cohen record and a case for the Super 8. I intended to take up filming. Was I falling for this bird from Hollywood? We ordered up salad and fish, being careful not to eat any crap. The waiter presented the simple food on white linen, the utensils of silver.

I put on Leonard's martyred music, so reminiscent of Greece. Leonard inspired me to write "dry-songs," just poems. While in Greece I had begun a letter to Leonard in answer to one I had received from him, somehow hand-delivered. The tough yellow envelope had contained a poem on a napkin—"Not having you is like feeling spring begin all over again"—plus some other items . . .

a fake gold-plated charm in a small white envelope (on which some words of wisdom were printed) from a mail-order spiritual company.

and . . .

a two-page catalog of other items from the same company: Holy Water in an aerosol can, canned incense, a battery-lit crucifix.

and . . .

a color reproduction of a lady saint of heavenly gaze, manacled and burning.

Sitting at the open window of the villa I had begun writing back to Leonard, stopped, continued, hesitated, shy. Shy? I had performed before one million people since my beginning in music.

> I got your napkin underneath the poem.
> I know your mournful fashion,
> your eyes for Greece
> wooden-shuttered
> rooms of coarse-sheeted only slept-in houses,
>
> the owls are calling to each other.
> Sometimes, as subtle twilight drifts, I catch a
> glimpse of their whiteness
> pale shadows, always in the corner of the eye.
>
> This is my first visit to Crete
> and there is such another feeling here
> that I have not felt in the other isles.
>
> It is only that I have not seen dawn
> that dusk for me is the most uplifting time.
> I feel so light, touched, illuminated,
> inspired, steady, balanced, joyful,
>
> and what beyond?
>
> Tomorrow I will see the dawn.
> I'm off with Janis to Iraklion to fly to Athens
> to meet a lady.
>
> —Donovan Leitch

Music floated around the suite as the Paris day faded. Karon parted the dusty curtains. Night had fallen on the city. It was raining and Renaults and Citroëns prowled in packs.

"Let's go out," I said, and slid Leonard back in his sleeve.

"Where to?"

"Anywhere, out into the street, let's get lost."

"OK, but I have to bathe," she said, as she walked out of her robe. My gaze followed her legs across the room.

Soon we were riding the rubber-wheeled Metro, then up into the rainy night I pulled her. We ran across the wet streets toward the lights of a small fair. All along one side of the boulevard we ran past bumper cars, rifle ranges, rockers, and sailors with groups of Arabs smoking Gauloises under the awnings.

8 July, Paris

We were in the Pigalle, and the hookers sat in their cars as we walked by the brightly lit cafés with steaming coffee, long loaves of bread, and ringing pinball machines. We stopped at a little cinema, garishly painted posters portraying lipsticked vampires sucking necks, monsters throttling damsels.

One film was called *Freaks,* starring dwarfs, Siamese twins, a torso with no arms or legs. We squeezed past the boards and paid some francs to a wizened old lady in a box (probably legless).

The lights were down already, and an usherette with a weak flashlight pushed us into the tiny fleapit. There was one aisle separating the seats, one side had more chairs. I didn't tip the lady, and she cursed us under her breath. Once seated in the broken-down chairs, springs out, stuffing loose, we watched the crazy foreign-language commercials. Two transvestites sat on the other side in the front row by the swing doors, carrying on and laughing at anything, totally unaware of themselves.

The ads finished and after a breakdown and boos, the film began. The black-and-white American movie from 1932 was subtitled in French: "Circus Special People" flickered and crackled on the old screen.

The first frame appeared, the transvestites screeched and clutched each other, the cinema audience laughed.

A showman addressing a fair crowd came into view. He introduced the latest addition to the show. The scene faded back in time. The film dissolved to a scene in the country, a tree, around which danced two of the special people. Again the transvestites screamed and clutched each other. The little cinema door burst open, and a little man in a short rain-coat, no trousers, with suspenders and shoes, leapt into the fleapit. The two transvestites screeched again, this time genuinely shocked. The little movie house was filling up with "freaks," there to see the special people.

On the screen the two little pointy-headed women danced, the legless man ran on his arms, the armless, legless black guy played harmonica and rolled cigarettes with his lips. A beautiful roly-poly woman mothered them all and called them her children.

Freaks is the strange tale of a trapeze artist (like a young Mae West) who plays a midget along for his money, when she really loves the strong-man. At the wedding of the little man and the trapeze artist, she insults all the special people and goes off with the strongman. She tries to poison the little guy, but his friends get wise.

Then, in a horrific rain scene, the trapeze artist is chased and punished by the special people. The scene fades to the present again, and the fair-ground barker about to show the latest exhibit to the frightened audience. Of course it is the villainess in a box of sawdust, turned into a human bird, limbless and tongueless.

As the film ended, we followed the Paris freaks out into the night. It was raining still, and we hurried down the Metro stairs. The platform was deserted. We sat on a bench and talked about the film. Across the tracks sat the little man with no trousers, unaware of his strangeness, it seemed. The underground train swished into the station and soon we were back in the somber bedchamber of the old hotel.

The next morning early, all the junk was thrown into the trunk. Down through the plush corridors of the Hotel Angélique we strolled and paused in front of the immaculate concierge. A large Turner oil painting hung on the silk-covered wall, the last remaining painting in this old hotel. The owner had been a patron of the arts, collecting paint-ings as rent perhaps, before he began to sell them. Big tip and door swing into the gaping limousine, and away to Orly airport and the flight to Toyko.

The Faerie

The star-shape of Paris faded far below as the jet passed through the clouds and headed north, to Russia and Japan. We passed the first part of the journey reading and meditating. Karon played at being a poor girl in the first-class cabin.

15 July

Three hours later the plane landed at Moscow airport. We passengers were herded in a line across the tarmac and into the transit building. Fat women drove trucks onto the airstrip. Spotty soldiers with automatic rifles oversaw our movements, in case we escaped from the terrible West to the perfect East.

In the hall regular passengers who knew the routine made for the few seats at the bar to eat black bread and drink beer. All along the tall glass wall overlooking the balcony displays stood depicting the life of Lenin, photos, paintings, and statements in English, free literature for oppressed readers. Karon took some travel brochures from a stand.

We stepped out onto the observation balcony for some fresh air and looked at the alien jets. The workmanship and construction of the buildings were of poor quality, cracking and in need of repair.

Fear lurked everywhere. It was a hot afternoon and flies bit as we sat on a bench and cuddled, scared to kiss in case it meant the salt mines.

OK, back on the plane, familiar capitalist bullshit, friendly chaos, and then, on arrival in Japan suddenly we were moving through the manic streets of Tokyo to our hotel. It was a letdown for me to see Japan turn out to be a giant suburb of the United States. Having been promised old-style inns, I was disappointed when the car pulled up at the Tokyo Hilton. One consolation, though, the room was Japanese, with tatami mats, lacquer table, paper lamps, and a wooden bath. The room smelled of fresh rushes. Peace and seclusion from the cares of the day, a little haven on the twenty-third floor. Green tea was ordered. Karon slid open a screen door, and there lay soft futons, silk-covered and green-leaved. Two small pillows filled with rice husks and covered with tiny floral-patterned cotton.

Shoes off, slipping silently on the rushes, I opened the trunk and pulled out the cassette player and put on a nice sound. Karon made up the beds on the floor, lit incense, and we fell into space.

16 July

It isn't a very bright day. It's a sort of a nothing day. Tokyo smog hangs low over the buildings, the worst in the world's statistics. Many old people gasp oxygen from dispensers at traffic lights. Below the room a tiny Japanese garden. On the aluminium roof of the Hilton, wires, poles, towers, sleeping neon, TV aerial, skyscrapers on and on.

And certainly across the city there must be little havens? Small room and silent, shoeless, and graceful . . .

But instead, my journal began to take on a morbid quality, entries wandering off into a blank verse of pessimistic despair.

I feel the world is dissolving before me. A sense of unreality. Each act seems not worth the effort and has no result other than further meaninglessness. Is there a word even to describe what is happening to me? Nothing is happening at all, and I must witness it; and if I try to withdraw from the world I can't see me anymore. Karon is real, though. I am falling for her in a most intense way. She lives and breathes and seems like the most real thing in the world.

"Women have operations to remove the slits from their eyes, to look more like Western faces," laughed the handsome Japanese tour manager from the driver's seat of our limo.

Karon shuddered next to me in the back.

"And we are getting taller, you know, because we no longer sit on the floor. We make lotsa cowboy movies, too."

We passed the Imperial Palace. Police stood around in space helmets, with sticks and Roman-style Plexiglas shields.

"For the students."

We arrived at our destination. I had hoped it would be an old pottery shop with a Zen master beaming behind his wheel. In reality it was the china department of a large store. Disgust.

Karon was becoming uptight with me. "You have no freedom on your tour," she exclaimed, "mixing with money mongers, staying in all the wrong places. Why not just walk the streets instead of the guided tour by people who don't know a chopstick from a pencil?"

My journal lapsed into the past, fragments of earlier dreams slid across my mind screen. I fell into blank verse:

> long-legged lazy lie
> corduroy soft shoe sigh
> miles and miles davis fly
> and denim blouse-breast
> campus green dinner time
> slowly emerging from
> "maybe" to "why not try"

I asked myself: What happened to my Beat dream?

Karon cooked some rice, and I flicked on the TV to watch the samurai serial, Clint Eastwood-style terror cool. American ads with slanted eyes.

18 July

Here in the room nothing else exists. The telephone rings, the door knocks with annoying inquiries about the concerts, the press, and radio interviews. I am pissed off. Karon tells me I am living a lie. "This isn't freedom; You're caught in a game. You don't meet any real people anymore."

She's half right, maybe she is *all* right. For the first time since the beginning I fail to handle my commitments.

I thought long on what Karon had said. I was heading for the big fold up. The very thing I was always about to do. Drop out of the fame game, the hit-bit baby.

I could just fuck off, right? Right? I dared myself to do it. Go on, do it!

And now here was a chick reflecting the truth which deep down I already knew. This casual affair—that's what it was meant to be—with the American actress had brought this to me, told me where it was at.

Yes, I thought. I'll piss off. With her, maybe? I wanted to take her back to the Scottish islands. I would show them to her.

And, yes, Karon saw I was becoming attached to her in an intense way, and I could see she did not know whether she liked the feeling or not. Then something happened that brought events to a head.

"What's going on? You seem more and more distracted," she said.

"Nothing's wrong, I'm fine," I lied.

"Well, I feel something. Is it the tour that is getting to you?"

"Look, I feel we are getting close, you and I, and I am not sure how to deal with it."

"Theo sent me a tape, you know; we do this sometimes when we travel." She looked uneasy, and I felt a shaft pierce my heart.

"I'm not sure about Scotland now," she said. She explained that across the Pacific her ex-lover was feeling a dull pain two inches below his collarbone, a dull weight in his chest.

I kissed her soft thigh as she lay in a faded turquoise kimono. She turned the full force of her eyes upon me and another strange shaft pierced me. I was becoming possessive.

I bought tickets for the Kabuki Theatre. The program begins in the morning and progresses through the day with intervals for food and drink, which the audience usually bring with them. I had tickets for the last acts of the day. We took our seats and looked around.

The black journal recorded my own emotional obituary:

19 July
The stage is in stereo. One long wide front stage and two slim side platforms that flank left and right, side stages, which are curtained as is the main stage. Tinky-Twanky music comes from behind the curtain on the left. "Clacks" and "clocks" of percussion, with occasional word sounds, come from somewhere up and behind us, a quadraphonic arrangement.

The curtains lift to show a large Japanese villa in the country. Steps rise to a patio. The side stages reveal the incidental musicians, who will sing the tale. They sit on their knees, hair slicked back, wearing wing-shouldered costumes, like the 1930s Hollywood idea of Martians. They hold large bone plectrums and all sit in a row. The singer (a colossal fat man) utters strained, high squeaks, slurring the notes. They are all in blue, and two of them look Western.

The music sets the strange scene. Center stage, from within the villa, a maid comes silent, attired in the most far-out kimono, lacquered hairpiece, white powdered face, slick lips, and doll pose, sliding out with marionette movements, tottering and staring with a fixed expression she comes.

At the far end of the patio a rush wall slips open to reveal the lady of the house, ailing on her couch, waited on by another serving maid in silk with incredible makeup and puppetlike gestures. Such amazing concentration and control.

Suddenly there appears from a trapdoor, stage left, a beautiful faerie who brings a curing herb for the lady. This vision is lacquered with spines of ivory in her hair, blanched white and dancing to the twangy sounds.

As the faerie pauses before the steps of the villa, we see two figures on their knees shuffle from the rear of the stage. They are dressed completely in black, hoods hiding their faces. They take up position behind the many folds of the faerie's kimono. The audience, of course, see the dark figures but are not distracted from the action; they are merely shadows compared to the brilliant colors of the other players.

The music builds, the hooded ones gather fine threads attached to the faerie's costume. Cymbals! Wham, totter, crash, scream! The other players all totter like distraught dolls. The hooded figures pull on the threads, and the top layers of the *faerie's* garment are whisked away in a puff of smoke from below the stage, to reveal her true form . . . she is an evil witch! She stands formidable, casting spells (tightly rolled streamers, very effective).

End of scene.

Reading it now, I see with extraordinary clarity I slid into my slow-motion breakdown even as I recorded this evening of Kabuki. I think I may have been seeing Karon as like the faerie in the play, casting a spell on me. Of course I can also see now that this most serene and sensitive girl had no such ambition.

Quite the reverse. I was far more interested in her than she was in me.

At the time it seemed to me that Karon was acting strange. Or was she pretending to be the actress Karon? I couldn't tell anymore. I felt fragmented. At the threshold. Of what?

The next morning a package awaited Joann Karon at the front desk. It was another cassette message from her lover in LA. She fitted the cartridge into her machine, plugged in the earpiece for privacy and pressed "play." A tear rolled down her cheek, and I was gripped by anxiety.

"I spoke with Theo."

This was it. I sat cross-legged on the tatami, waiting for the next bit.

"He wants me back." I could see that she was pleased. "He has asked me to marry him."

I tried for a smile, but it came out a smirk. "That's nice," I managed to say.

"Nice?" Karon retorted. "It's great, but I will believe it when it happens."

I tried to reason myself out of my misery. I had only met Karon a few weeks ago.

But Karon had other news. Enid had been talking to Theo about me. What could they have discussed?

"Did Theo say what they talked about?" I asked.

"I don't think you want to know," Karon replied. "Do you?"

I didn't.

"I hear Enid is seeing John Sebastian," said Karon. Then she smiled as she said, "Everyone likes to play the game of musical beds. We all do."

Had I fallen in love with a girl who loved another? She was returning to her own true love. I couldn't sleep, swimming in shallow seas of drowsiness. My ego was wide awake, though. She preferred someone else to me. I tried to win her, to persuade her, and eventually she agreed to a pact. She would journey to LA and check it out. I would return to London and await her call in five days' time. Then we both would know whom she had chosen. I was going back regardless of the canceled tour dates and the cost—tax free money, twenty million pounds. I did not care a fig for fame or money anymore.

At Tokyo airport my agent and my father pleaded with me not to board the BOAC jet. Once on the plane I was on British soil and the tax exile broken.

Gypsy Dave smiled at me and realized I was beyond convincing.

Gypsy, too, was going into a major change, fast becoming a skilled sculptor under the benign influence of David Wynne and his work.

Madness

On the plane, I wrote:

> There is no corner of every minute where she is not,
> her presence is everywhere. . . .

> When I fell in love I repeated "I love you"
> many, many times, each time
> the phrase held a different meaning.

Exaggeration. I fell into an uneasy sleep. After forty winks the air in the cabin stung my sinuses and I awoke, part of me happy to be feeling something after the last four years of fast affairs.

Karon had left Tokyo two hours before me, she east, me west.

Bad poetry flowed from the wound. I kept coming back to the question: what will she decide? I felt as if my life depended on her answer. I continued to search for the pattern of her thought.

An uneasy, fretful sleep—fleeting images of Karon, blue grapes in her mouth, bursting them between her teeth, the amber juice . . . a blond boy—child in a field of iris.

The jet circled over Moscow: stopover and refuel. A stewardess shook me gently and fastened my seat belt. I sat in the cabin completely detached from life. Down went the plane, out poured the cramped passengers, eager to stretch their legs. I followed, gliding down the stairs in a daze. I felt deathly and invisible. In fact, I *had* begun to die—my previous self was crinkling at the edges, my old skin puckering, ready to be discarded.

Back on the plane, I settled into my seat and watched as a new passenger came up the aisle looking at the numbers for her seat. She was in her early forties, English, from the North and loaded down with carrier bags. Chatting small talk with the odd passenger, she struggled along, loud and friendly. She was of slight but strong build, sort of short blonde hair and hard-working hands. A mother.

At last she spied the empty seat next to me and sat down with her bags on top of her. I took one of the bags.

"Here, let me put that down here."

"Are you sure it's OK?"

"Of course—there's plenty of room."

The plane took off and climbed high into the sky, dwarfing the cracked concrete airstrip. The woman penetrated my gloom, very slightly at first.

Some food came out of the galley on little trays, two kinds of nuts and a carnation. The woman ordered a drink and soon the meal arrived, steam heated and very unappetizing to me.

My neighbor tucked in, though. We engaged in small talk. The wine went to my head quickly, and I wanted to talk with this woman with the warm smile.

"Are you a singer?" She sort of recognized me.

"Yes, I am."

"I should know, shouldn't I?"

"No. In fact, it's a pleasure to talk with someone who doesn't know who I am. Then I'm taken at face value."

"Yes, yes, of course, I can see that." She had the warm northern character that I always took to.

"My children would know you, I bet—they buy lots of records."

"How many children do you have?"

Delighted to speak about her family, she began. "I've three. My oldest, Susan, she's twenty-one; there's John who's fifteen; and Andrew, he's eleven and he's . . ."

As she spoke, I imagined the children. It seemed to ease my pain, talking about someone else. We introduced ourselves. Her name was Claire. I just said my name was Don.

"Tell me." She leaned over. "I've always wanted to know something." She was about to ask a fan question. "What does it really feel like to be admired, you know, by so many fans?"

"Well, many things. In the beginning I was scared stiff—amazed at the reception. Up until I started getting paid for singing, I thought I was no good anyway. My parents backed me up. I would sit in the bathroom at home with my guitar (for the echo) and try to learn to play. Then I became confident as I learned my trade . . ." Slowly my heart opened up and then suddenly I spoke what was on my mind. "I'm going through some changes now—I think I'm in love with someone—she doesn't know whether she loves me."

Claire held her breath for a beat, evidently surprised at my confession—she was, after all, a complete stranger. But, tilting her head, she listened to the whole story intensely. After I had finished, I felt much better. I wanted her advice; she was a woman who knew how to console me; she was an older woman—experienced.

She spoke to me about how women are moved by emotion. "My opinion is that you will get your love; you deserve her."

After my confession Claire began her own. "I wouldn't ordinarily tell this to a stranger, but I feel we're friends now." She smiled, warmly. "I'm in some grief myself. I've left my husband in Moscow, where he is working, and my home life is all up in the air."

She spoke of her own troubles and felt relief. It seemed that her old man had prevented her being free. She had wanted to act once on the amateur stage. She'd even joined a small company when she was a girl, but had sacrificed her love of it for her man. He had seen how she enjoyed being with people and entertaining. He'd been jealous and put a stop to it.

I told her she should have continued doing her thing; her husband had been too selfish. I hope she felt better. We talked of how good it was to open up. We were friends.

Return

I stepped into the limousine. The black car sped through the suburbs, bound for the little lilac cottage in the woods. It was summer, I realized. Pale-skinned girls bared their arms and legs dressed in cotton prints and sandals.

Soon I was home. The lane opened leafy arms to me, yet I felt like a stranger as I knocked on the oak door. I was no longer the person who used to live there.

Serina opened the door, her brown body in soft, faded jeans and a Fair Isle sweater. I had rented the cottage to her and a friend, Angie—two American girls in Swinging England. I had rented it to them for a year, and now here I was, back after only a few months.

Serina put the kettle on. She had immediately sensed my gloom and came back in with hot lemon and honey. I told her all that had happened. My chest heaved. I wanted no sympathy from Serina, only recognition.

Angie was away, staying in Clapton's mansion for the long weekend, cooking for the party and courting Dave Mason. She had recently split with her old man and moved over the Atlantic to be a "Chelsea Girl."

During the sunny days that followed I spent my time up in the woods where I'd pitched a tent. There in the forest glade I lay on a green camp bed, gazing through the dappled leaves, listening to the birdsong, and waiting for Karon's call.

A visit to my parents' home on the third day was a disaster. When I laid all my pain before my mother, she could only feel hatred for the girl who had damaged her son. This was no consolation. My father was still reeling from my decision to cut short the tax exile, and he, too, had little comfort for me. What could anyone do, anyway? I felt empty of opinion.

On the fourth day—I was waiting impatiently for the next day, the day Karon would call—Serina asked me if she could invite some friends over. I answered that I was her guest, and she could do what she liked. She was sweetly respectful. So Pedro, Orange, Suave, and Veronica arrived. A Spanish dress designer, a red-haired blossom, a flint-featured young gallant, and an ex-"Living Theater" typist. Cynthia prepared rice and vegetables, and we ate up at my camp in the woods.

Businessmen called for me on the phone, and I told Serina to say I was no longer the person they wanted. It was a peaceful summer afternoon in the forest, friends dressing nice and eating rice.

The fifth day dawned—the day Karon had promised to call. The morning unfolded, slow and sunny. I reclined on Angie's bed of cushions and dozed in the early afternoon. I had not slept well.

Angie had called to say that she was returning, and soon the sound of her little Fiat came up the lane and cranked to a halt. Two doors slammed shut— she was with someone. Angie walked up the garden path to the front door. I came downstairs to meet her.

Serina opened the old oak door as I reached the tiny hall. Angie came in first, slightly bemused to find me there. Her friend was a young woman she had met at the weekend party.

"Do you two know each other at all?" Angie purred an introduction.

This young woman was in a long, green flowery dress and silver cowboy boots. Shafts of sunlight burnished her long hennaed hair as she paused on the threshold, a wide-eyed fawn in a forest glade. We were both embarrassed. We had never expected to see each other again. Angie and Serena withdrew discreetly.

"What brings you to England?" I asked.

"I am moving back to start a small boutique and bring up Julian here," Linda replied.

"Those are the boots, right?" I was sure I recognized them from back in Santa Monica in 1965.

"And this is the ring." She raised her delicate hand to show me the blood-stone band I had bought her in Portobello Road.

We walked up into the forest. There in a dappled glade a delicate atmosphere formed between us. Tenderly our gazes met. I felt a release. All my pain had not been for Karon. I saw this now.

"I . . . still feel for you," I breathed.

"I still feel the same," Linda sighed, softly.

We walked out of the woods into the field and lay on the grass. "This isn't going to be easy, you know," I said.

"If it was easy," she said, "we'd've been married in 1965."

Magically, a cow came over and gently licked Linda's face, which made us both laugh and broke the tension.

Later that night, in the little old-fashioned bedroom, we slept in each other's arms. She folded into me her long and slender body. I woke in the dark and knew I lay in Linda's red Egyptian hair.

As the 1960s came to a close, we two lovers were in each other's arms again. Like a Celtic pattern that returns to itself, we had returned to each other.

Epilogue

At the end of the 1960s, I dropped out of the music business and walked away from fame and millions of dollars. Linda had also chosen to turn away from Hollywood and a lucrative movie career for her son, Julian. The dream of the 1960s was becoming commercialized and I wanted no part of it.

I had also accomplished my aim, to help to introduce to my generation the Bohemian Manifesto of Change, and the "Doors of Perception" were now opened for anyone to enter. I thought to myself, I felt like I had been a teacher and the course I taught was over.

Music's fame had almost caught me in its web, as it had caught Brian, but I had escaped to find Linda waiting. Just in time I might add, as she had been offered marriage at the Clapton party by Bobbie Whitlock. True to herself, she knew she was not in love. Soon Brian and Linda's golden-haired boy would come to the cottage to live with us. I would be his father now. Linda also told me to see my son, Donno so that the same heartache would not happen as it had between young Julian and his father, Brian. Linda and I would finally marry and have two lovely little daughters, Astrella Celeste and Oriole Nebula. Unknown to each other I had returned from exile and Linda from Hollywood, both at the same time. Clearly we were meant to be. In time

I would see more of my American children by Enid, two wonderful spirits whom I love dearly.

In the years that followed I looked back at the thirteen hit singles, sell-out performances in all the great concert halls of the world, counting among my friends the important songwriters and creators of the day, two hundred of my own songs recorded by other artists, and I marveled at the fact that I was still only twenty-four years old.

The story you have just read is a tale of freedom won and lost and won again. I am blessed to have traveled the road with such compassionate and creative friends.

I finished writing shortly after the second war in Iraq. I look around me and see that the peace and love my friends and I called for in the 1960s are needed now more than ever.

Gypsy Dave and I stirred the cauldron of Bohemian power and Linda made the poet in me shine.

I thank the world for being there. I thank you all. Without you I would be singing in the dark.

www.donovan.ie